# THE ADVENTURES OF THEODORE ROOSEVELT

# The Adventures of Theodore Roosevelt

*

National Geographic
Adventure Classics

Washington, D.C.

Library of Congress Cataloging-in-Publication Data available upon request.

One of the world's largest nonprofit scientific and educational organizations, the National Geographic Society was founded in 1888 "for the increase and diffusion of geographic knowledge." Fulfilling this mission, the Society educates and inspires millions every day through its magazines, books, television programs, videos, maps and atlases, research grants, the National Geographic Bee, teacher workshops, and innovative classroom materials. The Society is supported through membership dues, charitable gifts, and income from the sale of its educational products. This support is vital to National Geographic's mission to increase global understanding and promote conservation of our planet through exploration, research, and education.

For more information, please call 1-800-NGS LINE (647-5463) or write to the following address:

National Geographic Society
1145 17th Street N.W.
Washington, DC 20036-4688 U.S.A.

Visit the Society's Web site at www.nationalgeographic.com.

# Contents

# FOREWORD

## by *Tweed Roosevelt*

OF COURSE I NEVER KNEW MY GREAT-GRANDFATHER, Theodore Roosevelt. He died more than twenty years before I was born. In fact the picture which appeared in most of the newspapers the day after he died showed TR holding my father as an infant with my grandmother, a very young woman, and other family members looking on.

Much of my childhood was spent with my grandparents, as my parents were frequently overseas in government service. My grandfather—Archie, TR's third son—lived close to Sagamore Hill, TR's home on the north shore of Long Island. My great-grandmother Edith was still alive and living in the house. We often went to Sagamore for Sunday dinners and holidays such as Christmas, which was celebrated as TR had when his children were young. The house is filled with TR—his office, his books, his hunting trophies and a great many other wonderful things fascinating to a young boy. Every time you opened a closet there was something of interest. The walls were covered with animal heads and the floors carpeted with the skins of bears, lions, and zebras.

One of my favorite places was the old gun room on the third floor overlooking Long Island Sound. Here were many mementos of TR's numerous adventure trips including, of course, his guns. Even as a small boy, my grandfather would occasionally let me shoot one of TR's rifles or pistols. When I spent the night, I stayed in the room where my grandfather had slept as a child. One of the great advantages of the room was that a young boy could scramble across a small shed to the lawn below, a useful escape route in those summer days when children were put to bed before dark. Although I was surrounded, so to speak, by my great-grandfather, very little mention of him was made. Contrary to popular belief, our family, just like every other family, did not spend much time at the dinner table or anywhere else for that matter, talking about a great-grandfather. Nonetheless, I was absorbing him without even realizing it.

Later I came to know TR through my own grandfather, not because of what he told me, but rather unintentionally and without attribution, by his behavior. Through my middle teens my grandfather, whenever he could spare time from his Wall Street career, would take me on hunting and camping trips, have me help him with various chores around his Cold Spring Harbor home, especially in the several acre kitchen garden. He taught me about the local birds including those "confusing fall warblers"; he quoted extensively from literature at the dinner table; he had me help prepare and roast a suckling pig before the enormous fireplace on holidays. On Christmas mornings he orchestrated the opening of presents, making notes on a pad of paper keeping track of whom to thank. He regaled me and my friends with stories from the old Norse sagas and from Roman history, and most memorably scared us with ghost stories before a roaring campfire on some remote, deserted island sandbar. It was not until years later, after I had read such books as Hermann Hagerdorn's wonderful account of TR's family life, *The Roosevelt Family of Sagamore Hill*, that I realized that most of what grandfather did in his recreation time with me came directly from his father. Without knowing it, I had absorbed another large dose of my great-grandfather.

It wasn't until I was well into my forties that I developed a completely new perspective on TR and especially the part of his life that he describes in his writings collected in this volume. It was then that I began to travel extensively to places he had visited. Particularly I retraced some of his adventures in the American West, East Africa, and the Brazilian Amazon. Although I am not much of a mystic, in these areas I often felt the presence of the ghost of TR, a very different ghost in each place.

In the Dakotas, Wyoming, and Montana, I could feel the optimism, enthusiasm, and energy of the young TR who wrote so lovingly of these open and wild spaces. Today, much of this land is almost exactly as it was in TR's day. I have been lucky enough to hike the badlands, ride the open prairie, and stalk elk in the Big Horn. When I first visited Medora, the little town nearest his ranches, I arose early one morning and drove to the Theodore Roosevelt National Park. Leaving my car by the side of the road, I splashed across the Little Missouri, just as TR had done on so many early mornings, for a day's hike in the unspoiled back country of the beautiful bad-lands. Not an easy hike but one well worth the trip. I did not see another per-son all day, only deer, prairie dogs, rattlesnakes, buffalo, hawks, and the meadowlark. The landscape, a fascinating combination of excruciatingly tor-tured buttes, deep draws, and open meadowlands, looked exactly as when TR rode through the area searching for elk, deer, or sheep for the pot. I could sense the energy and youth of America and I almost expected to see the young buckskin-clad figure of my great-grandfather at any moment riding up from one of the river bottoms. I began to understand better his unbound-ed love for this beautiful land.

Africa gave me a different TR. With a Masai warroir I stalked the same plains. I observed elephants mating, broke up a lion hunt in its very last stage before the kill, and watched huge herds of wildebeests, zebras, and gazelles slowly make their way across the plains. I visited Lake Naivasha where TR had shot hippos, and stayed with the grandson of the man who hosted TR when he was there in 1910. I spent several days on Lamu, an island off the coast of Kenya, which today is reminiscent of Mombasa when TR visited it at the start of his trip. Lamu is a Swahili port with dirt streets, no high rise hotels, and the only auto is owned by the island gov-ernor. The people, who are a mix of Arab and African and could serve as illustrations for Ali Baba and the forty thieves, earn their living in exactly the same way as their ancestors. Their little boats, Arab dhows, have not changed in design in hundreds of years and are identical to those TR noted. In this part of the world I frequently felt a mature ghost of TR, who knew more of the world, had lost some of his youthful innocence, but still possessed the same energy and purpose.

In Brazil, I experienced a totally different ghost of my great-grandfather. In 1992 I retraced his harrowing trip down an unexplored Amazon tributary about which you will read in this book. Through an extraordinary series of events, TR and his son Kermit joined Brazil's famous explorer Col. Candido Rondon on an expedition to discover the course of what was then known as the River of Doubt. It does not take much imagination to understand TR's delight at the opportunity to join an expedition that was, for Brazil, the mod-ern day equivalent of Lewis and Clark's famous trip. It turned out to be the most difficult and perilous adventure of his life. Rapids followed rapids, the danger of native attacks was ever present, the food ran out, disease struck, TR almost died, one person was killed in the rapids, another was murdered, and the murderer escaped to the jungle and was never seen again. The odds of the rest of them surviving seemed slim. But return they did, with a very sick and gaunt TR who had lost an incredible 55 pounds.

The river, renamed the Rio Roosevelt, was as wild and remote when I descended it as it was in TR's time. During the four weeks we were on the river, I often felt the presence of TR. He seemed everywhere—sometimes at night in camp while, just as he, I listened to the thunder of the wild rapids which lay before us, sometimes when sitting in the rafts lazily floating down the calm stretches enjoying the equatorial sun and watching the flocks of parrots, the clouds of multicolored butterflies, or listening to the howler monkeys. Perhaps I felt him most strongly when one day we found, with some difficulty, an extraordinary outcropping of rock where TR and Rondon had been photographed; the picture was used as the frontispiece for TR's book about his adventure. But this was a different TR—an older man close to the end of his life. The trip was an extremely unpleasant one for him. During most of the journey, all he wanted was to get through it and more importantly to get his son out alive. Although I had a marvelous time on my expedition, I continued to be aware of TR's presence and especially his discomfort and anxiety, so foreign to his optimistic nature. It was certainly not a happy place for him, and most historians believe that this trip played a major role in his early death a few years later.

I now think that perhaps I was wrong when I wrote that I never knew my great-grandfather. He has been all around me for many years. I hope this book will help you, the readers, to also get to know from TR's own words a little about the adventures that so defined his life.

## INTRODUCTION

# THE STRENUOUS LIFE

## *by Anthony Brandt*

YOU CANNOT SUM THEODORE ROOSEVELT UP. HE WAS TOO MANY MEN IN
*one, a naval historian and a historian of the American West, an ornithologist of the
first rank, an outdoorsman, a cattleman with ranches on the Little Missouri River in
the Dakota badlands, a writer of considerable talent, an explorer, a big game hunter,
one of the country's first and greatest conservationists, a New York City police
commissioner and, on the national level, a civil service reformer, a colonel who led his
regiment into battle, and of course the twenty-sixth President of the United States.*

*He was also once a deputy sheriff, serving under Hell Roaring Bill Jones, as he was
known, to distinguish him from Three Seven Bill Jones and Texas Bill Jones, also res-
ident in the Dakotas. In the late winter of 1886 three horse thieves stole his boat and
made off with it downstream. The thieves were suspected of a number of crimes—he calls
them hard cases, these three—but Roosevelt had no fear of them and was determined
to catch them and did. They had taken the only boat in the area so he had two of his
men, Sewall and Dow, quickly build another one. Then the three of them set out
downriver after the thieves. A few days later they surprised them in their camp.*

*So add lawman to the list above. And then reader. When he wasn't guarding these
particular thieves on the difficult trip to bring them to jail, he was reading a novel: Tolstoy's
Anna Karenina. It's an interesting thought: Anna Karenina, an urban creature if ever
there was one, in the badlands. "My surroundings were quite gray enough," he reported,
"to harmonize well with Tolstoy." He sometimes read a book a day and once complained
to someone who had sent him a history of early Greece that it wasn't long enough. When
a new ambassador from France came to introduce himself, Roosevelt discussed the
ambassador's works on medieval French history with him. He had, of course, read*

them. *He could identify birds by their song alone. He was a skilled taxidermist. When he was 22 years old and touring Europe he climbed the Matterhorn and had enough energy left the same day to have dinner at the hotel and then go out to visit friends staying in the area. He was a prodigy of energy, of intelligence, and of courage both physical and moral. He was the first President to invite a black man—Booker T. Washington, as it happened—to dinner in the White House. He took a great deal of grief for it. He won the Nobel Peace Prize for his work bringing the Russo-Japanese War of 1905 to an end. He was responsible for creating five National Parks, 51 federal bird refuges, and 150 national forests. He could speak German and French but regretted all his life that he did not know enough Greek and Latin to read Homer and Virgil in the original. He was largely responsible for the construction of the Panama Canal.*

*You cannot sum him up. You can only stand in awe of him.*

*This anthology collects some of Roosevelt's most interesting writings on his numerous experiences outdoors, including the episode with the boat thieves. His interest in nature, hunting, and outdoor adventure preceded his interest in politics and it never left him. Even as President he would get out as often as possible into the nearest thing to wilderness the District of Columbia had to offer, Rock Creek Park, taking various notables with him—the Secretary of the Interior, James Garfield, son of the former President; Major General Leonard Wood, who had been with him in Cuba at the charge up San Juan Hill during the Spanish-American War; Gifford Pinchot, chief of the Forest Service were a few—and scramble over cliff faces, swim Rock Creek itself or maybe the Potomac, even in winter with ice on the water. They would make point-to-point excursions in which all parties would agree beforehand to swim, to climb over, or to dig under any obstacle, but not to go around it.*

*Roosevelt was physically tough. In an exercise called "singlesticks" he and Leonard Wood would put on helmets and body pads and fight each other in the White House with large ash rods. He was foxhunting once on the north shore of Long Island near his home at Sagamore Hill when he fell off his horse, breaking his left arm, but he got back on his horse and finished the hunt anyway.*

*The toughness was an unexpected outcome for a child who had begun life with what seemed at the time insurmountable problems with his health. Born in New York City on October 27, 1858, he suffered from asthma almost from the beginning of his life and long successions of colds, fevers, and a kind of nervous diarrhea that the family called cholera morbus. He was not expected to live long. He lived sixty years, but he remained scrawny and frail through his early childhood. He was even then, however, a voracious reader, immersing himself in adventure stories and the battles of epic heroes, who became his models. When he was able to be outside he became fascinated by birds and other animals and read up on them until he had acquired a remarkable expertise for* a young boy. When he went to Harvard in the 1870s he went intending to become a naturalist, and was only persuaded not to when he fell in love and realized that he wanted a better life for his bride-to-be than any naturalist could ever afford.

He came from the moneyed, patrician class where going to Harvard or Yale or, if you were from the South, Princeton, was taken as a matter of course. The Roosevelts were an old, aristocratic New York City family, and his father, for whom he was named, was a highly respected member of what we would still call the Eastern Establishment. It was his father who inspired young Theodore—Teedie was his nickname—to try to work through his bad health and frailty by exercising and lifting weights. On an early trip to Europe that lasted over a year his father dragged him off on long walks in the Alps even as he was recovering from attacks of fever and asthma. Despite his illnesses he had amazing reserves of nervous energy. "You must make your body," his father told him, and the boy did just that, working out nearly every day for two years. He took up boxing after two other boys humiliated him in a fight. He had not just the energy but also the will to do whatever he set out to do. Over time, the illnesses began to recede. By his late teens they were more or less gone. By his late teens, indeed, so remarkable a person was he, people were already predicting that he would someday become President.

If he did not become a naturalist, or an explorer, or a rancher, or possibly a writer, instead. In fact he became all of these things. He was enough of a writer to make a living at it when he had to, and he sometimes did. His Harvard education turned him toward a political career, but he spent summers as a young man in the Adirondacks and his first published work was a catalog called "The Summer Birds of the Adirondacks." He was eighteen when he wrote it. He spent time in the northern Maine woods as well. There he met Messrs. Sewall and Dow, the woodsmen he would later bring to the Dakotas to work for him and the same men who joined him in the pursuit of the three thieves. They accompanied him when he climbed Mt. Katahdin and on other excursions into the Maine wilderness. They would remain lifelong friends as well as employees. He was in many respects a snob when he was a young man, but he knew natural aristocrats when he met them.

He found them all through the West. His first trip west was a hunting trip he took with his brother, Elliott, to Illinois, Iowa, and Minnesota, shooting deer, elk, and whatever else landed in his sights. He was fourteen when his father gave him his first gun, and he used it to shoot birds and other animals that he had learned to stuff. Hunting did not carry the social stigma it does in some quarters today. In the late 1870s and early 1880s there were still buffalo left on the Plains, still bounties on cougars in the woods of Pennsylvania. Passenger pigeons still filled the skies. Roosevelt would come to see during his lifetime the devastation over-hunting would cause in wildlife populations, and he would do something about it. Well before he became President of the United States he founded and was the first president of the Boone & Crockett Club, an organization devoted to the study and conservation of game animals. He was never sentimental about animals and seldom hesitated to shoot any game animal he was after. Nevertheless he was quick to understand the wastefulness of indiscriminate hunting. For him hunting was a manly sport that required a certain noblesse oblige in the hunter. The dangers and the difficulty had to be real, the odds at least reasonably fair. He once killed a cougar with a knife rather than risk shooting one of the hunting dogs that surrounded it. A grizzly bear he had shot and mortally wounded at close range almost took his head off with a swipe of its paw. A few inches closer and Roosevelt would have been dead.

This book is full of hunting stories, which he never tired of telling. It was one he did not tell, however, that created a legend. During his first term as President, in 1903, he took a hunting trip into the Yazoo River Valley in Mississippi in search of black bear, but for five days he and his guides could find no bears. When the dogs at last cornered a bear in a pond, one of the guides roped it and then stunned it with the butt of his rifle—and called for Roosevelt to come and shoot it. When he got there he found a small, bloody bear tied to a tree. He would not shoot and left in disgust. The incident got into the papers, and a political cartoonist for the Washington Post drew it up as a comment on Roosevelt's policies toward race, which were advanced for the time. Roosevelt the white man refused to shoot the black bear: he was "drawing the line in Mississippi." He followed that cartoon up with more, making the bear a symbol not just of Roosevelt's racial politics but of Roosevelt himself. That winter the Stieff toy factory in Germany shipped stuffed black bears to the stores of America. Someone had the wit to call it Teddy's Bear, after Roosevelt. A shortened version—Teddy Bear—stuck.

Four years later, it's worth noting, Roosevelt made the trip south again, this time to the canebrake country of Louisiana, and shot a bear.

But if he took pleasure in shooting animals, he also took pleasure in saving species and creating forest preserves and national parks where animals could find a refuge. In his capacity as president of the Boone & Crockett Club he lobbied Congress and helped de-commercialize Yellowstone National Park in the 1890s. He was a complicated man. The love of hunting and the insistence on conservation was just one of the contradictions he embodied. He loved war, too. The Spanish-American War of the late 1890s was at least in part his creation. As Assistant Secretary of the Navy he was instrumental in bringing the U. S. Navy up to fighting strength, and it was he who sent Admiral Dewey to the Philippines even before the war started, just in case war should break out, to destroy the Spanish fleet there. When war did break out he resigned his Navy post to form his own volunteer regiment, the Rough Riders, and he personally led it up San Juan Hill in Cuba while under heavy fire—while all around him, indeed, his comrades were falling. Yet while he loved war, he devoted much of his Presidency to making peace, first secretly heading off a threat to the Monroe Doctrine from Germany when it was planning to invade Venezuela to settle unpaid debts; then negotiating an end to the Russo-Japanese War. "Speak softly and carry a big stick" was his motto. It was a folk saying from a West African tribe; he adopted it and made it his own.

It was hunting that took him to Africa as soon as his second term as President came to an end in 1909. Since he had spent a good part of his Presidency reining in the big trusts that dominated the U. S. economy, Wall Street was glad to see him go. The great financier J. P. Morgan hoped that the lions he would hunt in Africa would "do their duty." The trip was ostensibly scientific in nature. He was planning to bring back untold numbers of "specimens" for the benefit of the Smithsonian Institution and he took no fewer than three naturalists with him on safari, but in truth the trip was more a chance for him to hunt the legendary animals of the African plains. In typical fashion he rode the cowcatcher on the train out to Nairobi so he wouldn't miss anything. He was irrepressible. He told one questioner, "I feel that this is my last chance for something in the nature of a great adventure."

He said much the same thing when he went to explore in the Amazon basin four years later. It was "my last chance to be a boy." An old English friend of his, advising someone who was going to have to deal with him as President, told him to remember that Roosevelt was really six years old. He was a boy who loved power and who used it sometimes impetuously, suddenly, without mature consideration, but the overwhelming force of his personality often carried the day regardless. He came back from Africa after a year abroad unable to stand being out of power, and ran for President again in 1912, as an independent. If he had won it's almost certain that the United States would have entered World War I long before 1917.

I have divided this collection into three main sections, corresponding to three rough divisions in his life—the years out West hunting; the Spanish-American War and the Presidency; and the major expeditions to Africa and the Amazon, with a chapter as well from his last book about his experiences in the wild. Roosevelt is such a good writer that the selections need little comment and I have tried to keep it to a minimum, with short introductions placing the selections in context. Roosevelt believed in what he called in a speech the strenuous life. Vigor was a word much on his lips. He believed in the "strong and brave and high-minded," he told his audience. "Our country calls," he went on, "not for the life of ease but for the life of strenuous endeavor."

He spent his life answering that call. But never grimly. What makes him so appealing a character is that he enjoyed himself so much. "The joy of living is his who has the heart to demand it," he wrote in his last book. Joy was another of his watchwords. It is hard to think of an American who achieved more, or lived more intensely, or took more pleasure in his life. He was one of a kind. This collection aims to celebrate the unique pleasure of reading him.

★

# PART ONE

# Out West

★

# Out West

Roosevelt made his first trip to the far West in 1883. His father had died and left him enough money to buy land on the north shore of Long Island and start to build his house there, at Sagamore Hill. He had married a woman from Boston named Alice Hathaway Lee, and he had already served a term in the New York State Assembly, where he rapidly became known as a reformer. He had made a name for himself at Harvard as a fashionable—almost laughably fashionable—dresser; but it was there that he did the preliminary work on his first major book, The Naval War of 1812, which historians still treat with respect. For all the high fashion of his dress, he was deeply addicted to exercise and the outdoors. He was already, in other words, the same bundle of contradictions he would always be. On his second trip to the Dakotas in 1884, one of his first orders of business was to dude himself up in the best possible buckskin shirt and pants, made to order, in the style worn by Davy Crockett. But that did not prevent him from becoming a highly skilled hunter and cowman capable of spending thirteen hours straight in the saddle.

He went west at the invitation of a Commander H. H. Gorringe, whom he met at a dinner party in New York. Gorringe was in the process of setting up a hunting ranch for wealthy Eastern dudes on the Little Missouri River in the Dakota Territory where they could hunt deer, buffalo, antelope, and other animals, and Roosevelt was eager to go hunting for big game. His brother, Elliott, had just returned from India with his own hunting trophies, so we can add to the mix a certain amount of sibling rivalry. The trip was set for the fall but at the last minute Gorringe backed out of the trip. Roosevelt went anyway. The train dropped him off very late at night at the town—town is too strong a word; it was no more than a collection of buildings—of Little Missouri. He banged on the door of the Pyramid Park Hotel, where Gorringe's name got him in, and was ushered to the dormitory at the top where guests slept on cots.

He stayed long enough on that first trip to fall in love with the place. The Little Missouri River runs through the Dakota Badlands, where the plains look as though some giant had taken an axe to them, and the beauty of the landscape has that raw strong feel to it of something primordial, something no one will ever succeed in domesticating. Before he had left he had managed, after sleeping in the open in the rain, falling off his horse, exhausting himself, and dragging his horse out of quicksand, to bag his first buffalo. He had also written a check for $14,000 to buy a share in a cattle ranching operation. He was definitely going to be back.

He came back the following summer, after suffering a terrible double loss: his young wife and his mother died on the same day. The West became for him that year a refuge from grief, if there is such a thing, and he spent a good deal of time there in 1884 and 1885. He began construction of a ranch house on the land he had acquired. He took a hunting trip into the Bighorn Mountains looking for grizzly. He literally learned the ropes and worked his cattle hard enough to win the respect of the men who worked for him. Then he wrote his first book about these Western experiences: Hunting Trips of a Ranchman. G. P. Putnam's Sons published it in the summer of 1885 and it did well, going through several printings. (The first edition had a picture of Roosevelt in his beloved buckskin outfit.) The reviewers liked it as well as the public. It was then, perhaps, that Roosevelt saw that he could make money as a writer. His style is full of charm and ease. The writing rambles, but it is not without direction. Our first selection illustrates this nicely. It is Chapter Six, "A Trip on the Prairie," and it describes one of the many solo trips Roosevelt took on his horse, Manitou, into the emptiness of this enormous landscape. The second selection from this book is Chapter Eight, "The Lordly Buffalo," which begins with an explanation of the fate of the buffalo since the coming of the white man and ends with Roosevelt's account of that first hunt for buffalo on his first trip to Dakota in 1883. This chapter contains the seeds of his later passion for conservation in its thorough examination of the depletion of buffalo on the plains, and the reasons for it. But it also shows no awareness on his part of the contradiction between believing in the preservation of the buffalo and shooting one of the last specimens of the animal in the Badlands. Roosevelt saw a real distinction, however, between hunters like himself, whom he thought of as sportsmen, and the "butchers" who killed for commercial reasons and in unconscionable numbers. It is a distinction we may find hard to make under the circumstances but he was firm in it. He also shows that he was developing a depth of knowledge about the game he shot that came close to the scientific. The hunter in him was never far from the naturalist.

Our third selection is Chapter Ten, "Old Ephraim," in which Roosevelt shoots his first grizzly bear. By the time Roosevelt went west grizzlies had retreated, for the most part, off the plains, although they were plains animals originally. Lewis and Clark encountered them from the Dakotas all the way to the Rockies, but not in the mountains. By Roosevelt's time you could only find them in the mountains.

# A Trip on the Prairie

*Hunting Trips of a Ranchman*

NO ANTELOPE ARE FOUND, EXCEPT RARELY, IMMEDIATELY ROUND MY ranch-house, where the ground is much too broken to suit them; but on the great prairies, ten or fifteen miles off, they are plentiful, though far from as abundant as they were a few years ago when the cattle were first driven into the land. By plainsmen they are called either prong-horn or antelope, but are most often known by the latter and much less descriptive title. Where they are found they are always very conspicuous figures in the landscape; for, far from attempting to conceal itself, an antelope really seems anxious to take up a prominent position, caring only to be able to itself see its foes. It is the smallest in size of the plains game, even smaller than a white-tail deer; and its hide is valueless, being thin and porous, and making very poor buckskin. In its whole appearance and structure it is a most singular creature. Unlike all other hollow-horned animals, it sheds its horns annually, exactly as the deer shed their solid antlers; but the shedding process in the prong-horn occupies but a very few days, so short a time, indeed, that many hunters stoutly deny that it takes place at all. The hair is of remarkable texture, very long, coarse, and brittle; in the spring it comes off in handfuls. In strong contrast to the reddish yellow of the other parts of the body, the rump is pure white, and when alarmed or irritated every hair in the white patch bristles up on end, greatly increasing the apparent area of the color. The flesh, unlike that of any other plains animal, is equally good all through the year. In the fall it is hardly so juicy as deer venison, but in the spring, when no other kind of game is worth eating, it is perfectly good; and at that time of the year, if we have to get fresh meat, we would rather kill antelope than any thing else; and as the bucks are always to be instantly distinguished from the does by their large horns, we confine ourselves to them, and so work no harm to the species.

The antelope is a queer-looking rather than a beautiful animal. The curious pronged horns, great bulging eyes, and strange bridle-like marks and bands on the face and throat are more striking, but less handsome, than the delicate head and branching antlers of a deer; and it entirely lacks the latter animal's grace of movement. In its form and look, when standing still, it is rather angular and goat-like, and its movements merely have the charm that comes from lightness, speed, and agility. Its gait is singularly regular and even, without any of the bounding, rolling movement of a deer; and it is, consequently, very easy to hit running, compared with other kinds of game.

Antelope possess a most morbid curiosity. The appearance of any thing out of the way, or to which they are not accustomed, often seems to drive them nearly beside themselves with mingled fright and desire to know what it is, a combination of feelings that throws them into a perfect panic, during whose continuance they will at times seem utterly unable to take care of themselves. In very remote, wild places, to which no white man often penetrates, the appearance of a white-topped wagon will be enough to excite this feeling in the prong-horn, and in such cases it is not unusual for a herd to come up and circle round the strange object heedless of rifle-shots. This curiosity is particularly strong in the bucks during rutting-time, and one method of hunting them is to take advantage of it, and "flag" them up to the hunters by waving a red handkerchief or some other object to and fro in the air. In very wild places they can sometimes be flagged up, even after they have seen the man; but, elsewhere, the latter must keep himself carefully concealed behind a ridge or hillock, or in tall grass, and keep cautiously waving the handkerchief overhead. The antelope will look fixedly at it, stamp, snort, start away, come nearer by fits and starts, and run from one side to the other, the better to see it. Sometimes a wary old buck will keep this up for half an hour, and at the end make off; but, again, the attraction may prove too strong, and the antelope comes slowly on until within rifle-shot. This method of hunting, however, is not so much practised now as formerly, as the antelope are getting continually shyer and more difficult to flag. I have never myself shot one in this manner, though I have often seen the feat performed, and have several times tried it myself, but always with the result that after I had made my arm really weak with waving the handkerchief to and fro, the antelope, which had been shifting about just out of range, suddenly took to its heels and made off.

No other kind of plains game, except the big-horn, is as shy and sharp-sighted as the antelope; and both its own habits and the open nature of the ground on which it is found render it peculiarly difficult to stalk. There is no cover, and if a man is once seen by the game the latter will not let him get out of sight again, unless it decides to go off at a gait that soon puts half a dozen miles between them. It shifts its position, so as to keep the hunter continually in sight. Thus, if it is standing on a ridge, and the hunter disappear into a ravine up which he intends to crawl, the antelope promptly gallops off to some other place of observation from which its foe is again visible; and this is repeated until the animal at last makes up its mind to start for good. It keeps up an incessant watch, being ever on the look-out for danger, far or near; and as it can see an immense distance, and has its home on ground so level that a horseman can be made out a mile off, its attention is apt to be attracted when still four or five rifle-shots beyond range, and after it has once caught a glimpse of the foe, the latter might as well give up all hopes of getting the game.

But while so much more wary than deer, it is also at times much more foolish, and has certain habits—some of which, such as its inordinate curiosity and liability to panic, have already been alluded to—that tend to its destruction. Ordinarily, it is a far more difficult feat to kill an antelope than it is to kill a deer, but there are times when the former can be slaughtered in such numbers that it becomes mere butchery.

The prong-horn is pre-eminently a gregarious animal. It is found in bands almost all the year through. During the two or three days after he has shed his horns and while the new ones are growing the buck retires to some out-of-the-way spot, and while bringing forth her fawns the doe stays by herself. But as soon as possible each again rejoins the band; and the fawns become members of it at a remarkably early age. In the late fall, when the bitter cold has begun, a large number of these bands collect together, and immense herds are formed which last throughout the winter. Thus at this season a man may travel for days through regions where antelope are most plentiful during the hot months and never see one; but if he does come across any they will be apt to be in great numbers, most probably along the edge of the Bad Lands, where the ground is rolling rather than broken, but where there is some shelter from the furious winter gales. Often they will even come down to the river bottom or find their way up to some plateau. They now always hang closely about the places they have chosen for their winter haunts, and seem very reluctant to leave them. They go in dense herds, and when starved and weak with cold are less shy; and can often be killed in great numbers by any one who has found out where they are—though a true sportsman will not molest them at this season.

Sometimes a small number of individuals will at this time get separated from the main herd and take up their abode in some place by themselves; and when they have once done so it is almost impossible to drive them away. Last winter a solitary prong-horn strayed into the river bottom at the mouth of a wide creek-valley, half a mile from my ranch, and stayed there for three months, keeping with the cattle, and always being found within a mile of the same spot. A little band at the same time established itself on a large plateau, about five miles long by two miles wide, some distance up the river above me, and afforded fine sport to a couple of ranchmen who lived not far from its base. The antelope, twenty or thirty in number, would not leave the plateau, which lies in the midst of broken ground; for it is a peculiarity of these animals, which will be spoken of further on, that they will try to keep in the open ground at any cost or hazard. The two ranchmen agreed never to shoot at the antelope on foot, but only to try to kill them from horseback, either with their revolvers or their Winchesters. They thus hunted them for the sake of the sport purely; and certainly they got plenty of fun out of them. Very few horses indeed are as fast as a prong-horn; and these few did not include any owned by either of my two friends. But the antelope were always being obliged to break back from the edge of the plateau, and so were forced constantly to offer opportunities for cutting them off; and these opportunities were still further increased by the two hunters separating. One of them would go to the upper end of the plateau and start the band, riding after them at full speed. They would distance him, but would be checked in their career by coming to the brink of the cliff; then they would turn at an angle and give their pursuer a chance to cut them off; and if they kept straight up the middle the other hunter would head them. When a favorable moment came the hunters would dash in as close as possible and empty their revolvers or repeaters into the herd; but it is astonishing how hard it is, when riding a horse at full speed, to hit any object, unless it is directly under the muzzle of the weapon. The number of cartridges spent compared to the number of prong-horn killed was enormous; but the fun and excitement of the chase were the main objects with my friends, to whom the actual killing of the game was of entirely secondary importance. They went out after them about a dozen times during the winter, and killed in all ten or fifteen prong-horns.

A prong-horn is by far the fleetest animal on the plains; one can outrun and outlast a deer with the greatest ease. Very swift greyhounds can overtake them, if hunted in leashes or couples; but only a remarkably good dog can run one down single-handed. Besides prong-horn are most plucky little creatures, and will make a most resolute fight against a dog or wolf, striking with their forefeet and punching with their not very formidable horns, and are so quick and wiry as to be really rather hard to master.

Antelope have the greatest objection to going on any thing but open ground, and seem to be absolutely unable to make a high jump. If a band is caught feeding in the bottom of a valley leading into a plain they invariably make a rush straight to the mouth, even if the foe is stationed there, and will run heedlessly by him, no matter how narrow the mouth is, rather than not try to reach the open country. It is almost impossible to force them into even a small patch of brush, and they will face almost certain death rather than try to leap a really very trifling obstacle. If caught in a glade surrounded by a slight growth of brushwood, they make no effort whatever to get through or over this growth, but dash frantically out through the way by which they got in. Often the deer, especially the black-tail, will wander out on the edge of the plain frequented by antelope; and it is curious to see the two animals separate the second there is an alarm, the deer making for the broken country, while the antelope scud for the level plains. Once two of my men nearly caught a couple of antelope in their hands. They were out driving in the buck-board, and saw two antelope, a long distance ahead, enter the mouth of a wash-out (a canyon *in petto*); they had strayed away from the prairie to the river bottom, and were evidently feeling lost. My two men did not think much of the matter but when opposite the mouth of the wash-out, which was only thirty feet or so wide, they saw the two antelope starting to come out, having found that it was a blind passage, with no outlet at the other end. Both men jumped out of the buck-board and ran to the entrance; the two antelope dashed frantically to and fro inside the wash-out. The sides were steep, but a deer would have scaled them at once; yet the antelope seemed utterly unable to do this, and finally broke out past the two men and got away. They came so close that the men were able to touch each of them, but their movements were too quick to permit of their being caught.

However, though unable to leap any height, an antelope can skim across a level jump like a bird, and will go over water-courses and wash-outs that very few horses indeed will face. A mountain-sheep, on the other hand, is a marvellous vertical leaper; the black-tail deer comes next; the white-tail is pretty good, and the elk is at any rate better than the antelope; but when it comes to horizontal jumping the latter can beat them all.

In May or early June the doe brings forth her fawns, usually two in number, for she is very prolific. She makes her bed in some valley or hollow, and keeps with the rest of the band, only returning to the fawns to feed them. They lie out in the grass or under some slight bush, but are marvellously hard to find. By instinct they at once know how to crouch down so as to be as inconspicuous as possible. Once we scared away a female prong-horn from an apparently perfectly level hill-side; and in riding along passed over the spot she had left and came upon two little fawns that could have been but a few hours old. They lay flat in the grass, with their legs doubled under them and their necks and heads stretched out on the ground. When we took them up and handled them, they soon got used to us and moved awkwardly round, but at any sudden noise or motion they would immediately squat flat down again. But at a very early age the fawns learn how to shift for themselves, and can then run almost as fast as their parents, even when no larger than a jack-rabbit. Once, while we were haying, a couple of my cowboys spent half an hour in trying to run down and capture a little fawn, but they were unable to catch it, it ran so fast and ducked about so quickly. Antelope fawns are very easily tamed and make most amusing pets. We have had two or three, but have never succeeded in rearing any of them; but some of the adjoining ranchmen have been more fortunate. They are not nearly so pretty as deer fawns, having long, gangling legs and angular bodies, but they are much more familiar and interesting. One of my neighbors has three live prong-horns, as well as two little spotted white-tail deer. The deer fawns are always skulking about, and are by no means such bold inquisitive little creatures as the small antelope are. The latter have a nurse in the shape of a fat old ewe; and it is funny to see her, when alarmed, running off at a waddling gait, while her ungainly little foster-children skip round and round her, cutting the most extraordinary antics. There are a couple of very large dogs, mastiffs, on the place, whose natural solemnity is completely disconcerted by the importunities and fearlessness of the little antelope fawns. Where one goes the other two always follow; and so one of the mastiffs, while solemnly blinking in the sun, will suddenly find himself charged at full speed by the three queer little creatures, who will often fairly butt up against him. The uneasy look of the dog, and his efforts to get out of the way without compromising his dignity, are really very comical.

Young fawns seem to give out no scent, and thus many of them escape from the numerous carnivorous beasts that are ever prowling about at night over the prairie, and which, during the spring months, are always fat from feeding on the bodies of the innocents they have murdered. If discovered by a fox or coyote during its first few days of existence a little fawn has no chance of life, although the mother, if present, will fight desperately for it; but after it has acquired the use of its legs it has no more to fear than have any of the older ones.

Sometimes the fawns fall victims to the great Golden Eagle. This grand bird, the War Eagle of the Sioux, is not very common in the Bad Lands, but is sometimes still seen with us; and, as everywhere else, its mere presence adds a certain grandeur to its lonely haunts. Two or three years ago a nest was found by one of my men on the face of an almost inaccessible cliff, and a young bird was taken out from it and reared in a roughly extemporized cage. Wherever the eagle exists it holds undisputed sway over every thing whose size does not protect it from the great bird's beak and talons; not only does it feed on hares, grouse, and ducks, but it will also attack the young fawns of the deer and antelope. Still, the eagle is but an occasional foe, and aside from man, the only formidable enemies the antelope has to fear are the wolves and coyotes. These are very destructive to the young, and are always lounging about the band to pick up any wounded straggler; in winter, when the ground is slippery and the antelope numbed and weak, they will often commit great havoc even among those that are grown up.

The voice of the antelope is not at all like that of the deer. Instead of bleating it utters a quick, harsh noise, a kind of bark; a little like the sound "kau," sharply and clearly repeated. It can be heard a long distance off; and is usually uttered when the animal is a little startled or surprised by the presence of something it does not understand.

The prong-horn cannot go without water any longer than a deer can, and will go great distances to get it; for space is nothing to a traveller with such speed and such last. No matter how dry and barren may be the desert in which antelope are found, it may be taken for granted that they are always within reaching distance of some spring or pool of water, and that they visit it once a day. Once or twice I have camped out by some pool, which was the only one for miles around, and in every such case have been surprised at night by the visits of the antelope, who, on finding that their drinking-place was tenanted, would hover round at a short distance, returning again and again and continually uttering the barking "kau, kau," until they became convinced that there was no hope of their getting in, when they would set off at a run for some other place.

Prong-horn perhaps prefer the rolling prairies of short grass as their home, but seem to do almost equally well on the desolate and monotonous wastes where the sage-brush and prickly pear and a few blades of coarse grass are the only signs of plant life to be seen. In such places, the prong-horn, the sage cock, the rattlesnake, and the horned frog alone are able to make out a livelihood.

The horned frog is not a frog at all, but a lizard,—a queer, stumpy little fellow with spikes all over the top of its head and back, and given to moving in the most leisurely manner imaginable. Nothing will make it hurry. If taken home it becomes a very tame and quaint but also very uninteresting little pet.

Rattlesnakes are only too plentiful everywhere; along the river bottoms, in the broken, hilly ground, and on the prairies and the great desert wastes alike. Every cowboy kills dozens each season. To a man wearing top-boots there is little or no danger while he is merely walking about, for the fangs cannot get through the leather, and the snake does not strike as high as the knee. Indeed the rattlesnake is not nearly as dangerous as are most poisonous serpents, for it always gives fair warning before striking, and is both sluggish and timid. If it can it will get out of the way, and only coils up in its attitude of defence when it believes that it is actually menaced. It is, of course, however, both a danger-ous and a disagreeable neighbor, and one of its annoying traits is the fondness it displays for crawling into a hut or taking refuge among the blankets left out on the ground. Except in such cases men are rarely in danger from it, unless they happen to be stooping over, as was the case with one of my cowboys who had leaned over to pick up a log, and was almost bitten by a snake which was underneath it; or unless the snake is encountered while stalking an animal. Once I was creeping up to an antelope under cover of some very low sage-brush—so low that I had to lie flat on my face and push myself along with my hands and feet. While cautiously moving on in this way I was electrified by hearing almost by my ears the well-known, ominous "whir-r-r" of a rattlesnake, and on hastily glancing up there was the reptile, not ten feet away from me, all coiled up and waiting. I backed off and crawled to one side, the rattler turn-ing its head round to keep watch over my movements; when the stalk was over (the antelope took alarm and ran off before I was within rifle-shot) I came back, hunted up the snake, and killed it. Although I have known of several men being bitten, I know of but one case where the bite caused the death of a human being. This was a girl who had been out milking, and was returning, in bare feet; the snake struck her just above the ankle, and in her fright she fell and was struck again in the neck. The double wound was too much for her, and the poison killed her in the course of a couple of hours.

Occasionally one meets a rattlesnake whose rattle has been lost or injured; and such a one is always dangerous, because it strikes without warning. I once nearly lost a horse by the bite of one of these snakes without rattles. I was riding along a path when my horse gave a tremendous start and jump; look-ing back I saw that it had been struck at by a rattlesnake with an injured tail, which had been lying hid in a bunch of grass, directly beside the path. Luckily it had merely hit the hard hoof, breaking one of its fangs.

Horses differ very much in their conduct toward snakes. Some show great fright at sight of them or on hearing their rattles, plunging and rearing and refusing to go anywhere near the spot; while others have no fear of them at all, being really perfectly stupid about them. Manitou does not lose his wits at all over them, but at the same time takes very good care not to come within striking distance.

Ranchmen often suffer some loss among their stock owing to snake-bites; both horned cattle and horses, in grazing, frequently coming on snakes and having their noses or cheeks bitten. Generally, these wounds are not fatal, though very uncomfortable; it is not uncommon to see a woe-begone looking mule with its head double the natural size, in consequence of having incau-tiously browsed over a snake. A neighbor lost a weak pony in this way; and one of our best steers also perished from the same cause. But in the latter case, the animal, like the poor girl spoken of above, had received two wounds with the poison fangs; apparently it had, while grazing with its head down, been first struck in the nose, and been again struck in the foreleg as it started away.

Of all kinds of hunting, the chase of the antelope is pre-eminently that requiring skill in the use of the rifle at long range. The distance at which shots have to be taken in antelope hunting is at least double the ordinary distance at which deer are fired at. In pursuing most other kinds of game, a hunter who is not a good shot may still do excellent work; but in prong-horn hunting, no man can make even a fairly good record unless he is a skilful marksman. I have myself done but little hunting after antelopes, and have not, as a rule, been very successful in the pursuit.

Ordinary hounds are rarely, or never, used to chase this game; but coursing it with greyhounds is as manly and exhilarating a form of sport as can be imagined,—a much better way of hunting it than is shooting it with the rifle, which latter, though needing more skill in the actual use of the weapon, is in every other respect greatly inferior as a sport to still-hunting the black-tail or big-horn.

I never but once took a trip of any length with antelope hunting for its chief object. This was one June, when all the men were away on the round-up. As is usual during the busy half of the ranchman's year, the spring and summer, when men have no time to hunt and game is out of condition, we had been living on salt pork, beans, potatoes, and bread; and I had hardly had a rifle in my hand for months;

so, finding I had a few days to spare, I thought I should take a short trip on the prairie, in the beautiful June weather, and get a little sport and a little fresh meat out of the bands of prong-horn bucks, which I was sure to encounter. Intending to be gone but a couple of days, it was not necessary to take many articles. Behind my saddle I carried a blanket for bedding, and an oil-skin coat to ward off the wet; a large metal cup with the handle riveted, not soldered, on, so that water could be boiled in it; a little tea and salt, and some biscuits; and a small water-proof bag containing my half dozen personal necessaries—not forgetting a book. The whole formed a small, light pack, very little encumbrance to stout old Manitou. In June, fair weather can generally be counted on in the dry plains country.

I started in the very earliest morning, when the intense brilliancy of the stars had just begun to pale before the first streak of dawn. By the time I left the river bottom and struck off up the valley of a winding creek, which led through the Bad Lands, the eastern sky was growing rosy; and soon the buttes and cliffs were lit up by the level rays of the cloudless summer sun. The air was fresh and sweet, and odorous with the sweet scents of the spring-time that was but barely passed; the dew lay heavy, in glittering drops, on the leaves and the blades of grass, whose vivid green, at this season, for a short time brightens the desolate and sterile-looking wastes of the lonely western plains. The rose-bushes were all in bloom, and their pink blossoms clustered in every point and bend of the stream; and the sweet, sad songs of the hermit thrushes rose from the thickets, while the meadow larks perched boldly in sight as they uttered their louder and more cheerful music. The round-up had passed by our ranch, and all the cattle with our brands, the maltese cross and cut dewlap, or the elk-horn and triangle, had been turned loose; they had not yet worked away from the river, and I rode by long strings of them, walking in single file off to the hills, or standing in groups to look at me as I passed.

Leaving the creek I struck off among a region of scoria buttes, the ground rising into rounded hills through whose grassy covering the red volcanic rock showed in places, while boulder-like fragments of it were scattered all through the valleys between. There were a few clumps of bushes here and there, and near one of them were two magpies, who lit on an old buffalo skull, bleached white by sun and snow. Magpies are birds that catch the eye at once from their bold black and white plumage and long tails; and they are very saucy and at the same time very cunning and shy. In spring we do not often see them; but in the late fall and winter they will come close round the huts and out-buildings on the look-out for any thing to eat. If a deer is hung up and they can get at it they will pick it to pieces with their sharp bills; and their carnivorous tastes and their habit of coming round hunters' camps after the game that is left out, call to mind their kinsman, the whiskey-jack or moose-bird of the northern forests.

After passing the last line of low, rounded scoria buttes, the horse stepped out on the border of the great, seemingly endless stretches of rolling or nearly level prairie, over which I had planned to travel and hunt for the next two or three days. At intervals of ten or a dozen miles this prairie was crossed by dry creeks, with, in places in their beds, pools or springs of water, and alongside a spindling growth of trees and bushes; and my intention was to hunt across these creeks, and camp by some water-hole in one of them at night.

I rode over the land in a general southerly course, bending to the right or left according to the nature of the ground and the likelihood of finding game. Most of the time the horse kept on a steady single-foot, but this was varied by a sharp lope every now and then, to ease the muscles of both steed and rider. The sun was well up, and its beams beat fiercely down on our heads from out of the cloudless sky; for at this season, though the nights and the early morning and late evening are cool and pleasant, the hours around noon are very hot. My glass was slung alongside the saddle, and from every one of the scattered hillocks the country was scanned carefully far and near; and the greatest caution was used in riding up over any divide, to be sure that no game on the opposite side was scared by the sudden appearance of my horse or myself.

Nowhere, not even at sea, does a man feel more lonely than when riding over the far-reaching, seemingly never-ending plains; and, after a man has lived a little while on or near them, their very vastness and loneliness and their melancholy monotony have a strong fascination for him. The landscape seems always the same, and after the traveller has plodded on for miles and miles he gets to feel as if the distance was indeed boundless. As far as the eye can see there is no break; either the prairie stretches out into perfectly level flats, or else there are gentle, rolling slopes, whose crests mark the divides between the drainage systems of the different creeks; and when one of these is ascended, immediately another precisely like it takes its place in the distance, and so roll succeeds roll in a succession as interminable as that of the waves of the ocean. Nowhere else does one seem so far off from all mankind; the plains stretch out in death-like and measure-less expanse, and as he journeys over them they will for many miles be lacking in all signs of life. Although he can see so far, yet all objects on the outermost verge of the horizon, even though within the ken of his vision, look unreal and strange; for there is no shade to take away from the bright glare, and at a little distance things seem to shimmer and dance in the hot rays of the sun. The ground is scorched to a dull brown, and against its monotonous expanse any objects stand out with a prominence that makes it difficult to judge of the distance at which they are. A mile off one can see, through the strange shimmering haze, the shadowy white outlines of something which looms vaguely up till it looks as large as the canvas-top of a prairie wagon; but as the horseman comes nearer it shrinks and dwindles and takes clearer form, until at last it changes into the ghastly staring skull of some mighty buffalo, long dead and gone to join the rest of his vanished race.

When the grassy prairies are left and the traveller enters a region of alkali desert and sage-brush, the look of the country becomes even more grim and forbidding. In places the alkali forms a white frost on the ground that glances in the sunlight like the surface of a frozen lake; the dusty little sage-brush, stunted and dried up, sprawls over the parched ground, from which it can hardly extract the small amount of nourishment necessary for even its weazened life; the spiny cactus alone seems to be really in its true home. Yet even in such places antelope will be found, as alert and as abounding with vivacious life as elsewhere. Owing to the magnifying and distorting power of the clear, dry plains air, every object, no matter what its shape or color or apparent distance, needs the closest examination. A magpie sitting on a white skull, or a couple of ravens, will look, a quarter of a mile off, like some curious beast; and time and again a raw hunter will try to stalk a lump of clay or a burnt stick; and after being once or twice disappointed he is apt to rush to the other extreme, and conclude too hastily that a given object is not an antelope, when it very possibly is.

During the morning I came in sight of several small bands or pairs of antelope. Most of them saw me as soon as or before I saw them, and after watching me with intense curiosity as long as I was in sight and at a distance, made off at once as soon as I went into a hollow or appeared to be approaching too near. Twice, in scanning the country narrowly with the glasses, from behind a sheltering divide, bands of prong-horn were seen that had not discovered me. In each case the horse was at once left to graze, while I started off after the game, nearly a mile distant. For the first half mile I could walk upright or go along half stooping; then, as the distance grew closer, I had to crawl on all fours and keep behind any little broken bank, or take advantage of a small, dry watercourse; and toward the end work my way flat on my face, wriggling like a serpent, using every stunted sage-brush or patch of cactus as a cover, bare-headed under the blazing sun. In each case, after nearly an hour's irksome, thirsty work, the stalk failed. One band simply ran off without a second's warning, alarmed at some awkward movement on my part, and without giving a chance for a shot. In the other instance, while still at very long and uncertain range, I heard the sharp barking alarm-note of one of the prong-horn; the whole band instantly raising their heads and gazing intently at their would-be destroyer. They were a very long way off; but, seeing it was hopeless to try to get nearer I rested my rifle over a little mound of earth and fired. The dust came up in a puff to one side of the nearest antelope; the whole band took a few jumps and turned again; the second shot struck at their feet, and they went off like so many race-horses, being missed again as they ran. I sat up by a sage-brush thinking they would of course not come back, when to my surprise I saw them wheel round with the precision of a cavalry squadron, all in line and fronting me, the white and brown markings on their heads and throats showing like the facings on soldiers' uniforms; and then back they came charging up till again within long range, when they wheeled their line as if on a pivot and once more made off, this time for good, not heeding an ineffectual fusillade from the Winchester. Antelope often go through a series of regular evolutions, like so many trained horsemen, wheeling, turning, halting, and running as if under command; and their coming back to again run the (as it proved very harmless) gauntlet of my fire was due either to curiosity or to one of those panicky freaks which occasionally seize those ordinarily wary animals, and cause them to run into danger easily avoided by creatures commonly much more readily approached than they are. I had fired half a dozen shots without effect; but while no one ever gets over his feeling of self-indignation at missing an easy shot at close quarters, any one who hunts antelope and is not of a disposition so timid as never to take chances, soon learns that he has to expect to expend a good deal of powder and lead before bagging his game.

By mid-day we reached a dry creek and followed up its course for a mile or so, till a small spot of green in the side of a bank showed the presence of water, a little pool of which lay underneath. The ground was so rotten that it was with difficulty I could get Manitou down where he could drink; but at last both of us satisfied our thirst, and he was turned loose to graze, with his saddle off, so as to cool his back, and I, after eating a biscuit, lay on my face on the ground—there was no shade of any sort near—and dozed until a couple of hours' rest and feed had put the horse in good trim for the afternoon ride. When it came to crossing over the dry creek on whose bank we had rested, we almost went down in a quicksand, and it was only by frantic struggles and flounderings that we managed to get over.

On account of these quicksands and mud-holes, crossing the creeks on the prairie is often very disagreeable work. Even when apparently perfectly dry the bottom may have merely a thin crust of hard mud and underneath a fathomless bed of slime. If the grass appears wet and with here and there a few tussocks of taller blades in it, it is well to avoid it. Often a man may have to go along a creek nearly a mile before he can find a safe crossing, or else run the risk of seeing his horse mired hard and fast. When a horse is once in a mud-hole it will perhaps so exhaust itself by its first desperate and fruitless strug-gle that it is almost impossible to get it out. Its bridle and saddle have to be taken off; if another horse is along the lariat is drawn from the pommel of the latter's saddle to the neck of the one that is in, and it is hauled out by main force. Otherwise a man may have to work half a day, fixing the horse's legs in the right position and then taking it by the forelock and endeavoring to get it to make a plunge; each plunge bringing it perhaps a few inches nearer the firm ground. Quicksands are even more dangerous than these mud-holes, as, if at all deep, a creature that cannot get out immediately is sure to be speed-ily engulfed. Many parts of the Little Missouri are impassable on account of these quicksands. Always in crossing unknown ground that looks dangerous it is best to feel your way very cautiously along, and, if possible, to find out some cattle trail or even game trail which can be followed.

For some time after leaving the creek nothing was seen; until, on coming over the crest of the next great divide, I came in sight of a band of six or eight prong-horn about a quarter of a mile off to my right hand. There was a slight breeze from the southeast, which blew diagonally across my path towards the antelopes. The latter, after staring at me a minute, as I rode slowly on, suddenly started at full speed to run directly up wind, and therefore in a direction that would cut the line of my course less than half a mile ahead of where I was. Knowing that when antelope begin running in a straight line they are very hard to turn, and seeing that they would have to run a longer distance than my horse would to intercept them, I clapped spurs into Manitou, and the game old fel-low, a very fleet runner, stretched himself down to the ground and seemed to go almost as fast as the quarry. As I had expected, the latter, when they saw me running, merely straightened themselves out and went on, possibly even faster than before, without changing the line of their flight, keeping right up wind. Both horse and antelope fairly flew over the ground, their courses being at an angle that would certainly bring them together. Two of the antelope led, by some fifty yards or so, the others, who were all bunched together. Nearer and nearer we came, Manitou, in spite of carrying myself and the pack behind the saddle, gamely holding his own, while the antelope, with outstretched necks, went at an even, regular gait that offered a strong contrast to the springing bounds with which a deer runs. At last the two leading animals crossed the line of my flight ahead of me; when I pulled short up, leaped from Manitou's back, and blazed into the band as they went by not forty yards off, aiming well ahead of a fine buck who was on the side nearest me. An antelope's gait is so even that it offers a good running mark; and as the smoke blew off I saw the buck roll over like a rabbit, with both shoulders broken. I then emptied the Winchester at the rest of the band, breaking one hind leg of a young buck. Hastily cutting the throat of, and opening, the dead buck, I again mounted and started off after the wounded one. But, though only on three legs, it went astonishingly fast, having had a good start; and after following it over a mile I gave up the pursuit, though I had gained a good deal; for the heat was very great, and I did not deem it well to tire the horse at the beginning of the trip. Returning to the carcass, I cut off the hams and strung them beside the saddle; an antelope is so spare that there is very little more meat on the body.

This trick of running in a straight line is another of the antelope's peculiar characteristics which frequently lead it into danger. Although with so much sharper eyes than a deer, antelope are in many ways far stupider animals, more like sheep, and they especially resemble the latter in their habit of following a leader, and in their foolish obstinacy in keeping to a course they have once adopted. If a horseman starts to head off a deer the latter will always turn long before he has come within range, but quite often an antelope will merely increase his speed and try to pass ahead of his foe. Almost always, however, one if alone will keep out of gunshot, owing to the speed at which he goes, but if there are several in a band which is well strung out, the leader only cares for his own safety and passes well ahead himself. The others follow like sheep, without turning in the least from the line the first followed, and thus may pass within close range. If the leader bounds into the air, those following will often go through exactly the same motions; and if he turns, the others are very apt to each in succession run up and turn in the same place, unless the whole band are manoeuvring together, like a squadron of cavalry under orders, as has already been spoken of.

After securing the buck's hams and head (the latter for the sake of the horns, which were unusually long and fine), I pushed rapidly on without stopping to hunt, to reach some large creek which should contain both wood and water, for even in summer a fire adds greatly to the comfort and cosiness of a night camp. When the sun had nearly set we went over a divide and came in sight of a creek fulfilling the required conditions. It wound its way through a valley of rich bottom land, cotton-wood trees of no great height or size growing in thick groves along its banks, while its bed contained many deep pools of water, some of it fresh and good. I rode into a great bend, with a grove of trees on its right and containing excellent feed. Manitou was loosed, with the lariat round his neck, to feed where he wished until I went to bed, when he was to be taken to a place where the grass was thick and succulent, and tethered out for the night. There was any amount of wood with which a fire was started for cheerfulness, and some of the coals were soon raked off apart to cook over. The horse blanket was spread on the ground, with the oil-skin over it as a bed, underneath a spreading cotton-wood tree, while the regular blanket served as covering. The metal cup was soon filled with water and simmering over the coals to make tea, while an antelope steak was roasting on a forked stick. It is wonderful how cosy a camp, in clear weather, becomes if there is a good fire and enough to eat, and how sound the sleep is afterwards in the cool air, with the brilliant stars glimmering through the branches overhead. In the country where I was there was absolutely no danger from Indian horse-thieves, and practically none from white ones, for I felt pretty sure no one was anywhere within a good many miles of me, and none could have seen me come into the valley. Besides, in the cattle country stealing horses is a hazardous profession, as any man who is found engaged in it is at once, and very properly, strung up to the nearest tree, or shot if no trees are handy; so very few people follow it, at least for any length of time, and a man's horses are generally safe.

Near where we had halted for the night camp was a large prairie-dog town. Prairie-dogs are abundant all over the cattle country; they are in shape like little woodchucks, and are the most noisy and inquisitive animals imaginable. They are never found singly, but always in towns of several hundred inhabitants; and these towns are found in all kinds of places where the country is flat and treeless. Sometimes they will be placed on the bottoms of the creeks or rivers, and again far out on the prairie or among the Bad Lands, a long distance from any water. Indeed, so dry are some of the localities in which they exist, that it is a marvel how they can live at all; yet they seem invariably plump and in good condition. They are exceedingly destructive to grass, eating away every thing round their burrows, and thus each town is always extending at the borders, while the holes in the middle are deserted; in many districts they have become a perfect bane to the cattlemen, for the incoming of man has been the means of causing a great falling off in the ranks of their four-footed foes, and this main check to their increase being gone, they multiply at a rate that threatens to make them a serious pest in the future. They are among the few plains animals who are benefited instead of being injured by the presence of man; and it is most difficult to exterminate them or to keep their number in any way under, as they are prolific to a most extraordinary degree; and the quantity of good feed they destroy is very great, and as they eat up the roots of the grass it is a long time before it grows again. Already in many districts the stockmen are seriously considering the best way in which to take steps against them. Prairie-dogs wherever they exist are sure to attract attention, all the more so because, unlike most other rodents, they are diurnal and not nocturnal, offering therein a curious case of parallelism to their fellow denizen of the dry plains, the antelope, which is also a creature loving to be up and stirring in the bright daylight, unlike its relatives, the dusk-loving deer. They are very noisy, their shrill yelping resounding on all sides whenever a man rides through a town. None go far from their homes, always keeping close enough to be able to skulk into them at once; and as soon as a foe appears they take refuge on the hillocks beside their burrows, yelping continuously, and accompanying each yelp by a spasmodic jerking of the tail and body. When the man comes a little nearer they disappear inside and then thrust their heads out, for they are most inquisitive. Their burrows form one of the chief dangers to riding at full speed over the plains country; hardly any man can do much riding on the prairie for more than a year or two without coming to grief on more than one occasion by his horse putting its foot in a prairie-dog hole. A badger hole is even worse. When a horse gets his foot in such a hole, while going at full speed, he turns a complete somersault, and is lucky if he escape without a broken leg, while I have time and again known the rider to be severely injured. There are other smaller animals whose burrows sometimes cause a horseman to receive a sharp tumble. These are the pocket-gophers, queer creatures, shaped like moles and having the same subterranean habits, but with teeth like a rat's, and great pouches on the outside of their jaws, whose long, rambling tunnels cover the ground in certain places, though the animals themselves are very rarely seen; and the little striped gophers and gray gophers, entirely different animals, more like ground squirrels. But the prairie-dog is always the main source of danger to the horseman, as well as of mischief to the cattle-herder.

Around the prairie-dog towns it is always well to keep a look-out for the smaller carnivora, especially coyotes and badgers, as they are very fond of such neighborhoods, and almost always it is also a favorite resort for the larger kinds of hawks, which are so numerous throughout the cattle country. Rattlesnakes are quite plenty, living in the deserted holes, and the latter are also the homes of the little burrowing owls, which will often be seen standing at the opening, ready to run in as quick as any of the prairie-dogs if danger threatens. They have a funny habit of gravely bowing or posturing at the passer-by, and stand up very erect on their legs. With the exception of this species, owls are rare in the cattle country.

A prairie-dog is rather a difficult animal to get, as it stands so close to its burrow that a spasmodic kick, even if at the last gasp, sends the body inside, where it cannot be recovered. The cowboys are always practising at them with their revolvers, and as they are pretty good shots, mortally wound a good many, but unless the force of the blow fairly knocks the prairie-dog away from the mouth of the burrow, it almost always manages to escape inside. But a good shot with the rifle can kill any number by lying down quietly and waiting a few minutes until the dogs get a little distance from the mouths of their homes.

Badgers are more commonly found round prairie-dog towns than anywhere else; and they get their chief food by digging up the prairie-dogs and gophers with their strong forearms and long, stout claws. They are not often found wandering away from their homes in the daytime, but if so caught are easily run down and killed. A badger is a most desperate fighter, and an overmatch for a coyote, his hide being very thick and his form so squat and strong that it is hard to break his back or legs, while his sharp teeth grip like a steel trap. A very few seconds allow him to dig a hole in the ground, into which he can back all except his head; and when placed thus, with his rear and flanks protected, he can beat off a dog many times his own size. A young badger one night came up round the ranch-house, and began gnawing at some bones that had been left near the door. Hearing the noise one of my men took a lantern and went outside. The glare of the light seemed to make the badger stupid, for after looking at the lantern a few moments, it coolly turned and went on eating the scraps of flesh on the bones, and was knocked on the head without attempting to escape.

To come back to my trip. Early in the morning I was awakened by the shrill yelping of the prairie-dogs whose town was near me. The sun had not yet risen, and the air had the peculiar chill it always takes on toward morning, while little wreaths of light mist rose from the pools. Getting up and loosing Manitou to let him feed round where he wished and slake his thirst, I took the rifle, strolled up the creek valley a short distance, and turned off out on the prairie. Nothing was in sight in the way of game; but overhead a skylark was singing, soaring up above me so high that I could not make out his form in the gray morning light. I listened for some time, and the music never ceased for a moment, coming down clear, sweet, and tender from the air above. Soon the strains of another answered from a little distance off, and the two kept soaring and singing as long as I stayed to listen; and when I walked away I could still hear their notes behind me. In some ways the skylark is the sweetest singer we have; only certain of the thrushes rival it, but though the songs of the latter have perhaps even more melody, they are far from being as uninterrupted and well sustained, being rather a succession of broken bursts of music.

The sun was just appearing when I walked back to the creek bottom. Coming slowly out of a patch of brushwood, was a doe, going down to drink; her great, sensitive ears thrown forward as she peered anxiously and timidly round. She was very watchful, lifting her head and gazing about between every few mouthfuls. When she had drunk her fill she snatched a hasty mouthful or two of the wet grass, and then cantered back to the edge of the brush, when a little spotted fawn came out and joined her. The two stood together for a few moments, and then walked off into the cover. The little pond at which they had drunk was within fifty yards of my night bed; and it had other tenants in the shape of a mallard duck, with a brood of little ducklings, balls of fuzzy yellow down, that bobbed off into the reeds like little corks as I walked by.

Breaking camp is a simple operation for one man; and but a few minutes after breakfast Manitou and I were off; the embers of the fire having been extinguished with the care that comes to be almost second nature with the cattle-man, one of whose chief dreads is the prairie fire, that sometimes robs his stock of such an immense amount of feed. Very little game was seen during the morning, as I rode in an almost straight line over the hot, parched plains, the ground cracked and seamed by the heat, and the dull brown blades bending over as if the sun was too much even for them. The sweat drenched the horse even when we were walking; and long before noon we halted for rest by a bitter alkaline pool with border so steep and rotten that I had to bring water up to the horse in my hat; having taken some along in a canteen for my own use. But there was a steep bank near, overgrown with young trees, and thus giving good shade; and it was this that induced me to stop. When leaving this halting-place, I spied three figures in the distance, loping towards me; they turned out to be cowboys, who had been out a couple of days looking up a band of strayed ponies, and as they had exhausted their supply of food, I gave them the antelope hams, trusting to shoot another for my own use.

Nor was I disappointed. After leaving the cowboys I headed the horse towards the more rolling country where the prairies begin to break off into the edges of the Bad Lands. Several bands of antelope were seen, and I tried one unsuccessful stalk, not being able to come within rifle range; but towards evening, when only about a mile from a wooded creek on whose banks I intended to sleep, I came across a solitary buck, just as I was topping the ridge of the last divide. As I was keeping a sharp lookout at the time, I reined in the horse the instant the head of the antelope came in sight, and jumping off crept up till I could see his whole body, when I dropped on my knee and took steady aim. He was a long way off (three hundred yards by actual pacing), and not having made out exactly what we were he stood still, looking intently in our direction and broadside to us. I held well over his shoulder, and at the report he dropped like a shot, the ball having broken his neck. It was a very good shot; the best I ever made at antelope, of which game, as already said, I have killed but very few individuals. Taking the hams and saddle I rode on down to the creek and again went into camp among timber. Thus on this trip I was never successful in outwitting antelope on the several occasions when I pitted my craft and skill against their wariness and keen senses, always either failing to get within range or else missing them; but nevertheless I got two by taking advantage of the stupidity and curiosity which they occasionally show.

The middle part of the days having proved so very hot, and as my store of biscuits was nearly gone, and as I knew, moreover, that the antelope meat would not keep over twenty-four hours, I decided to push back home next day; and accordingly I broke camp at the first streak of dawn, and took Manitou back to the ranch at a smart lope.

A solitary trip such as this was, through a comparatively wild region in which game is still plentiful, always has great attraction for any man who cares for sport and for nature, and who is able to be his own companion, but the pleasure after all depends a good deal on the weather. To be sure, after a little experience in roughing it, the hardships seem a good deal less formidable than they formerly did, and a man becomes able to roll up in a wet blanket and sleep all night in a pelting rain without hurting himself—though he will shiver a good deal, and feel pretty numb and stiff in those chill and dreary hours just before dawn. But when a man's clothes and bedding and rifle are all wet, no matter how philosophically he may bear it, it may be taken for granted that he does not enjoy it. So fair weather is a very vital and important element among those that go to make up the pleasure and success of such a trip. Luckily fair weather can be counted on with a good deal of certainty in late spring and throughout most of the summer and fall on the northern cattle plains. The storms that do take place, though very violent, do not last long.

Every now and then, however, there will be in the fall a three-days' storm in which it is almost impossible to travel, and then the best thing to be done is to lie up under any shelter that is at hand until it blows over. I remember one such camp which was made in the midst of the most singular and picturesque surroundings. It was toward the end of a long wagon trip that we had been taking, and all of the horses were tired by incessant work. We had come through country which was entirely new to us, passing nearly all day in a long flat prairie through which flowed a stream that we supposed to be either the Box Alder or the Little Beaver. In leaving this we had struck some heavy sand-hills, and while pulling the loaded wagon up them one of the team played out completely, and we had to take her out and put in one of the spare saddle-ponies, a tough little fellow. Night came on fast, and the sun was just setting when we crossed the final ridge and came in sight of as singular a bit of country as I have ever seen. The cowboys, as we afterward found, had christened the place "Medicine Buttes." In plains dialect, I may explain, "Medicine" has been adopted from the Indians, among whom it means any thing supernatural or very unusual. It is used in the sense of "magic," or "out of the common."

Over an irregular tract of gently rolling sandy hills, perhaps about three quarters of a mile square, were scattered several hundred detached and isolated buttes or cliffs of sandstone, each butte from fifteen to fifty feet high, and from thirty to a couple of hundred feet across. Some of them rose as sharp peaks or ridges, or as connected chains, but much the greater number had flat tops like little table-lands. The sides were perfectly perpendicular, and were cut and channelled by the weather into the most extraordinary forms; caves, columns, battlements, spires, and flying buttresses were mingled in the strangest confusion. Many of the caves were worn clear through the buttes, and they were at every height in the sides, while ledges ran across the faces, and shoulders and columns jutted out from the corners. On the tops and at the bases of most of the cliffs grew pine trees, some of considerable height, and the sand gave every thing a clean, white look.

Altogether it was as fantastically beautiful a place as I have ever seen: it seemed impossible that the hand of man should not have had something to do with its formation. There was a spring of clear cold water a few hundred yards off, with good feed for the horses round it; and we made our camp at the foot of one of the largest buttes, building a roaring pine-log fire in an angle in the face of the cliff, while our beds were under the pine trees. It was the time of the full moon, and the early part of the night was clear. The flame of the fire leaped up the side of the cliff, the red light bringing out into lurid and ghastly relief the bold corners and strange-looking escarpments of the rock, while against it the stiff limbs of the pines stood out like rigid bars of iron. Walking off out of sight of the circle of firelight, among the tall crags, the place seemed almost as unreal as if we had been in fairy-land. The flood of clear moonlight turned the white faces of the cliffs and the grounds between them into shining silver, against which the pines showed dark and sombre, while the intensely black shadows of the buttes took on forms that were grimly fantastic. Every cave or cranny in the crags looked so black that it seemed almost to be thrown out from the surface, and when the branches of the trees moved, the bright moonlight danced on the ground as if it were a sheet of molten metal. Neither in shape nor in color did our surroundings seem to belong to the dull gray world through which we had been travelling all day.

But by next morning every thing had changed. A furious gale of wind was blowing, and we were shrouded in a dense, drizzling mist, through which at times the rain drove in level sheets. Now and then the fog would blow away, and then would come on thicker than ever; and when it began to clear off a steady rain took its place, and the wind increased to a regular hurricane. With its canvas top on, the wagon would certainly have been blown over if on open ground, and it was impossible to start or keep a fire except under the sheltered lee of the cliff. Moreover, the wind kept shifting, and we had to shift too, as fast as ever it started to blow from a new quarter; and thus in the course of the twenty-four hours we made a complete circle of the cliff at whose base we were. Our blankets got wet during the night; and they got no drier during the day; and the second night, as we slept on them they got steadily damper. Our provisions were pretty nearly out, and so, with little to eat and less to do, wet and uncomfortable, we cowered over the sputtering fire, and whiled the long day away as best we might with our own thoughts; fortunately we had all learned that no matter how bad things are, grumbling and bad temper can always be depended upon to make them worse, and so bore our ill-fortune, if not with stoical indifference, at least in perfect quiet. Next day the storm still continued, but the fog was gone and the wind somewhat easier; and we spent the whole day looking up the horses, which had drifted a long distance before the storm; nor was it till the morning of the third day that we left our beautiful but, as events had made it, uncomfortable camping-ground.

In midsummer the storms are rarely of long duration, but are very severe while they last. I remember well one day when I was caught in such a storm. I had gone some twenty-five miles from the ranch to see the round-up, which had reached what is known as the Oxbow of the Little Missouri, where the river makes a great loop round a flat grassy bottom, on which the cattle herd was gathered. I stayed, seeing the cattle cut out and the calves branded, until after dinner; for it was at the time of the year when the days were longest.

At last the work was ended, and I started home in the twilight. The horse splashed across the shallow ford, and then spent half an hour in climbing up through the rugged side hills, till we reached the top of the first great plateau that had to be crossed. As soon as I got on it I put in the spurs and started off at a gallop. In the dusk the brown level land stretched out in formless expanse ahead of me, unrelieved, except by the bleached white of a buffalo's skull, whose outlines glimmered indistinctly to one side of the course I was riding. On my left the sun had set behind a row of jagged buttes, that loomed up in sharp relief against the western sky; above them it had left a bar of yellow light, which only made more intense the darkness of the surrounding heavens. In the quarter towards which I was heading there had gathered a lowering mass of black storm-clouds, lit up by the incessant play of the lightning. The wind had totally died away, and the death-like stillness was only broken by the continuous, measured beat of the horse's hoofs as he galloped over the plain, and at times by the muttered roll of the distant thunder.

Without slacking pace I crossed the plateau, and as I came to the other edge the storm burst in sheets and torrents of water. In five minutes I was drenched through, and to guide myself had to take advantage of the continual flashes of lightning; and I was right glad, half an hour afterward, to stop and take shelter in the log hut of a couple of cowboys, where I could get dry and warm.

# The Lordly Buffalo

*Hunting Trips of a Ranchman*

GONE FOREVER ARE THE MIGHTY HERDS OF THE LORDLY BUFFALO. A few solitary individuals and small bands are still to be found scattered here and there in the wilder parts of the plains; and though most of these will be very soon destroyed, others will for some years fight off their doom and lead a precarious existence either in remote and almost desert portions of the country near the Mexican frontier, or else in the wildest and most inaccessible fastnesses of the Rocky Mountains; but the great herds, that for the first three quarters of this century formed the distinguishing and characteristic feature of the Western plains, have vanished forever.

It is only about a hundred years ago that the white man, in his march westward, first encroached upon the lands of the buffalo, for these animals had never penetrated in any number to the Appalachian chain of mountains. Indeed, it was after the beginning of the century before the inroads of the whites upon them grew at all serious. Then, though constancy driven westward, the diminution in their territory, if sure, was at least slow, although growing progressively more rapid. Less than a score of years ago the great herds, containing many millions of individuals, ranged over a vast expanse of country that stretched in an unbroken line from near Mexico to far into British America; in fact, over almost all the plains that are now known as the cattle region. But since that time their destruction has gone on with appalling rapidity and thoroughness; and the main factors in bringing it about have been the railroads, which carried hordes of hunters into the land and gave them means to transport their spoils to market. Not quite twenty years since, the range was broken in two, and the buffalo herds in the middle slaughtered or thrust aside; and thus there resulted two ranges, the northern and the southern. The latter was the larger, but being more open to the hunters, was the sooner to be depopulated; and the last of the great southern herds was destroyed in 1878, though scattered bands escaped and wandered into the desolate wastes to the southwest. Meanwhile equally savage war was waged on the northern herds, and five years later the last of these was also destroyed or broken up. The bulk of this slaughter was done in the dozen years from 1872 to 1883; never before in all history were so many large wild animals of one species slain in so short a space of time.

The extermination of the buffalo has been a veritable tragedy of the animal world. Other races of animals have been destroyed within historic times, but these have been species of small size, local distribution, and limited numbers, usually found in some particular island or group of islands; while the huge buffalo, in countless myriads, ranged over the greater part of a continent. Its nearest relative, the Old World aurochs, formerly found all through the forests of Europe, is almost as near the verge of extinction, but with the latter the process has been slow, and has extended over a period of a thousand years, instead of being compressed into a dozen. The destruction of the various larger species of South African game is much more local, and is proceeding at a much slower rate. It may truthfully be said that the sudden and complete extermination of the vast herds of the buffalo is without a parallel in historic times.

No sight is more common on the plains than that of a bleached buffalo skull; and their countless numbers attest the abundance of the animal at a time not so very long past. On those portions where the herds made their last stand, the carcasses, dried in the clear, high air, or the mouldering skeletons, abound. Last year, in crossing the country around the heads of the Big Sandy, O'Fallon Creek, Little Beaver, and Box Alder, these skeletons or dried carcasses were in sight from every hillock, often lying over the ground so thickly that several score could be seen at once. A ranchman who at the same time had made a journey of a thousand miles across Northern Montana, along the Milk River, told me that, to use his own expression, during the whole distance he was never out of sight of a dead buffalo, and never in sight of a live one.

Thus, though gone, the traces of the buffalo are still thick over the land. Their dried dung is found everywhere, and is in many places the only fuel afforded by the plains; their skulls, which last longer than any other part of the animal, are among the most familiar of objects to the plainsman; their bones are in many districts so plentiful that it has become a regular industry, followed by hundreds of men (christened "bone hunters" by the frontiersmen), to go out with wagons and collect them in great numbers for the sake of the phosphates they yield; and Bad Lands, plateaus, and prairies alike, are cut up in all directions by the deep ruts which were formerly buffalo trails.

These buffalo trails were made by the herds travelling strung out in single file, and invariably taking the same route each time they passed over the same piece of ground. As a consequence, many of the ruts are worn so deeply into the ground that a horseman riding along one strikes his stirrups on the earth. In moving through very broken country they are often good guides; for though buffalo can go easily over the roughest places, they prefer to travel where it is smooth, and have a remarkable knack at finding out the best passage down a steep ravine, over a broken cliff, or along a divide. In a pass, or, as it is called in the West, "draw," between two feeding grounds, through which the buffalo were fond of going, fifteen or twenty deep trails may be seen; and often, where the great beasts have travelled in parallel files, two ruts will run side by side over the prairie for a mile's length. These old trails are frequently used by the cattle herds at the present time, or are even turned into pony paths by the ranchmen. For many long years after the buffalo die out from a place, their white skulls and well-worn roads remain as melancholy monuments of their former existence.

The rapid and complete extermination of the buffalo affords an excellent instance of how a race, that has thriven and multiplied for ages under conditions of life to which it has slowly fitted itself by a process of natural selection continued for countless generations, may succumb at once when these surrounding conditions are varied by the introduction of one or more new elements, immediately becoming the chief forces with which it has to contend in the struggle for life. The most striking characteristics of the buffalo, and those which had been found most useful in maintaining the species until the white man entered upon the scene, were its phenomenal gregariousness—surpassed by no other four-footed beast, and only equalled, if equalled at all, by one or two kinds of South African antelope,—its massive bulk, and unwieldy strength. The fact that it was a plains and not a forest or mountain animal was at that time also greatly in its favor. Its toughness and hardy endurance fitted it to contend with purely natural forces: to resist cold and the winter blasts, or the heat of a thirsty summer, to wander away to new pastures when the feed on the old was exhausted, to plunge over broken ground, and to plough its way through snow-drifts or quagmires. But one beast of prey existed sufficiently powerful to conquer it when full grown and in health; and this, the grizzly bear, could only be considered an occasional foe. The Indians were its most dangerous enemies, but they were without horses, and their weapons, bows and arrows, were only available at close range; so that a slight degree of speed enabled buffalo to get out of the way of their human foes when discovered, and on the open plains a moderate development of the senses was sufficient to warn them of the approach of the latter before they had come up to the very close distance required for their primitive weapons to take effect. Thus the strength, size, and gregarious habits of the brute were sufficient for a protection against most foes; and a slight degree of speed and moderate development of the senses served as adequate guards against the grizzlies and bow-bearing foot Indians. Concealment and the habit of seeking lonely and remote places for a dwelling would have been of no service.

But the introduction of the horse, and shortly afterwards the incoming of white hunters carrying long-range rifles, changed all this. The buffaloes' gregarious habits simply rendered them certain to be seen, and made it a matter of perfect ease to follow them up; their keeping to the open plains heightened their conspicuousness, while their senses were too dull to discover their foes at such a distance as to nullify the effects of the long rifles; their speed was not such as to enable them to flee from a horseman; and their size and strength merely made them too clumsy either to escape from or to contend with their foes. Add to this the fact that their hides and flesh were valuable, and it is small wonder that under the new order of things they should have vanished with such rapidity.

The incoming of the cattle-men was another cause of the completeness of their destruction. Wherever there is good feed for a buffalo, there is good feed for a steer or cow; and so the latter have penetrated into all the pastures of the former; and of course the cowboys follow. A cowboy is not able to kill a deer or antelope unless in exceptional cases, for they are too fleet, too shy, or keep themselves too well hidden. But a buffalo neither tries nor is able to do much in the way of hiding itself; its senses are too dull to give it warning in time; and it is not so swift as a horse, so that a cowboy, riding round in the places where cattle, and therefore buffalo, are likely to be, is pretty sure to see any of the latter that may be about, and then can easily approach near enough to be able to overtake them when they begin running. The size and value of the animal makes the chase after it very keen. Hunters will follow the trail of a band for days, when they would not follow that of deer or antelope for a half hour.

Events have developed a race of this species, known either as the wood or mountain buffalo, which is acquiring, and has already largely acquired, habits widely different from those of the others of its kind. It is found in the wooded and most precipitous portions of the mountains, instead of on the level and open plains; it goes singly or in small parties, instead of in huge herds; and it is more agile and infinitely more wary than is its prairie cousin. The formation of this race is due solely to the extremely severe process of natural selection that has been going on among the buffalo herds for the last sixty or seventy years; the vast majority of the individuals were utterly unable to accommodate themselves to the sudden and complete change in the surrounding forces with which they had to cope, and therefore died out; while a very few of the more active and wary, and of those most given to wandering off into mountainous and out-of-the-way places, in each generation survived, and among these the wariness continually increased, partly by personal experience, and still more by inheriting an increasingly suspicious nature from their ancestors. The sense of smell always was excellent in the buffalo; the sense of hearing becomes much quicker in any woods animal than it is in one found on the plains; while in beasts of the forest the eyesight does not have to be as keen as is necessary for their protection in open country. On the mountains the hair grows longer and denser, and the form rather more thickset. As a result, a new race has been built up; and we have an animal far better fitted to "harmonize with the environment," to use the scientific cant of the day. Unfortunately this race has developed too late. With the settlement of the country it will also disappear, unless very stringent laws are made for its protection; but at least its existence will for some years prevent the total extermination of the species as a whole. It must be kept in mind that even this shyer kind of buffalo has not got the keen senses of other large game, such as moose; and it is more easily followed and much more keenly and eagerly sought after than would be any other animal smaller and less valuable to the hunter than itself.

While the slaughter of the buffalo has been in places needless and brutal, and while it is to be greatly regretted that the species is likely to become extinct, and while, moreover, from a purely selfish standpoint many, including myself, would rather see it continue to exist as the chief feature in the unchanged life of the Western wilderness; yet, on the other hand, it must be remembered that its continued existence in any numbers was absolutely incompatible with any thing but a very sparse settlement of the country; and that its destruction was the condition precedent upon the advance of white civilization in the West, and was a positive boon to the more thrifty and industrious frontiersmen. Where the buffalo were plenty, they ate up all the grass that could have supported cattle. The country over which the huge herds grazed during the last year or two of their existence was cropped bare, and the grass did not grow to its normal height and become able to support cattle for, in some cases two, in others three, seasons. Every buffalo needed as much food as an ox or cow; and if the former abounded, the latter perforce would have to be scarce. Above all, the extermination of the buffalo was the only way of solving the Indian question. As long as this large animal of the chase existed, the Indians simply could not be kept on reservations, and always had an ample supply of meat on hand to support them in the event of a war; and its disappearance was the only method of forcing them to at least partially abandon their savage mode of life. From the standpoint of humanity at large, the extermination of the buffalo has been a blessing. The many have been benefited by it; and I suppose the comparatively few of us who would have preferred the continuance of the old order of things, merely for the sake of our own selfish enjoyment, have no right to complain.

The buffalo is easier killed than is any other kind of plains game; but its chase is very far from being the tame amusement it has been lately represented. It is genuine sport; it needs skill, marksmanship, and hardihood in the man who follows it, and if he hunts on horseback, it needs also pluck and good riding. It is in no way akin to various forms of so-called sport in vogue in parts of the East, such as killing deer in a lake or by fire hunting, or even by watching at a runaway. No man who is not of an adventurous temper, and able to stand rough food and living, will penetrate to the haunts of the buffalo. The animal is so tough and tenacious of life that it must be hit in the right spot; and care must be used in approaching it, for its nose is very keen, and though its sight is dull, yet, on the other hand, the plains it frequents are singularly bare of cover; while, finally, there is just a faint spice of danger in the pursuit, for the bison, though the least dangerous of all bovine animals, will, on occasions, turn upon the hunter, and though its attack is, as a rule, easily avoided, yet in rare cases it manages to charge home. A ranchman of my acquaintance once, many years ago, went out buffalo hunting on horseback, together with a friend who was unused to the sport, and who was mounted on a large, untrained, nervous horse. While chasing a bull, the friend's horse became unmanageable, and when the bull turned, proved too clumsy to get out of the way, and was caught on the horns, one of which entered its flank, while the other inflicted a huge, bruised gash across the man's thigh, tearing the muscles all out. Both horse and rider were flung to the ground with tremendous violence. The horse had to be killed, and the man died in a few hours from the shock, loss of blood, and internal injuries. Such an accident, however, is very exceptional.

My brother was in at the death of the great southern herds in 1877, and had a good deal of experience in buffalo hunting; and once or twice was charged by old bulls, but never had any difficulty in either evading the charge or else killing the brute as it came on. My cousin, John Roosevelt, also had one adventure with a buffalo, in which he received rather a fright. He had been out on foot with a dog and had severely wounded a buffalo bull, which nevertheless, with the wonderful tenacity of life and ability to go over apparently inaccessible places that this species shows, managed to clamber up a steep, almost perpendicular, cliff. My cousin climbed up after it, with some difficulty; on reaching the top he got his elbows over and drew himself up on them only to find the buffalo fronting him with lowered head not a dozen feet off. Immediately upon seeing him it cocked up its tail and came forward. He was clinging with both hands to the edge and could not use his rifle; so, not relishing what was literally a tête-à-tête, he promptly let go and slid or rather rolled head over heels to the foot of the cliff, not hurting himself much in the sand, though of course a good deal jarred by the fall. The buffalo came on till its hoofs crumbled the earth at the brink, when the dog luckily got up and distracted its attention; meanwhile, my cousin, having bounced down to the bottom, picked himself up, shook himself, and finding that nothing was broken, promptly scrambled up the bluff at another place a few yards off and shot his antagonist.

When my cattle first came on the Little Missouri three of my men took a small bunch of them some fifty miles to the south and there wintered with them, on what were then the outskirts of the buffalo range, the herds having been pressed up northwards. In the intervals of tending the cattle—work which was then entirely new to them—they occupied themselves in hunting buffalo, killing during the winter sixty or seventy, some of them on horseback, but mostly by still-hunting them on foot. Once or twice the bulls when wounded turned to bay; and a couple of them on one occasion charged one of the men and forced him to take refuge upon a steep isolated butte. At another time the three of them wounded a cow so badly that she broke down and would run no farther, turning to bay in a small clump of thick trees. As this would have been a very bad place in which to skin the body, they wished to get her out and tried to tease her into charging; but she seemed too weak to make the effort. Emboldened by her apathy one of the men came up close to her behind, while another was standing facing her; and the former finally entered the grove of trees and poked her with a long stick. This waked her up most effectually, and instead of turning on her assailant she went headlong at the man in front. He leaped to one side just in time, one of her horns grazing him, ripping away his clothes and knocking him over; as he lay she tried to jump on him with her forefeet, but he rolled to one side, and as she went past she kicked at him like a vicious mule. The effort exhausted her, however, and she fell before going a dozen yards farther. The man who was charged had rather a close shave; thanks to the rashness and contempt of the game's prowess which they all felt—for all three are very quiet men and not afraid of any thing. It is always a good rule to be cautious in dealing with an apparently dead or dying buffalo. About the time the above incident occurred a party of hunters near my ranch killed a buffalo, as they thought, and tied a pony to its foreleg, to turn it over, as its position was a very bad one for skinning. Barely had the pony been tied when the buffalo came to with a jump, killed the unfortunate pony, and needed a dozen more balls before he fell for good.

At that time the buffalo would occasionally be scattered among the cattle, but, as a rule, avoided the latter and seemed to be afraid of them; while the cattle, on the contrary, had no apparent dread of the buffalo, unless it happened that on some occasion they got caught by a herd of the latter that had stampeded. A settler or small ranchman, not far from my place, was driving in a team of oxen in a wagon one day three years since, when, in crossing a valley, he encountered a little herd of stampeded buffalo, who, in their blind and heedless terror, ran into him and knocked over the wagon and oxen. The oxen never got over the fright the rough handling caused them, and ever afterward became unmanageable and tore off at sight or smell of a buffalo. It is said that the few buffalo left in the country through which the head waters of the Belle Fourche flow, have practically joined themselves to the great herds of cattle now found all over that region.

Buffalo are very easily tamed. On a neighboring ranch there are four which were taken when very young calves. They wander about with the cattle, and are quite as familiar as any of them, and do not stray any farther away. One of them was captured when a yearling, by the help of a large yellow hound. The cowboy had been chasing it some time and, finally, fearing it might escape, hied on the hound, which dashed in, caught the buffalo by the ear, and finally brought it down to its knees, when the cowboy, by means of his lariat secured it, and, with the help of a companion, managed to get it back to the ranch. Buffalo can be trained to draw a wagon, and are valuable for their great strength; but they are very headstrong and stupid. If thirsty, for instance, and they smell or see water, it is absolutely impossible to prevent their going to it, no matter if it is in such a place that they have to upset the wagon to get down to it, nor how deep the mud is. When tamed they do not seem to be as ferocious as ordinary cattle that are allowed to go free; but they are such strong, blundering brutes that very few fences will hold them.

My men, in hunting buffalo, which was with them an occasional occupation and not a regular pursuit, used light Winchesters; but the professional buffalo hunters carried either 40-90 or 45-120 Sharps, than which there are in the
world no rifles more accurate or powerful; with the larger calibred ones (45 or
50) a man could easily kill an elephant. These weapons are excellent for very
long range work, being good for half a mile and over; and sometimes the
hunters were able to kill very many buffalo at a time, owing to their curious
liability to fits of stupid, panic terror. Sometimes when these panics seize
them they stampede and run off in headlong, heedless flight, going over any
thing in their way. Once, in mid-winter, one of my men was lying out in the
open, under a heavy roll of furs, the wagon sheet over all. During the night a
small herd of stampeded buffalo passed by, and one of them jumped on the bed,
almost trampling on the sleeper, and then bounded off, as the latter rose with
a yell. The others of the herd passed almost within arm's length on each side.

Occasionally these panic fits have the opposite effect and make them run
together and stand still in a stupid, frightened manner. This is now and then
the result when a hunter fires at a herd while keeping himself concealed; and
on rare occasions (for buffalo act very differently at different times, according
to their moods) it occurs even when he is in full sight. When they are made
to act thus it is called in hunters' parlance getting a "stand" on them; and often
thirty or forty have been killed in one such stand, the hunter hardly shifting
his position the whole time. Often, with their long-range heavy rifles, the
hunters would fire a number of shots into a herd half a mile off, and on
approaching would find that they had bagged several—for the Sharps rifle has
a very long range, and the narrow, heavy conical bullets will penetrate almost
any thing. Once while coming in over the plains with an ox wagon two of my
cowboys surprised a band of buffaloes, which on being fired at ran clear round
them and then made a stand in nearly their former position; and there they
stood until the men had fired away most of their ammunition, but only half
a dozen or so were killed, the Winchesters being too light for such a distance.
Hunting on foot is much the most destructive way of pursuing buffaloes; but
it lacks the excitement of chasing them with horses.

When in Texas my brother had several chances to hunt them on horseback,
while making a trip as guest of a captain of United States cavalry. The country
through which they hunted was rolling and well watered, the buffalo being scattered over it in bands of no great size. While riding out to look for the game they
were mounted on large horses; when a band was spied they would dismount and
get on the smaller buffalo ponies which the orderlies had been leading behind

them. Then they would carefully approach from the leeward side, if possible keeping behind some hill or divide. When this was no longer possible they trotted gently towards the game, which usually gathered together and stood for a moment looking at them. The instant the buffalo turned, the spurs were put in and the ponies raced forward for all there was in them, it being an important point to close as soon as possible, as buffalo, though not swift, are very enduring. Usually a half a mile took the hunters up to the game, when each singled out his animal, rode alongside on its left flank, so close as almost to be able to touch it with the hand, and fired the heavy revolver into the loins or small of the back, the bullet ranging forward. At the instant of firing, the trained pony swerved off to the left, almost at right angles to its former course, so as to avoid the lunging charge sometimes made by the wounded brute. If the animal kept on, the hunter, having made a half circle, again closed up and repeated the shot; very soon the buffalo came to a halt, then its head dropped, it straddled widely with its forelegs, swayed to and fro, and pitched heavily forward on its side. The secret of success in this sort of hunting is to go right up by the side of the buffalo; if a man stays off at a distance of fifteen or twenty feet he may fire a score of shots and not kill or cripple his game.

While hunting this, the largest of American animals, on horseback is doubtless the most exciting way in which its chase can be carried on, we must beware of crying down its pursuit on foot. To be sure, in the latter case, the actual stalking and shooting the buffalo does not need on the part of the hunter as much skill and as good marksmanship as is the case in hunting most other kinds of large game, and is but a trifle more risky; yet, on the other hand, the fatigue of following the game is much greater, and the country is usually so wild as to call for some hardihood and ability to stand rough work on the part of the man who penetrates it.

One September I determined to take a short trip after bison. At that time I was staying in a cow-camp a good many miles up the river from my ranch; there were then no cattle south of me, where there are now very many thousand head, and the buffalo had been plentiful in the country for a couple of winters past, but the last of the herds had been destroyed or driven out six months before, and there were only a few stragglers left. It was one of my first hunting trips; previously I had shot with the rifle very little, and that only at deer or antelope. I took as a companion one of my best men, named Ferris (a brother of the Ferris already mentioned); we rode a couple of ponies, not very good ones, and each carried his roll of blankets and a very small store of food in a pack behind the saddle.

Leaving the cow-camp early in the morning, we crossed the Little Missouri and for the first ten miles threaded our way through the narrow defiles and along the tortuous divides of a great tract of Bad Lands. Although it was fall and the nights were cool the sun was very hot in the middle of the day, and we jogged along at a slow pace, so as not to tire our ponies. Two or three black-tail deer were seen, some distance off, and when we were a couple of hours on our journey, we came across the fresh track of a bull buffalo. Buffalo wander a great distance, for, though they do not go fast, yet they may keep travelling, as they graze, all day long; and though this one had evidently passed but a few hours before, we were not sure we would see him. His tracks were easily followed as long as he had kept to the soft creek bottom, crossing and recrossing the narrow wet ditch which wound its way through it; but when he left this and turned up a winding coulie that branched out in every direction, his hoofs scarcely made any marks in the hard ground. We rode up the ravine, carefully examining the soil for nearly half an hour, however; finally, as we passed the mouth of a little side coulie, there was a plunge and crackle through the bushes at its head, and a shabby-looking old bull bison galloped out of it and, without an instant's hesitation, plunged over a steep bank into a patch of rotten, broken ground which led around the base of a high butte. So quickly did he disappear that we had not time to dismount and fire. Spurring our horses we galloped up to the brink of the cliff down which he had plunged; it was remarkable that he should have gone down it unhurt. From where we stood we could see nothing; so, getting our horses over the broken ground as fast as possible, we ran to the butte and rode round it, only to see the buffalo come out of the broken land and climb up the side of another butte over a quarter of a mile off. In spite of his great weight and cumbersome, heavy-looking gait, he climbed up the steep bluff with ease and even agility, and when he had reached the ridge stood and looked back at us for a moment; while so doing he held his head high up, and at that distance his great shaggy mane and huge fore-quarter made him look like a lion. In another second he again turned away and made off; and, being evidently very shy and accustomed to being harassed by hunters, must have travelled a long distance before stopping, for we followed his trail for some miles until it got on such hard, dry ground that his hoofs did not leave a scrape in the soil, and yet did not again catch so much as a glimpse of him.

Soon after leaving his trail we came out on the great, broken prairies that lie far back from the river. These are by no means everywhere level. A flat space of a mile or two will be bounded by a low cliff or a row of small round-topped buttes; or will be interrupted by a long, gently sloping ridge, the divide between two creeks; or by a narrow canyon, perhaps thirty feet deep and not a dozen wide, stretching for miles before there is a crossing place. The smaller creeks were dried up, and were merely sinuous hollows in the prairie; but one or two of the larger ones held water here and there, and cut down through the land in bold, semicircular sweeps, the outside of each curve being often bounded by a steep bluff with trees at its bottom, and occasionally holding a miry pool. At one of these pools we halted, about ten o'clock in the morning, and lunched; the banks were so steep and rotten that we had to bring water to the more clumsy of the two ponies in a hat.

Then we remounted and fared on our way, scanning the country far and near from every divide, but seeing no trace of game. The air was hot and still, and the brown, barren land stretched out on every side for leagues of dreary sameness. Once we came to a canyon which ran across our path, and followed along its brink for a mile to find a place where we could get into it; when we finally found such a place, we had to back the horses down to the bottom and then lead them along it for some hundred yards before finding a break through which we could climb out.

It was late in the afternoon before we saw any game; then we made out in the middle of a large plain three black specks, which proved to be buffalo—old bulls. Our horses had come a good distance, under a hot sun, and as they had had no water except from the mud-hole in the morning they were in no condition for running. They were not very fast anyhow; so, though the ground was unfavorable, we made up our minds to try to creep up to the buffalo. We left the ponies in a hollow half a mile from the game, and started off on our hands and knees, taking advantage of every sage-brush as cover. After a while we had to lie flat on our bodies and wriggle like snakes; and while doing this I blundered into a bed of cactus, and filled my hands with the spines. After taking advantage of every hollow, hillock, or sage-brush, we got within about a hundred and twenty-five or fifty yards of where the three bulls were unconsciously feeding, and as all between was bare ground I drew up and fired. It was the first time I ever shot at buffalo, and, confused by the bulk and shaggy hair of the beast, I aimed too far back at one that was standing nearly broadside on towards me. The bullet told on his body with a loud crack, the dust flying up from his hide; but it did not work him any immediate harm, or in the least hinder him from making off; and away went all three, with their tails up, disappearing over a slight rise in the ground.

Much disgusted, we trotted back to where the horses were picketed, jumped on them, a good deal out of breath, and rode after the flying game. We thought that the wounded one might turn out and leave the others; and so followed them, though they had over a mile's start. For seven or eight miles we loped our jaded horses along at a brisk pace, occasionally seeing the buffalo far ahead; and finally, when the sun had just set, we saw that all three had come to a stand in a gentle hollow. There was no cover anywhere near them; and, as a last desperate resort, we concluded to try to run them on our worn-out ponies.

As we cantered toward them they faced us for a second and then turned round and made off, while with spurs and quirts we made the ponies put on a burst that enabled us to close in with the wounded one just about the time that the lessening twilight had almost vanished; while the rim of the full moon rose above the horizon. The pony I was on could barely hold its own, after getting up within sixty or seventy yards of the wounded bull; my companion, better mounted, forged ahead, a little to one side. The bull saw him coming and swerved from his course, and by cutting across I was able to get nearly up to him. The ground over which we were running was fearful, being broken into holes and ditches, separated by hillocks; in the dull light, and at the speed we were going, no attempt could be made to guide the horses, and the latter, fagged out by their exertions, floundered and pitched forward at every stride, hardly keeping their legs. When up within twenty feet I fired my rifle, but the darkness, and especially the violent, labored motion of my pony, made me miss; I tried to get in closer, when suddenly up went the bull's tail, and wheeling, he charged me with lowered horns. My pony, frightened into momentary activity, spun round and tossed up his head; I was holding the rifle in both hands, and the pony's head, striking it, knocked it violently against my forehead, cutting quite a gash, from which, heated as I was, the blood poured into my eyes. Meanwhile the buffalo, passing me, charged my companion, and followed him as he made off, and, as the ground was very bad, for some little distance his lowered head was unpleasantly near the tired pony's tail. I tried to run in on him again, but my pony stopped short, dead beat; and by no spurring could I force him out of a slow trot. My companion jumped off and took a couple of shots at the buffalo, which missed in the dim moonlight; and to our unutterable chagrin the wounded bull labored off and vanished in the darkness. I made after him on foot, in hopeless and helpless wrath, until he got out of sight.

Our horses were completely done out; we did not mount them again, but led them slowly along, trembling, foaming, and sweating. The ground was moist in places, and after an hour's search we found in a reedy hollow a little mud-pool, with water so slimy that it was almost gelatinous. Thirsty though we were, for we had not drunk for twelve hours, neither man nor horse could swallow more than a mouthful or two of this water. We unsaddled the horses, and made our beds by the hollow, each eating a biscuit; there was not a twig with which to make a fire, nor any thing to which we might fasten the horses. Spreading the saddle-blankets under us, and our own over us, we lay down, with the saddles as pillows, to which we had been obliged to lariat our steeds.

The ponies stood about almost too tired to eat; but in spite of their fatigue they were very watchful and restless, continually snorting or standing with their ears forward, peering out into the night; wild beasts, or some such things, were about. The day before we had had a false alarm from supposed hostile Indians, who turned out to be merely half-breed Crees; and, as we were in a perfectly lonely part of the wilderness, we knew we were in the domain of both white and red horse-thieves, and that the latter might in addition to our horses try to take our scalps. It was some time before we dozed off; waking up with a start whenever we heard the horses stop grazing and stand motionless with heads raised, looking out into the darkness. But at last, tired out, we fell sound asleep.

About midnight we were rudely wakened by having our pillows whipped out from under our heads; and as we started from the bed we saw, in the bright moonlight, the horses galloping madly off with the saddles, tied to the lariats whose other ends were round their necks, bounding and trailing after them. Our first thought was that they had been stampeded by horse-thieves, and we rolled over and crouched down in the grass with our rifles; but nothing could be seen, except a shadowy four-footed form in the hollow, and in the end we found that the horses must have taken alarm at a wolf or wolves that had come up to the edge of the bank and looked over at us, not being able at first to make out what we were.

We did not expect to find the horses again that night, but nevertheless took up the broad trail made by the saddles as they dragged through the dewy grass, and followed it well in the moonlight. Our task proved easier than we had feared; for they had not run much over half a mile, and we found them standing close together and looking intently round when we came up. Leading them back we again went to sleep; but the weather was rapidly changing, and by three o'clock a fine rain began to come steadily down, and we cowered and shivered under our wet blankets till morning. At the first streak of dawn, having again eaten a couple of biscuits, we were off, glad to bid good-bye to the inhospitable pool, in whose neighborhood we had spent such a comfortless night. A fine, drizzling mist shrouded us and hid from sight all distant objects; and at times there were heavy downpours of rain. Before we had gone any distance we became what is termed by backwoodsmen or plainsmen, "turned round," and the creeks suddenly seemed to be running the wrong way; after which we travelled purely by the compass.

For some hours we kept a nearly straight course over the formless, shapeless plain, drenched through, and thoroughly uncomfortable; then as we rose over a low divide the fog lifted for a few minutes, and we saw several black objects slowly crossing some rolling country ahead of us, and a glance satisfied us they were buffalo. The horses were picketed at once, and we ran up as near the game as we dared, and then began to stalk them, creeping forward on our hands and knees through the soft, muddy prairie soil, while a smart shower of rain blew in our faces, as we advanced up wind. The country was favorable, and we got within less than a hundred yards of the nearest, a large cow, though we had to creep along so slowly that we were chilled through, and our teeth chattered behind our blue lips. To crown my misfortunes, I now made one of those misses which a man to his dying day always looks back upon with wonder and regret. The rain was beating in my eyes, and the drops stood out in the sights of the rifle so that I could hardly draw a bead; and I either overshot or else at the last moment must have given a nervous jerk and pulled the rifle clear off the mark. At any rate I missed clean, and the whole band plunged down into a hollow and were off before, with my stiffened and numbed fingers, I could get another shot; and in wet, sullen misery we plodded back to the ponies.

All that day the rain continued, and we passed another wretched night. Next morning, however, it had cleared off, and as the sun rose brightly we forgot our hunger and sleepiness, and rode cheerily off up a large dry creek, in whose bottom pools of rain-water still stood. During the morning, however, our ill-luck continued. My companion's horse almost trod on a rattlesnake, and narrowly escaped being bitten. While riding along the face of a steeply-inclined bluff the sandy soil broke away under the ponies' hoofs, and we slid and rolled down to the bottom, where we came to in a heap, horses and men. Then while galloping through a brush-covered bottom my pony put both forefeet in a hole made by the falling and uprooting of a tree, and turned a complete somersault, pitching me a good ten feet beyond his head. And finally, while crossing what looked like the hard bed of a dry creek, the earth gave way under my horse as if he had stepped on a trap-door, and let him down to his withers in soft, sticky mud. I was off at once and floundered to the bank, loosening the lariat from the saddle-bow; and both of us turning to with a will, and bringing the other pony in to our aid, hauled him out by the rope, pretty nearly strangling him in so doing, and he looked rather a melancholy object as he stood up, trembling and shaking, and plastered with mire from head to tail.

So far the trip had certainly not been a success, although sufficiently varied as regards its incidents; we had been confined to moist biscuits for three days as our food; had been wet and cold at night, and sunburned till our faces peeled in the day; were hungry and tired, and had met with bad weather, and all kinds of accidents; in addition to which I had shot badly. But a man who is fond of sport, and yet is not naturally a good hunter, soon learns that if he wishes any success at all he must both keep in memory and put in practice Anthony Trollope's famous precept: "It 's dogged as does it." And if he keeps doggedly on in his course the odds are heavy that in the end the longest lane will prove to have a turning. Such was the case on this occasion.

Shortly after mid-day we left the creek bottom, and skirted a ridge of broken buttes, cut up by gullies and winding ravines, in whose bottoms grew bunch grass. While passing near the mouth, and to leeward of one of these ravines, both ponies threw up their heads, and snuffed the air, turning their muzzles towards the head of the gully. Feeling sure that they had smelt some wild beast, either a bear or a buffalo, I slipped off my pony, and ran quickly but cautiously up along the valley. Before I had gone a hundred yards, I noticed in the soft soil at the bottom the round prints of a bison's hoofs; and immediately afterwards got a glimpse of the animal himself, as he fed slowly up the course of the ravine, some distance ahead of me. The wind was just right, and no ground could have been better for stalking. Hardly needing to bend down, I walked up behind a small sharp-crested hillock, and peeping over, there below me, not fifty yards off, was a great bison bull. He was walking along, grazing as he walked. His glossy fall coat was in fine trim, and shone in the rays of the sun; while his pride of bearing showed him to be in the lusty vigor of his prime. As I rose above the crest of the hill, he held up his head and cocked his tail in the air. Before he could go off, I put the bullet in behind his shoulder. The wound was an almost immediately fatal one, yet with surprising agility for so large and heavy an animal, he bounded up the opposite side of the ravine, heedless of two more balls, both of which went into his flank and ranged forwards, and disappeared over the ridge at a lumbering gallop, the blood pouring from his mouth and nostrils. We knew he could not go far, and trotted leisurely along on his bloody trail; and in the next gully we found him stark dead, lying almost on his back, having pitched over the side when he tried to go down it. His head was a remarkably fine one, even for a fall buffalo. He was lying in a very bad position, and it was most tedious and tiresome work to cut it off and pack it out. The flesh of a cow or calf is better eating than is that of a bull; but the so-called hump meat—that is, the strip of steak on each side of the backbone—is excellent, and tender and juicy. Buffalo meat is with difficulty to be distinguished from ordinary beef. At any rate, the flesh of this bull tasted uncommonly good to us, for we had been without fresh meat for a week; and until a healthy, active man has been without it for some little time, he does not know how positively and almost painfully hungry for flesh he becomes, no matter how much farinaceous food he may have. And the very toil I had been obliged to go through, in order to procure the head, made me feel all the prouder of it when it was at last in my possession.

A year later I made another trip, this time with a wagon, through what had once been a famous buffalo range, the divide between the Little Missouri and the Powder, at its northern end, where some of the creeks flowing into the Yellowstone also head up; but though in most places throughout the range the grass had not yet grown from the time a few months before when it had been cropped off down close to the roots by the grazing herds, and though the ground was cut up in all directions by buffalo trails, and covered by their innumerable skulls and skeletons, not a living one did we see, and only one moderately fresh track, which we followed until we lost it. Some of the sharper ridges were of soft, crumbling sand-stone, and when a buffalo trail crossed such a one, it generally made a curious, heart-shaped cut, the feet of the animals sinking the narrow path continually deeper and deeper, while their bodies brushed out the sides. The profile of a ridge across which several trails led had rather a curious look when seen against the sky.

Game was scarce on this broken plains country, where the water supply was very scanty, and where the dull brown grass that grew on the parched, sun-cracked ground had been already cropped close; still we found enough to keep us in fresh meat; and though no buffalo were seen, the trip was a pleasant one. There was a certain charm in the very vastness and the lonely, melancholy desolation of the land over which every day we galloped far and wide from dawn till nightfall; while the heavy canvas-covered wagon lumbered slowly along to the appointed halting-place. On such a trip one soon gets to feel that the wagon is home; and after a tiresome day it is pleasant just to lie still in the twilight by the side of the smouldering fire and watch the men as they busy themselves cooking or arranging the beds, while the solemn old ponies graze around or stand quietly by the great white-topped prairie schooner.

The blankets and rubbers being arranged in a carefully chosen spot to leeward of the wagon, we were not often bothered at night, even by quite heavy rainfalls; but once or twice, when in peculiarly exposed places, we were struck by such furious gusts of wind and rain that we were forced to gather up our bedding and hastily scramble into the wagon, where we would at least be dry, even though in pretty cramped quarters.

# Old Ephraim

*Hunting Trips of a Ranchman*

But few bears are found in the immediate neighborhood of my ranch; and though I have once or twice seen their tracks in the Bad Lands, I have never had any experience with the animals themselves except during the elk-hunting trip on the Bighorn Mountains, described in the preceding chapter. The grizzly bear undoubtedly comes in the category of dangerous game, and is, perhaps, the only animal in the United States that can be fairly so placed, unless we count the few jaguars found north of the Rio Grande. But the danger of hunting the grizzly has been greatly exaggerated, and the sport is certainly very much safer than it was at the beginning of this century. The first hunters who came into contact with this great bear were men belonging to that hardy and adventurous class of backwoodsmen which had filled the wild country between the Appalachian Mountains and the Mississippi. These men carried but one weapon: the long-barrelled, small-bored pea-rifle, whose bullets ran seventy to the pound, the amount of powder and lead being a little less than that contained in the cartridge of a thirty-two calibre Winchester. In the Eastern States almost all the hunting was done in the woodland; the shots were mostly obtained at short distance, and deer and black bear were the largest game; moreover, the pea-rifles were marvellously accurate for close range, and their owners were famed the world over for their skill as marksmen. Thus these rifles had so far proved plenty good enough for the work they had to do, and indeed had done excellent service as military weapons in the ferocious wars that the men of the border carried on with their Indian neighbors, and even in conflict with more civilized foes, as at the battles of King's Mountain and New Orleans.

But when the restless frontiersmen pressed out over the Western plains, they encountered in the grizzly a beast of far greater bulk and more savage temper than any of those found in the Eastern woods, and their small-bore rifles were utterly inadequate weapons with which to cope with him. It is small wonder that he was considered by them to be almost invulnerable, and extraordinarily tenacious of life. He would be a most unpleasant antagonist now to a man armed only with a thirty-two calibre rifle, that carried but a single shot and was loaded at the muzzle. A rifle, to be of use in this sport, should carry a ball weighing from half an ounce to an ounce. With the old pea-rifles the shot had to be in the eye or heart; and accidents to the hunter were very common. But the introduction of heavy breech-loading repeaters has greatly lessened the danger, even in the very few and far-off places where the grizzlies are as ferocious as formerly. For nowadays these great bears are undoubtedly much better aware of the death-dealing power of men, and, as a consequence, much less fierce, than was the case with their forefathers, who so unhesitatingly attacked the early Western travellers and explorers. Constant contact with rifle-carrying hunters, for a period extending over many generations of bear-life, has taught the grizzly by bitter experience that man is his undoubted overlord, as far as fighting goes; and this knowledge has become an hereditary characteristic. No grizzly will assail a man now unprovoked, and one will almost always rather run than fight; though if he is wounded or thinks himself cornered he will attack his foes with a headlong, reckless fury that renders him one of the most dangerous of wild beasts. The ferocity of all wild animals depends largely upon the amount of resistance they are accustomed to meet with, and the quantity of molestation to which they are subjected.

The change in the grizzly's character during the last half century has been precisely paralleled by the change in the characters of his northern cousin, the polar bear, and of the South African lion. When the Dutch and Scandinavian sailors first penetrated the Arctic seas, they were kept in constant dread of the white bear, who regarded a man as simply an erect variety of seal, quite as good eating as the common kind. The records of these early explorers are filled with examples of the ferocious and man-eating propensities of the polar bears; but in the accounts of most of the later Arctic expeditions they are portrayed as having learned wisdom, and being now most anxious to keep out of the way of the hunters. A number of my sporting friends have killed white bears, and none of them were ever even charged. And in South Africa the English sportsmen and Dutch boers have taught the lion to be a very different creature from what it was when the first white man reached that continent. If the Indian tiger had been a native of the United States, it would now be one of the most shy of beasts. Of late years our estimate of the grizzly's ferocity has been lowered; and we no longer accept the tales of uneducated hunters as being proper authority by which to judge it. But we should make a parallel reduction in the cases of many foreign animals and their describers. Take, for example, that purely melodramatic beast, the North African lion, as portrayed by Jules Gérard, who bombastically describes himself as "le tueur des lions." Gérard's accounts are self-evidently in large part fictitious, while if true they would prove less for the bravery of the lion than for the phenomenal cowardice, incapacity, and bad marksmanship of the Algerian Arabs. Doubtless Gérard was a great hunter; but so is many a Western plainsman, whose account of the grizzlies he has killed would be wholly untrustworthy. Take for instance the following from page 223 of "La Chasse au Lion": "The inhabitants had assembled one day to the number of two or three hundred with the object of killing (the lion) or driving it out of the country. The attack took place at sunrise; at mid-day five hundred cartridges had been expended; the Arabs carried off one of their number dead and six wounded, and the lion remained master of the field of battle." Now if three hundred men could fire five hundred shots at a lion without hurting him, it merely shows that they were wholly incapable of hurting any thing, or else that M. Gérard was more expert with the long-bow than with the rifle. Gérard's whole book is filled with equally preposterous nonsense; yet a great many people seriously accept this same book as trustworthy authority for the manners and ferocity of the North African lion. It would be quite as sensible to accept M. Jules Verne's stories as being valuable contributions to science. A good deal of the lion's reputation is built upon just such stuff.

How the prowess of the grizzly compares with that of the lion or tiger would be hard to say; I have never shot either of the latter myself, and my brother, who has killed tigers in India, has never had a chance at a grizzly. Any one of the big bears we killed on the mountains would, I should think, have been able to make short work of either a lion or a tiger; for the grizzly is greatly superior in bulk and muscular power to either of the great cats, and its teeth are as large as theirs, while its claws, though blunter, are much longer; nevertheless, I believe that a lion or a tiger would be fully as dangerous to a hunter or other human being, on account of the superior speed of its charge, the lightning-like rapidity of its movements, and its apparently sharper senses. Still, after all is said, the man should have a thoroughly trustworthy weapon and a fairly cool head, who would follow into his own haunts and slay grim Old Ephraim.

A grizzly will only fight if wounded or cornered, or, at least, if he thinks himself cornered. If a man by accident stumbles on to one close up, he is almost certain to be attacked really more from fear than from any other motive; exactly the same reason that makes a rattlesnake strike at a passer-by. I have personally known of but one instance of a grizzly turning on a hunter before being wounded. This happened to a friend of mine, a Californian ranchman, who, with two or three of his men, was following a bear that had carried off one of his sheep. They got the bear into a cleft in the mountain from which there was no escape, and he suddenly charged back through the line of his pursuers, struck down one of the horsemen, seized the arm of the man in his jaws and broke it as if it had been a pipestem, and was only killed after a most lively fight, in which, by repeated charges, he at one time drove every one of his assailants off the field.

But two instances have come to my personal knowledge where a man has been killed by a grizzly. One was that of a hunter at the foot of the Bighorn Mountains who had chased a large bear and finally wounded him. The animal turned at once and came straight at the man, whose second shot missed. The bear then closed and passed on, after striking only a single blow; yet that one blow, given with all the power of its thick, immensely muscular forearm, armed with nails as strong as so many hooked steel spikes, tore out the man's collar-bone and snapped through three or four ribs. He never recovered from the shock, and died that night.

The other instance occurred to a neighbor of mine—who has a small ranch on the Little Missouri—two or three years ago. He was out on a mining trip, and was prospecting with two other men near the head-water of the Little Missouri, in the Black Hills country. They were walking down along the river, and came to a point of land, thrust out into it, which was densely covered with brush and fallen timber. Two of the party walked round by the edge of the stream, but the third, a German, and a very powerful fellow, followed a well-beaten game trail, leading through the bushy point. When they were some forty yards apart the two men heard an agonized shout from the German, and at the same time the loud coughing growl, or roar, of a bear. They turned just in time to see their companion struck a terrible blow on the head by a grizzly, which must have been roused from its lair by his almost stepping on it; so close was it that he had no time to fire his rifle, but merely held it up over his head as a guard. Of course it was struck down, the claws of the great brute at the same time shattering his skull like an egg-shell. Yet the man staggered on some ten feet before he fell; but when he did he never spoke or moved again. The two others killed the bear after a short, brisk struggle, as he was in the midst of a most determined charge.

In 1872, near Fort Wingate, New Mexico, two soldiers of a cavalry regiment came to their death at the claws of a grizzly bear. The army surgeon who attended them told me the particulars, as far as they were known. The men were mail carriers, and one day did not come in at the appointed time. Next day, a relief party was sent out to look for them, and after some search found the bodies of both, as well as that of one of the horses. One of the men still showed signs of life; he came to his senses before dying, and told the story. They had seen a grizzly and pursued it on horseback, with their Spencer rifles. On coming close, one had fired into its side, when it turned with marvellous quickness for so large and unwieldy an animal, and struck down the horse, at the same time inflicting a ghastly wound on the rider. The other man dismounted and came up to the rescue of his companion. The bear then left the latter and attacked the other. Although hit by the bullet, it charged home and threw the man down, and then lay on him and deliberately bit him to death, while his groans and cries were frightful to hear. Afterward it walked off into the bushes without again offering to molest the already mortally wounded victim of its first assault.

At certain times the grizzly works a good deal of havoc among the herds of the stockmen. A friend of mine, a ranchman in Montana, told me that one fall bears became very plenty around his ranches, and caused him severe loss, killing with ease even full-grown beef-steers. But one of them once found his intended quarry too much for him. My friend had a stocky, rather vicious range stallion, which had been grazing one day near a small thicket of bushes, and, towards evening, came galloping in with three or four gashes in his haunch, that looked as if they had been cut with a dull axe. The cowboys knew at once that he had been assailed by a bear, and rode off to the thicket near which he had been feeding. Sure enough a bear, evidently in a very bad temper, sallied out as soon as the thicket was surrounded, and, after a spirited fight and a succession of charges, was killed. On examination, it was found that his under jaw was broken, and part of his face smashed in, evidently by the stallion's hoofs. The horse had been feeding when the bear leaped out at him but failed to kill at the first stroke; then the horse lashed out behind, and not only freed himself, but also severely damaged his opponent.

Doubtless, the grizzly could be hunted to advantage with dogs, which would not, of course, be expected to seize him, but simply to find and bay him, and distract his attention by barking and nipping. Occasionally a bear can be caught in the open and killed with the aid of horses. But nine times out of ten the only way to get one is to put on moccasins and still-hunt it in its own haunts, shooting it at close quarters. Either its tracks should be followed until the bed wherein it lies during the day is found, or a given locality in which it is known to exist should be carefully beaten through, or else a bait should be left out and a watch kept on it to catch the bear when he has come to visit it.

For some days after our arrival on the Bighorn range we did not come across any grizzly.

Although it was still early in September, the weather was cool and pleasant, the nights being frosty; and every two or three days there was a flurry of light snow, which rendered the labor of tracking much more easy. Indeed, throughout our stay on the mountains, the peaks were snow-capped almost all the time. Our fare was excellent, consisting of elk venison, mountain grouse, and small trout; the last caught in one of the beautiful little lakes that lay almost up by timber line. To us, who had for weeks been accustomed to make small fires from dried brush, or from sage-brush roots, which we dug out of the ground, it was a treat to sit at night before the roaring and crackling pine logs; as the old teamster quaintly put it, we had at last come to a land "where the wood grew on trees." There were plenty of black-tail deer in the woods, and we came across a number of bands of cow and calf elk, or of young bulls; but after several days' hunting, we were still without any head worth taking home, and had seen no sign of grizzly, which was the game we were especially anxious to kill; for neither Merrifield nor I had ever seen a wild bear alive.

Sometimes we hunted in company; sometimes each of us went out alone; the teamster, of course, remaining in to guard camp and cook. One day we had separated; I reached camp early in the afternoon, and waited a couple of hours before Merrifield put in an appearance.

At last I heard a shout—the familiar long-drawn Ei-koh-h-h of the cattle-men,—and he came in sight galloping at speed down an open glade, and waving his hat, evidently having had good luck; and when he reined in his small, wiry, cow-pony, we saw that he had packed behind his saddle the fine, glossy pelt of a black bear. Better still, he announced that he had been off about ten miles to a perfect tangle of ravines and valleys where bear sign was very thick; and not of black bear either but of grizzly. The black bear (the only one we got on the mountains) he had run across by accident, while riding up a valley in which there was a patch of dead timber grown up with berry bushes. He noticed a black object which he first took to be a stump; for during the past few days we had each of us made one or two clever stalks up to charred logs which our imagination converted into bears. On coming near, however, the object suddenly took to its heels; he followed over frightful ground at the pony's best pace, until it stumbled and fell down. By this time he was close on the bear, which had just reached the edge of the wood. Picking himself up, he rushed after it, hearing it growling ahead of him; after running some fifty yards the sounds stopped, and he stood still listening. He saw and heard nothing, until he happened to cast his eyes upwards, and there was the bear, almost overhead, and about twenty-five feet up a tree; and in as many seconds afterwards it came down to the ground with a bounce, stone dead. It was a young bear, in its second year, and had probably never before seen a man, which accounted for the ease with which it was treed and taken. One minor result of the encounter was to convince Merrifield—the list of whose faults did not include lack of self-confidence—that he could run down any bear; in consequence of which idea we on more than one subsequent occasion went through a good deal of violent exertion.

Merrifield's tale made me decide to shift camp at once, and go over to the spot where the bear-tracks were so plenty. Next morning we were off, and by noon pitched camp by a clear brook, in a valley with steep, wooded sides, but with good feed for the horses in the open bottom. We rigged the canvas wagon sheet into a small tent, sheltered by the trees from the wind, and piled great pine logs near by where we wished to place the fire; for a night camp in the sharp fall weather is cold and dreary unless there is a roaring blaze of flame in front of the tent.

That afternoon we again went out, and I shot a fine bull elk. I came home alone toward nightfall, walking through a reach of burnt forest, where there was nothing but charred tree-trunks and black mould. When nearly through it I came across the huge, half-human footprints of a great grizzly, which must have passed by within a few minutes. It gave me rather an eerie feeling in the silent, lonely woods, to see for the first time the unmistakable proofs that I was in the home of the mighty lord of the wilderness. I followed the tracks in the fading twilight until it became too dark to see them any longer, and then shouldered my rifle and walked back to camp.

That evening we almost had a visit from one of the animals we were after. Several times we had heard at night the musical calling of the bull elk—a sound to which no writer has as yet done justice. This particular night, when we were in bed and the fire was smouldering, we were roused by a ruder noise—a kind of grunting or roaring whine, answered by the frightened snorts of the ponies. It was a bear which had evidently not seen the fire, as it came from behind the bank, and had probably been attracted by the smell of the horses. After it made out what we were it stayed round a short while, again uttered its peculiar roaring grunt, and went off; we had seized our rifles and had run out into the woods, but in the darkness could see nothing; indeed it was rather lucky we did not stumble across the bear, as he could have made short work of us when we were at such a disadvantage.

Next day we went off on a long tramp through the woods and along the sides of the canyons. There were plenty of berry bushes growing in clusters; and all around these there were fresh tracks of bear. But the grizzly is also a flesh-eater, and has a great liking for carrion. On visiting the place where Merrifield had killed the black bear, we found that the grizzlies had been there before us, and had utterly devoured the carcass, with cannibal relish. Hardly a scrap was left, and we turned our steps toward where lay the bull elk I had killed. It was quite late in the afternoon when we reached the place. A grizzly had evidently been at the carcass during the preceding night, for his great footprints were in the ground all around it, and the carcass itself was gnawed and torn, and partially covered with earth and leaves—for the grizzly has a curious habit of burying all of his prey that he does not at the moment need. A great many ravens had been feeding on the body, and they wheeled about over the tree tops above us, uttering their barking croaks.

The forest was composed mainly of what are called ridge-pole pines, which grow close together, and do not branch out until the stems are thirty or forty feet from the ground. Beneath these trees we walked over a carpet of pine needles, upon which our moccasined feet made no sound. The woods seemed vast and lonely, and their silence was broken now and then by the strange noises always to be heard in the great forests, and which seem to mark the sad and everlasting unrest of the wilderness. We climbed up along the trunk of a dead tree which had toppled over until its upper branches struck in the limb crotch of another, that thus supported it at an angle half-way in its fall. When above the ground far enough to prevent the bear's smelling us, we sat still to wait for his approach; until, in the gathering gloom, we could no longer see the sights of our rifles, and could but dimly make out the carcass of the great elk. It was useless to wait longer; and we clambered down and stole out to the edge of the woods. The forest here covered one side of a steep, almost canyon-like ravine, whose other side was bare except of rock and sage-brush. Once out from under the trees there was still plenty of light, although the sun had set, and we crossed over some fifty yards to the opposite hill-side, and crouched down under a bush to see if perchance some animal might not also leave the cover. To our right the ravine sloped downward toward the valley of the Bighorn River, and far on its other side we could catch a glimpse of the great main chain of the Rockies, their snow peaks glinting crimson in the light of the set sun. Again we waited quietly in the growing dusk until the pine trees in our front blended into one dark, frowning mass. We saw nothing; but the wild creatures of the forest had begun to stir abroad. The owls hooted dismally from the tops of the tall trees, and two or three times a harsh wailing cry, probably the voice of some lynx or wolverine, arose from the depths of the woods. At last, as we were rising to leave, we heard the sound of the breaking of a dead stick, from the spot where we knew the carcass lay. It was a sharp, sudden noise, perfectly distinct from the natural creaking and snapping of the branches; just such a sound as would be made by the tread of some heavy creature. "Old Ephraim" had come back to the carcass. A minute afterward, listening with strained ears, we heard him brush by some dry twigs. It was entirely too dark to go in after him; but we made up our minds that on the morrow he should be ours.

Early next morning we were over at the elk carcass, and, as we expected, found that the bear had eaten his fill at it during the night. His tracks showed him to be an immense fellow, and were so fresh that we doubted if he had left long before we arrived; and we made up our minds to follow him up and try to find his lair. The bears that lived on these mountains had evidently been little disturbed; indeed, the Indians and most of the white hunters are rather chary of meddling with "Old Ephraim," as the mountain men style the grizzly, unless they get him at a disadvantage; for the sport is fraught with some danger and but small profit. The bears thus seemed to have very little fear of harm, and we thought it likely that the bed of the one who had fed on the elk would not be far away.

My companion was a skilful tracker, and we took up the trail at once. For some distance it led over the soft, yielding carpet of moss and pine needles, and the footprints were quite easily made out, although we could follow them but slowly; for we had, of course, to keep a sharp look-out ahead and around us as we walked noiselessly on in the sombre half-light always prevailing under the great pine trees, through whose thickly interlacing branches stray but few beams of light, no matter how bright the sun may be outside. We made no sound ourselves, and every little sudden noise sent a thrill through me as I peered about with each sense on the alert. Two or three of the ravens that we had scared from the carcass flew overhead, croaking hoarsely; and the pine tops moaned and sighed in the slight breeze—for pine trees seem to be ever in motion, no matter how light the wind.

After going a few hundred yards the tracks turned off on a well-beaten path made by the elk; the woods were in many places cut up by these game trails, which had often become as distinct as ordinary foot-paths. The beast's footprints were perfectly plain in the dust, and he had lumbered along up the path until near the middle of the hill-side, where the ground broke away and there were hollows and boulders. Here there had been a windfall, and the dead trees lay among the living, piled across one another in all directions; while between and around them sprouted up a thick growth of young spruces and other evergreens. The trail turned off into the tangled thicket, within which it was almost certain we would find our quarry. We could still follow the tracks, by the slight scrapes of the claws on the bark, or by the bent and broken twigs; and we advanced with noiseless caution, slowly climbing over the dead tree trunks and upturned stumps, and not letting a branch rustle or catch on our clothes. When in the middle of the thicket we crossed what was almost a breastwork of fallen logs, and Merrifield, who was leading, passed by the upright stem of a great pine. As soon as he was by it he sank suddenly on one knee, turning half round, his face fairly aflame with excitement; and as I strode past him, with my rifle at the ready, there, not ten steps off, was the great bear, slowly rising from his bed among the young spruces. He had heard us, but apparently hardly knew exactly where or what we were, for he reared up on his haunches sideways to us. Then he saw us and dropped down again on all fours, the shaggy hair on his neck and shoulders seeming to bristle as he turned toward us. As he sank down on his forefeet I had raised the rifle; his head was bent slightly down, and when I saw the top of the white bead fairly between his small, glittering, evil eyes, I pulled trigger. Half-rising up, the huge beast fell over on his side in the death throes, the ball having gone into his brain, striking as fairly between the eyes as if the distance had been measured by a carpenter's rule.

The whole thing was over in twenty seconds from the time I caught sight of the game; indeed, it was over so quickly that the grizzly did not have time to show fight at all or come a step toward us. It was the first I had ever seen, and I felt not a little proud, as I stood over the great brindled bulk, which lay stretched out at length in the cool shade of the evergreens. He was a monstrous fellow, much larger than any I have seen since, whether alive or brought in dead by the hunters. As near as we could estimate (for of course we had nothing with which to weigh more than very small portions) he must have weighed about twelve hundred pounds, and though this is not as large as some of his kind are said to grow in California, it is yet a very unusual size for a bear. He was a good deal heavier than any of our horses; and it was with the greatest difficulty that we were able to skin him. He must have been very old, his teeth and claws being all worn down and blunted; but nevertheless he had been living in plenty, for he was as fat as a prize hog, the layers on his back being a finger's length in thickness. He was still in the summer coat, his hair being short, and in color a curious brindled brown, somewhat like that of certain bull-dogs; while all the bears we shot afterward had the long thick winter fur, cinnamon or yellowish brown. By the way, the name of this bear has reference to its character and not to its color, and should, I suppose, be properly spelt grisly—in the sense of horrible, exactly as we speak of a "grisly spectre"—and not grizzly; but perhaps the latter way of spelling it is too well established to be now changed.

In killing dangerous game steadiness is more needed than good shooting. No game is dangerous unless a man is close up, for nowadays hardly any wild beast will charge from a distance of a hundred yards, but will rather try to run off; and if a man is close it is easy enough for him to shoot straight if he does not lose his head. A bear's brain is about the size of a pint bottle; and any one can hit a pint bottle off-hand at thirty or forty feet. I have had two shots at bears at close quarters, and each time I fired into the brain, the bullet in one case striking fairly between the eyes, as told above, and in the other going in between the eye and ear. A novice at this kind of sport will find it best and safest to keep in mind the old Norse viking's advice in reference to a long sword: "If you go in close enough your sword will be long enough." If a poor shot goes in close enough he will find that he shoots straight enough.

I was very proud over my first bear; but Merrifield's chief feeling seemed to be disappointment that the animal had not had time to show fight. He was rather a reckless fellow, and very confident in his own skill with the rifle; and he really did not seem to have any more fear of the grizzlies than if they had been so many jack-rabbits. I did not at all share his feelings, having a hearty respect for my foes' prowess, and in following and attacking them always took all possible care to get the chances on my side. Merrifield was sincerely sorry that we never had to stand a regular charge; while on this trip we killed five grizzlies with seven bullets, and except in the case of the she and cub, spoken of further on, each was shot about as quickly as it got sight of us. The last one we got was an old male, which was feeding on an elk carcass. We crept up to within about sixty feet, and as Merrifield had not yet killed a grizzly purely to his own gun, and I had killed three, I told him to take the shot. He at once whispered gleefully: "I'll break his leg, and we'll see what he'll do!" Having no ambition to be a participator in the antics of a three-legged bear, I hastily interposed a most emphatic veto; and with a rather injured air he fired, the bullet going through the neck just back of the head. The bear fell to the shot, and could not get up from the ground, dying in a few minutes; but first he seized his left wrist in his teeth and bit clean through it, completely separating the bones of the paw and arm. Although a smaller bear than the big one I first shot, he would probably have proved a much more ugly foe, for he was less unwieldy, and had much longer and sharper teeth and claws. I think that if my companion had merely broken the beast's leg he would have had his curiosity as to its probable conduct more than gratified.

We tried eating the grizzly's flesh but it was not good, being coarse and not well flavored; and besides, we could not get over the feeling that it had belonged to a carrion feeder. The flesh of the little black bear, on the other hand, was excellent; it tasted like that of a young pig. Doubtless, if a young grizzly, which had fed merely upon fruits, berries, and acorns, was killed, its flesh would prove good eating; but even then, it would probably not be equal to a black bear.

A day or two after the death of the big bear, we went out one afternoon on horseback, intending merely to ride down to see a great canyon lying some six miles west of our camp; indeed, we went more to look at the scenery than for any other reason, though, of course, neither of us ever stirred out of camp without his rifle. We rode down the valley in which we had camped, through alternate pine groves and open glades, until we reached the canyon, and then skirted its brink for a mile or so. It was a great chasm, many miles in length, as if the table-land had been rent asunder by some terrible and unknown force; its sides were sheer walls of rock, rising three or four hundred feet straight up in the air, and worn by the weather till they looked like the towers and battlements of some vast fortress. Between them at the bottom was a space, in some places nearly a quarter of a mile wide, in others very narrow, through whose middle foamed a deep, rapid torrent of which the sources lay far back among the snow-topped mountains around Cloud Peak. In this valley, dark-green, sombre pines stood in groups, stiff and erect; and here and there among them were groves of poplar and cotton-wood, with slender branches and trembling leaves, their bright green already changing to yellow in the sharp fall weather. We went down to where the mouth of the canyon opened out, and rode our horses to the end of a great jutting promontory of rock, thrust out into the plain; and in the cold, clear air we looked far over the broad valley of the Bighorn as it lay at our very feet, walled in on the other side by the distant chain of the Rocky Mountains.

Turning our horses, we rode back along the edge of another canyon-like valley, with a brook flowing down its centre, and its rocky sides covered with an uninterrupted pine forest—the place of all others in whose inaccessible wildness and ruggedness a bear would find a safe retreat. After some time we came to where other valleys, with steep, grass-grown sides, covered with sage-brush, branched out from it, and we followed one of these out. There was plenty of elk sign about, and we saw several black-tail deer. These last were very common on the mountains, but we had not hunted them at all, as we were in no need of meat. But this afternoon we came across a buck with remarkably fine antlers, and accordingly I shot it, and we stopped to cut off and skin out the horns, throwing the reins over the heads of the horses and leaving them to graze by themselves. The body lay near the crest of one side of a deep val-ley, or ravine, which headed up on the plateau a mile to our left. Except for scat-tered trees and bushes the valley was bare; but there was heavy timber along the crests of the hills on its opposite side. It took some time to fix the head prop-erly, and we were just ending when Merrifield sprang to his feet and exclaimed: "Look at the bears!" pointing down into the valley below us. Sure enough there were two bears (which afterwards proved to be an old she and a nearly full-grown cub) travelling up the bottom of the valley, much too far off for us to shoot. Grasping our rifles and throwing off our hats we started off as hard as we could run, diagonally down the hill-side, so as to cut them off. It was some little time before they saw us, when they made off at a lumbering gallop up the valley. It would seem impossible to run into two grizzlies in the open, but they were going up-hill and we down, and moreover the old one kept stopping. The cub would forge ahead and could probably have escaped us, but the mother now and then stopped to sit up on her haunches and look round at us, when the cub would run back to her. The upshot was that we got ahead of them, when they turned and went straight up one hill-side as we ran straight down the other behind them. By this time I was pretty nearly done out, for running along the steep ground through the sage-brush was most exhausting work; and Merrifield kept gaining on me and was well in front. Just as he disappeared over a bank, almost at the bottom of the valley, I tripped over a bush and fell full-length. When I got up I knew I could never make up the ground I had lost, and besides, could hardly run any longer; Merrifield was out of sight below, and the bears were laboring up the steep hill-side directly opposite and about three hun-dred yards off, so I sat down and began to shoot over Merrifield's head, aim-ing at the big bear. She was going very steadily and in a straight line, and each bullet sent up a puff of dust where it struck the dry soil, so that I could keep correcting my aim; and the fourth ball crashed into the old bear's flank. She lurched heavily forward, but recovered herself and reached the timber, while Merrifield, who had put on a spurt, was not far behind.

I toiled up the hill at a sort of trot, fairly gasping and sobbing for breath; but before I got to the top I heard a couple of shots and a shout. The old bear had turned as soon as she was in the timber, and came towards Merrifield, but he gave her the death wound by firing into her chest, and then shot at the young one, knocking it over. When I came up he was just walking towards the latter to finish it with the revolver, but it suddenly jumped up as lively as ever and made off at a great pace—for it was nearly full-grown. It was impossible to fire where the tree trunks were so thick, but there was a small opening across which it would have to pass, and collecting all my energies I made a last run, got into position, and covered the opening with my rifle. The instant the bear appeared I fired, and it turned a dozen somersaults downhill, rolling over and over; the ball had struck it near the tail and had ranged forward through the hollow of the body. Each of us had thus given the fatal wound to the bear into which the other had fired the first bullet. The run, though short, had been very sharp, and over such awful country that we were completely fagged out, and could hardly speak for lack of breath. The sun had already set, and it was too late to skin the animals; so we merely dressed them, caught the ponies—with some trouble, for they were frightened at the smell of the bear's blood on our hands,—and rode home through the darkening woods. Next day we brought the teamster and two of the steadiest pack-horses to the carcasses, and took the skins into camp.

The feed for the horses was excellent in the valley in which we were camped, and the rest after their long journey across the plains did them good. They had picked up wonderfully in condition during our stay on the mountains; but they were apt to wander very far during the night, for there were so many bears and other wild beasts around that they kept getting frightened and running off. We were very loath to leave our hunting grounds, but time was pressing, and we had already many more trophies than we could carry; so one cool morning, when the branches of the evergreens were laden with the feathery snow that had fallen overnight, we struck camp and started out of the mountains, each of us taking his own bedding behind his saddle, while the pack-ponies were loaded down with bearskins, elk and deer antlers, and the hides and furs of other game. In single file we moved through the woods, and across the canyons to the edge of the great table-land, and then slowly down the steep slope to its foot, where we found our canvas-topped wagon; and next day saw us setting out on our long journey homewards, across the three hundred weary miles of treeless and barren-looking plains country.

Last spring, since the above was written, a bear killed a man not very far from my ranch. It was at the time of the floods. Two hunters came down the river, by our ranch, on a raft, stopping to take dinner. A score or so of miles below, as we afterwards heard from the survivor, they landed, and found a bear in a small patch of brushwood. After waiting in vain for it to come out, one of the men rashly attempted to enter the thicket, and was instantly struck down by the beast, before he could so much as fire his rifle. It broke in his skull with a blow of its great paw, and then seized his arm in its jaws, biting it through and through in three places, but leaving the body and retreating into the bushes as soon as the unfortunate man's companion approached. We did not hear of the accident until too late to go after the bear, as we were just about starting to join the spring round-up.

*Roosevelt tells another story about hunting grizzly in his 1913 Autobiography. It's the story mentioned in the Introduction about the bear's paw just missing his face; it speaks to his character and it's worth repeating. He had been talking in the book about his African game experiences and the dangers of hunting big game animals:*

But, as I said above, the only narrow escape I met with was not from one of those dangerous African animals, but from a grizzly bear. It was about twenty-four years ago. I had wounded the bear just at sunset, in a wood of lodge-pole pines, and, following him, I wounded him again, as he stood on the other side of a thicket. He then charged through the brush, coming with such speed and with such an irregular gait that, try as I would, I was not able to get the sight of my rifle on the brain-pan, though I hit him very hard with both the remaining barrels of my magazine Winchester. It was in the days of black powder, and the smoke hung. After my last shot, the first thing I saw was the bear's left paw as he struck at me, so close that I made a quick movement to one side. He was, however, practically already dead, and after another jump, and while in the very act of trying to turn to come at me, he collapsed like a shot rabbit.

*Roosevelt then explains how hard it was, working alone, to bring the bear's skin back on his horse. Then he goes on:*

The reason why I was alone in the mountains on this occasion was because, for the only time in all my experience, I had a difficulty with my guide. He was a crippled old mountain man, with a profound contempt for "tenderfeet," a contempt that in my case was accentuated by the fact that I wore spectacles—which at that day and in that region were usually held to indicate a defective moral character in the wearer. He had never previously acted as guide, or, as he expressed it, "trundled a tenderfoot," and though a good hunter, who showed me much game, our experience together was not happy. He was very rheumatic and liked to lie abed late, so that I usually had to get breakfast, and, in fact, do most of the work around camp. Finally one day he declined to go out with me, saying that he had a pain. When, that afternoon, I got back to camp, I speedily found out what the "pain" was. We were traveling very light indeed, I having practically nothing but my buffalo sleeping-bag, my wash kit, and a pair of socks. I had also taken a flask of whisky for emergencies—although, as I found that emergencies never arose and that tea was better than whisky when a man was cold or done out, I abandoned the practice of taking whisky on hunting trips twenty years ago. When I got back to camp the old fellow was sitting on a tree-trunk, very erect, with his rifle across his knees, and in response to my nod of greeting he merely leered at me. I leaned my rifle against a tree, walked over to where my bed was lying, and, happening to rummage in it for something, I found the whisky flask was empty. I turned on him at once and accused him of having drunk it, to which he merely responded by asking what I was going to do about it. There did not seem much to do, so I said that we would part company—we were only four or five days from a settlement—and I would go in alone, taking one of the horses. He responded by cocking his rifle and saying that I could go alone and be damned to me, but I could not take any horse. I answered "all right," that if I could not I could not, and began to move around to get some flour and salt pork. He was misled by my quietness and by the fact that I had not in any way resented either his actions or his language during the days we had been together, and did not watch me as closely as he ought to have done. He was sitting with the cocked rifle across his knees, the muzzle to the left. My rifle was leaning against a tree near the cooking things to his right. Managing to get near it, I shipped it up and threw the bead on him, calling, "Hands up!" He, of course, put up his hands, and then said, "Oh, come, I was only joking"; to which I answered, "Well, I am not. Now straighten your legs and let your rifle go to the ground." He remonstrated, saying the rifle would go off, and I told him to let it go off. However, he straightened his legs in such fashion that it came to the ground without a jar. I then made him move back, and picked up the rifle. By this time he was quite sober, and really did not seem angry, looking at me quizzically. He told me that if I would give him back his rifle, he would call it quits and we could go on together. I did not think it best to trust him, so I told him that our hunt was pretty well through, anyway, and that I would go home. There was a blasted pine on the trail, in plain view of the camp, about a mile off, and I told him that I would leave his rifle at that blasted pine if I could see him in camp, but that he must not come after me, for if he did I should assume that it was with hostile intent and would shoot. He said he had no intention of coming after me; and as he was very much crippled with rheumatism, I did not believe he would do so.

Accordingly I took the little mare, with nothing but some flour, bacon, and tea, and my bed-roll, and started off. At the blasted pine I looked round, and as I could see him in camp, I left his rifle there. I then traveled till dark, and that night, for the only time in my experience, I used in camping a trick of the old-time trappers in the Indian days. I did not believe I would be followed, but still it was not possible to be sure, so, after getting supper, while my pony fed round, I left the fire burning, repacked the mare and pushed ahead until it literally became so dark that I could not see. Then I picketed the mare, slept where I was without a fire until the first streak of dawn, and then pushed on for a couple of hours before halting to take breakfast and to let the little mare have a good feed. No plainsman needs to be told that a man should not lie near a fire if there is danger of an enemy creeping up on him, and that above all a man should not put himself in a position where he can be ambushed at dawn. On this second day I lost the trail, and toward nightfall gave up the effort to find it, camped where I was, and went out to shoot a grouse for supper. It was while hunting in vain for a grouse that I came on the bear and killed it as above described.

When I reached the settlement and went into the store, the storekeeper identified me by remarking: "You're the tenderfoot that old Hank was trundling, ain't you?" I admitted that I was. A good many years later, after I had been elected Vice-President, I went on a cougar hunt in northwestern Colorado with Johnny Goff, a famous hunter and mountain man. It was midwinter. I was rather proud of my achievements, and pictured myself as being known to the few settlers in the neighborhood as a successful mountain-lion hunter. I could not help grinning when I found out that they did not even allude to me as the Vice-President-elect, let alone as a hunter, but merely as "Johnny Goff's tourist."

*By the time he was done with the West nobody could have called him a tourist any more.*

*Late in 1885 he met an old friend from his childhood days again, Edith Carow. She was not quite a childhood sweetheart but she was close, and an elegant beautiful young woman now. They were engaged secretly that November and they married in England in December of the following year. He had had one child by Alice Hathaway, a daughter. He would have five more, four boys and a girl, by Edith Carow. Early in 1886 he went back to his ranch, which he had named Elkhorn Ranch, to work on a biography of Thomas Hart Benton, the pioneer senator from Missouri. In the late summer he went to northern Idaho to hunt, then he was back in New York, where he ran* for mayor and lost. Emotionally this was a difficult loss for him and he retired from politics for a time. He sailed for Europe, where Edith Carow was waiting, after the election and married her in London. He came back to the Dakotas in the spring of 1887 to find a disaster of epic proportions: "the worst winter," says Roosevelt's biographer Edmund Morris, "in frontier history." Temperatures dropped to 40 degrees below zero F, the storms were relentless; snow covered the plains so deep that cattle could not find grass, they became so weak from hunger the wind blew them over and they died where they lay; cattle that survived invaded the towns, thrusting their heads through the windows of houses in a desperate search for food. The coulees in the Badlands filled with snow to depths, Morris reports, of a hundred feet or more. When it was over nobody could guess the numbers of cattle dead. But it was in the tens, perhaps the hundreds of thousands. By then Roosevelt had invested $80,000 in his Elkhorn Ranch. A substantial fraction of it was now a dead loss. From then on he wanted only to get out of the business.

Late that year he did manage to get in another hunt in the Dakotas, but his mind was turning to more financially rewarding activities—writing. Early in 1888 he signed a contract to produce a four-volume epic called The Winning of the West that would take him some eight years to finish. He had already, besides the biography of Thomas Hart Benton, written one of Gouverneur Morris, a lesser known Founding Father, and he would now produce the book we take our next selections from, Ranch Life and the Hunting Trail. This is in several ways a more engaging book than the earlier Hunting Trips of a Ranchman. He is less interested in hunting, for one thing, than in life on the plains and in the Badlands and the men living that life. And he is an even better writer, more focused, not relying so much on his charm. This selection contains three chapters of the book: Chapter V, "Winter Weather," which describes with poetic force the weather the cattle endured that terrible winter; Chapter VII, "Red and White on the Border," which tells the story of Roosevelt's own encounter with Indians while riding alone on the plains and is revealing of Western attitudes at the time toward Indians; and Chapter VIII, "Sheriff's Work on a Ranch," in which we find the story of his capture of the three boat thieves.

# Winter Weather

*Ranch Life and the Hunting Trail*

WHEN THE DAYS HAVE DWINDLED TO THEIR SHORTEST, AND THE NIGHTS seem never ending, then all the great northern plains are changed into an abode of iron desolation. Sometimes furious gales blow out of the north, driving before them the clouds of blinding snow-dust, wrapping the mantle of death round every unsheltered being that faces their unshackled anger. They roar in a thunderous bass as they sweep across the prairie or whirl through the naked cañons; they shiver the great brittle cottonwoods, and beneath their rough touch the icy limbs of the pines that cluster in the gorges sing like the chords of an Æolian harp. Again, in the coldest midwinter weather, not a breath of wind may stir; and then the still, merciless, terrible cold that broods over the earth like the shadow of silent death seems even more dreadful in its gloomy rigor than is the lawless madness of the storms. All the land is like granite; the great rivers stand still in their beds, as if turned to frosted steel. In the long nights there is no sound to break the lifeless silence. Under the ceaseless, shifting play of the Northern Lights, or lighted only by the wintry brilliance of the stars, the snow-clad plains stretch out into dead and endless wastes of glimmering white.

Then the great fire-place of the ranch house is choked with blazing logs, and at night we have to sleep under so many blankets that the weight is fairly oppressive. Outside, the shaggy ponies huddle together in the corral, while long icicles hang from their lips, and the hoar-frost whitens the hollow backs of the cattle. For the ranchman the winter is occasionally a pleasant holiday, but more often an irksome period of enforced rest and gloomy foreboding.

In the winter there is much less work than at any other season, but what there is involves great hardship and exposure. Many of the men are discharged after the summer is over, and during much of the cold weather there is little to do except hunt now and then, and in very bitter days lounge listlessly about the house. But some of the men are out in the line camps, and the ranchman has occasionally to make the round of these; and besides that, one or more of the cowboys who are at home ought to be out every day when the cattle have become weak, so as to pick up and drive in any beast that will otherwise evidently fail to get through the season—a cow that has had an unusually early calf being particularly apt to need attention. The horses shift for themselves and need no help. Often, in winter, the Indians cut down the cottonwood trees and feed the tops to their ponies; but this is not done to keep them from starving, but only to keep them from wandering off in search of grass. Besides, the ponies are very fond of the bark of the young cottonwood shoots, and it is healthy for them.

The men in the line camps lead a hard life, for they have to be out in every kind of weather, and should be especially active and watchful during the storms. The camps are established along some line which it is proposed to make the boundary of the cattle's drift in a given direction. For example, we care very little whether our cattle wander to the Yellowstone; but we strongly object to their drifting east and south-east towards the granger country and the Sioux reservation, especially as when they drift that way they come out on flat, bare plains where there is danger of perishing. Accordingly, the cowmen along the Little Missouri have united in establishing a row of camps to the east of the river, along the line where the broken ground meets the prairie. The camps are usually for two men each, and some fifteen or twenty miles apart; then, in the morning, its two men start out in opposite ways, each riding till he meets his neighbor of the next camp nearest on that side, when he returns. The camp itself is sometimes merely a tent pitched in a sheltered coulée, but ought to be either made of logs or else a dug-out in the ground. A small corral and horse-shed is near by, with enough hay for the ponies, of which each rider has two or three. In riding over the beat each man drives any cattle that have come near it back into the Bad Lands, and if he sees by the hoof-marks that a few have strayed out over the line very recently, he will follow and fetch them home. They must be shoved well back into the Bad Lands before a great storm strikes them; for if they once begin to drift in masses before an icy gale it is impossible for a small number of men to hold them, and the only thing is to let them go, and then to organize an expedition to follow them as soon as possible. Line riding is very cold work, and dangerous too, when the men have to be out in a blinding snow-storm, or in a savage blizzard that takes the spirit in the thermometer far down below zero. In the worst storms it is impossible for any man to be out.

But other kinds of work besides line riding necessitate exposure to bitter weather. Once, while spending a few days over on Beaver Creek hunting up a lost horse, I happened to meet a cowboy who was out on the same errand, and made friends with him. We started home together across the open prairies, but were caught in a very heavy snow-storm almost immediately after leaving the ranch where we had spent the night. We were soon completely turned round, the great soft flakes—for, luckily, it was not cold—almost blinding us, and we had to travel entirely by compass. After feeling our way along for eight or nine hours, we finally got down into the broken country near Sentinel Butte and came across an empty hut, a welcome sight to men as cold, hungry, and tired as we were. In this hut we passed the night very comfortably, picketing our horses in a sheltered nook near by, with plenty of hay from an old stack. To while away the long evening, I read Hamlet aloud, from a little pocket Shakspere. The cowboy, a Texan,—one of the best riders I have seen, and also a very intelligent as well as a thoroughly good fellow in every way,—was greatly interested in it and commented most shrewdly on the parts he liked, especially Polonius's advice to Laertes, which he translated into more homely language with great relish, and ended with the just criticism that "old Shakspere saveyed human natur' some"—savey being a verb presumably adapted into the limited plains' vocabulary from the Spanish.

Even for those who do not have to look up stray horses, and who are not forced to ride the line day in and day out, there is apt to be some hardship and danger in being abroad during the bitter weather; yet a ride in midwinter is certainly fascinating. The great white country wrapped in the powdery snow-drift seems like another land; and the familiar landmarks are so changed that a man must be careful lest he lose his way, for the discomfort of a night in the open during such weather is very great indeed. When the sun is out the glare from the endless white stretches dazzles the eyes; and if the gray snow-clouds hang low and only let a pale, wan light struggle through, the lonely wastes become fairly appalling in their desolation. For hour after hour a man may go on and see no sign of life except, perhaps, a big white owl sweeping noiselessly by, so that in the dark it looks like a snow-wreath; the cold gradually chilling the rider to the bones, as he draws his fur cap tight over his ears and muffles his face in the huge collar of his wolf-skin coat, and making the shaggy little steed drop head and tail as it picks its way over the frozen soil. There are few

moments more pleasant than the home-coming, when, in the gathering darkness, after crossing the last chain of ice-covered buttes, or after coming round
the last turn in the wind-swept valley, we see, through the leafless trees, or across
the frozen river, the red gleam of the firelight as it shines through the ranch
windows and flickers over the trunks of the cottonwoods outside, warming a
man's blood by the mere hint of the warmth awaiting him within.

The winter scenery is especially striking in the Bad Lands, with their
queer fantastic formations. Among the most interesting features are the burning mines. These are formed by the coal seams that get on fire. They vary greatly
in size. Some send up smoke-columns that are visible miles away, while others are not noticeable a few rods off. The old ones gradually burn away, while
new ones unexpectedly break out. Thus, last fall, one suddenly appeared but
half a mile from the ranch house. We never knew it was there until one cold
moonlight night, when we were riding home, we rounded the corner of a ravine
and saw in our path a tall white column of smoke rising from a rift in the snowy
crags ahead of us. As the trail was over perfectly familiar ground, we were for
a moment almost as startled as if we had seen a ghost.

The burning mines are uncanny places, anyhow. A strong smell of sulphur
hangs round them, the heated earth crumbles and cracks, and through the long
clefts that form in it we can see the lurid glow of the subterranean fires, with here
and there tongues of blue or cherry colored flame dancing up to the surface.

The winters vary greatly in severity with us. During some seasons
men can go lightly clad even in January and February, and the cattle
hardly suffer at all; during others there will be spells of bitter weather,
accompanied by furious blizzards, which render it impossible for days and
weeks at a time for men to stir out-of-doors at all, save at the risk of their
lives. Then line rider, ranchman, hunter, and teamster alike all have to keep
within doors. I have known of several cases of men freezing to death
when caught in shelterless places by such a blizzard, a strange fact being
that in about half of them the doomed man had evidently gone mad
before dying, and had stripped himself of most of his clothes, the body
when found being nearly naked. On our ranch we have never had any bad
accidents, although every winter some of us get more or less frost-bitten.
My last experience in this line was while returning by moonlight from a
successful hunt after mountain sheep. The thermometer was 26° below zero,
and we had had no food for twelve hours. I became numbed, and before
I was aware of it had frozen my face, one foot, both knees, and one hand.
Luckily, I reached the ranch before serious damage was done.

About once every six or seven years we have a season when these storms follow one another almost without interval throughout the winter months, and then the loss among the stock is frightful. One such winter occurred in 1880-81. This was when there were very few ranchmen in the country. The grass was so good that the old range stock escaped pretty well; but the trail herds were almost destroyed. The next severe winter was that of 1886-87, when the rush of incoming herds had overstocked the ranges, and the loss was in consequence fairly appalling, especially to the outfits that had just put on cattle.

The snow-fall was unprecedented, both for its depth and for the way it lasted; and it was this, and not the cold, that caused the loss. About the middle of November the storms began. Day after day the snow came down, thawing and then freezing and piling itself higher and higher. By January the drifts had filled the ravines and coulées almost level. The snow lay in great masses on the plateaus and river bottoms; and this lasted until the end of February. The preceding summer we had been visited by a prolonged drought, so that the short, scanty grass was already well cropped down; the snow covered what pasturage there was to the depth of several feet, and the cattle could not get at it at all, and could hardly move round. It was all but impossible to travel on horseback—except on a few well-beaten trails. It was dangerous to attempt to penetrate the Bad Lands, whose shape had been completely altered by the great white mounds and drifts. The starving cattle died by scores of thousands before their helpless owners' eyes. The bulls, the cows who were suckling calves, or who were heavy with calf, the weak cattle that had just been driven up on the trail, and the late calves suffered most; the old range animals did better, and the steers best of all; but the best was bad enough. Even many of the horses died. An outfit near me lost half its saddle-band, the animals having been worked so hard that they were very thin when fall came.

In the thick brush the stock got some shelter and sustenance. They gnawed every twig and bough they could get at. They browsed the bitter sage brush down to where the branches were the thickness of a man's finger. When near a ranch they crowded into the outhouses and sheds to die, and fences had to be built around the windows to keep the wild-eyed, desperate beasts from thrusting their heads through the glass panes. In most cases it was impossible either to drive them to the haystacks or to haul the hay out to them. The deer even were so weak as to be easily run down; and on one or two of the plateaus where there were bands of antelope, these wary creatures grew so numbed and feeble that they could have been slaughtered like rabbits. But the hunters could hardly get out, and could bring home neither hide nor meat, so the game went unharmed.

The way in which the cattle got through the winter depended largely on the different localities in which the bands were caught when the first heavy snows came. A group of animals in a bare valley, without underbrush and with steepish sides, would all die, weak and strong alike; they could get no food and no shelter, and so there would not be a hoof left. On the other hand, hundreds wintered on the great thickly wooded bottoms near my ranch house with little more than ordinary loss, though a skinny sorry-looking crew by the time the snow melted. In intermediate places the strong survived and the weak perished.

It would be impossible to imagine any sight more dreary and melancholy than that offered by the ranges when the snow went off in March. The land was a mere barren waste; not a green thing could be seen; the dead grass eaten off till the country looked as if it had been shaved with a razor. Occasionally among the desolate hills a rider would come across a band of gaunt, hollow-flanked cattle feebly cropping the sparse, dry pasturage, too listless to move out of the way; and the blackened carcasses lay in the sheltered spots, some stretched out, others in as natural a position as if the animals had merely lain down to rest. It was small wonder that cheerful stockmen were rare objects that spring.

Our only comfort was that we did not, as usual, suffer a heavy loss from weak cattle getting mired down in the springs and mud-holes when the ice broke up—for all the weak animals were dead already. The truth is, ours is a primitive industry, and we suffer the reverses as well as enjoy the successes only known to primitive peoples. A hard winter is to us in the north what a dry summer is to Texas or Australia—what seasons of famine once were to all peoples. We still live in an iron age that the old civilized world has long passed by. The men of the border reckon upon stern and unending struggles with their iron-bound surroundings; against the grim harshness of their existence they set the strength and the abounding vitality that come with it. They run risks to life and limb that are unknown to the dwellers in cities; and what the men freely brave, the beasts that they own must also sometimes suffer.

# RED AND WHITE ON THE BORDER

*Ranch Life and the Hunting Trail*

UP TO 1880 THE COUNTRY THROUGH WHICH THE LITTLE MISSOURI flows remained as wild and almost as unknown as it was when the old explorers and fur traders crossed it in the early part of the century. It was the last great Indian hunting-ground, across which Grosventres and Mandans, Sioux and Cheyennes, and even Crows and Rees wandered in chase of game, and where they fought one another and plundered the small parties of white trappers and hunters that occasionally ventured into it. Once or twice generals like Sully and Custer had penetrated it in the course of the long, tedious, and bloody campaigns that finally broke the strength of the northern Horse Indians; indeed, the trail made by Custer's baggage train is to this day one of the well-known landmarks, for the deep ruts worn by the wheels of the heavy wagons are in many places still as distinctly to be seen as ever.

In 1883, a regular long-range skirmish took place just south of us between some Cheyennes and some cowboys, with bloodshed on both sides, while about the same time a band of Sioux plundered a party of buffalo hunters of everything they owned, and some Crows who attempted the same feat with another party were driven off with the loss of two of their number. Since then there have been in our neighborhood no stand-up fights or regular raids; but the Indians have at different times proved more or less troublesome, burning the grass, and occasionally killing stock or carrying off horses that have wandered some distance away. They have also themselves suffered somewhat at the hands of white horse-thieves.

Bands of them, accompanied by their squaws and children, often come into the ranch country, either to trade or to hunt, and are then, of course, perfectly meek and peaceable. If they stay any time they build themselves quite comfortable tepees (wigwams, as they would be styled in the East), and an Indian camp is a rather interesting, though very dirty, place to visit. On our ranch we get along particularly well with them, as it is a rule that they shall be treated as fairly as if they were whites: we neither wrong them ourselves nor allow others to wrong them. We have always, for example, been as keen in putting down horse-stealing from Indians as from whites—which indicates rather an advanced stage of frontier morality, as theft from the "redskins" or the "Government" is usually held to be a very trivial matter compared with the heinous crime of theft from "citizens."

There is always danger in meeting a band of young bucks in lonely, uninhabited country—those that have barely reached manhood being the most truculent, insolent, and reckless. A man meeting such a party runs great risk of losing his horse, his rifle, and all else he has. This has happened quite frequently during the past few years to hunters or cowboys who have wandered into the debatable territory where our country borders on the Indian lands; and in at least one such instance, that took place three years ago, the unfortunate individual lost his life as well as his belongings. But a frontiersman of any experience can generally "stand off" a small number of such assailants, unless he loses his nerve or is taken by surprise.

My only adventure with Indians was of a very mild kind. It was in the course of a solitary trip to the north and east of our range, to what was then practically unknown country, although now containing many herds of cattle. One morning I had been traveling along the edge of the prairie, and about noon I rode Manitou up a slight rise and came out on a plateau that was perhaps half a mile broad. When near the middle, four or five Indians suddenly came up over the edge, directly in front of me. The second they saw me they whipped their guns out of their slings, started their horses into a run, and came on at full tilt, whooping and brandishing their weapons. I instantly reined up and dismounted. The level plain where we were was of all places the one on which such an onslaught could best be met. In any broken country, or where there is much cover, a white man is at a great disadvantage if pitted against such adepts in the art of hiding as Indians; while, on the other hand, the latter will rarely rush in on a foe who, even if overpowered in the end, will probably inflict severe loss on his assailants. The fury of an Indian charge, and the whoops by which it is accompanied, often scare horses so as to stampede them; but in Manitou I had perfect trust, and the old fellow stood as steady as a rock, merely cocking his ears and looking round at the noise. I waited until the Indians were a hundred yards off, and then threw up my rifle and drew a bead on the foremost. The effect was like magic. The whole party scattered out as wild pigeons or teal ducks sometimes do when shot at, and doubled back on their tracks, the men bending over alongside their horses. When some distance off they halted and gathered together to consult, and after a minute one came forward alone, ostentatiously dropping his rifle and waving a blanket over his head. When he came to within fifty yards I stopped him, and he pulled out a piece of paper—all Indians, when absent from their reservations, are supposed to carry passes—and called out, "How! Me good Indian!" I answered, "How," and assured him most sincerely I was very glad he *was* a good Indian, but I would not let him come closer; and when his companions began to draw near, I covered him with the rifle and made him move off, which he did with a sudden lapse into the most canonical Anglo-Saxon profanity. I then started to lead my horse out to the prairie; and after hovering round a short time they rode off, while I followed suit, but in the opposite direction. It had all passed too quickly for me to have time to get frightened; but during the rest of my ride I was exceedingly uneasy, and pushed tough, speedy old Manitou along at a rapid rate, keeping well out on the level. However, I never saw the Indians again. They may not have intended any mischief beyond giving me a fright; but I did not dare to let them come to close quarters, for they would have probably taken my horse and rifle, and not impossibly my scalp as well. Towards nightfall I fell in with two old trappers who lived near Killdeer Mountains, and they informed me that my assailants were some young Sioux bucks, at whose hands they themselves had just suffered the loss of two horses.

A few cool, resolute whites, well armed, can generally beat back a much larger number of Indians if attacked in the open. One of the first cattle outfits that came to the Powder River country, at the very end of the last war with the Sioux and Cheyennes, had an experience of this sort. There were six or eight whites, including the foreman, who was part owner, and they had about a thousand head of cattle. These they intended to hold just out of the dangerous district until the end of the war, which was evidently close at hand. They would thus get first choice of the new grazing grounds. But they ventured a little too far, and one day while on the trail were suddenly charged by fifty or sixty Indians. The cattle were scattered in every direction, and many of them slain in wantonness, though most were subsequently recovered. All the loose horses were driven off. But the men themselves instantly ran together and formed a ring, fighting from behind the pack and saddle ponies. One of their number was killed, as well as two or three of the animals composing their living breastwork;

but being good riflemen, they drove off their foes. The latter did not charge them directly, but circled round, each rider concealed on the outside of his horse; and though their firing was very rapid, it was, naturally, very wild. The whites killed a good many ponies, and got one scalp, belonging to a young Sioux brave who dashed up too close, and whose body in consequence could not be carried off by his comrades, as happened to the two or three others who were seen to fall. Both the men who related the incident to me had been especially struck by the skill and daring shown by the Indians in thus carrying off their dead and wounded the instant they fell.

The relations between the white borderers and their red-skinned foes and neighbors are rarely pleasant. There are incessant quarrels, and each side has to complain of bitter wrongs. Many of the frontiersmen are brutal, reckless, and overbearing; most of the Indians are treacherous, revengeful, and fiendishly cruel. Crime and bloodshed are the only possible results when such men are brought in contact. Writers usually pay heed only to one side of the story; they recite the crimes committed by one party, whether whites or Indians, and omit all reference to the equally numerous sins of the other. In our dealings with the Indians we have erred quite as often through sentimentality as through willful wrong-doing. Out of my own short experience I could recite a dozen instances of white outrages which, if told alone, would seem to justify all the outcry raised on behalf of the Indian; and I could also tell of as many Indian atrocities which make one almost feel that not a single one of the race should be left alive.

The chief trouble arises from the feeling alluded to in this last sentence—the tendency on each side to hold the race, and not the individual, responsible for the deeds of the latter. The skirmish between the cowboys and the Cheyennes, spoken of above, offers a case in point. It was afterwards found out that two horse-thieves had stolen some ponies from the Cheyennes. The latter at once sallied out and attempted to take some from a cow camp, and a fight resulted. In exactly the same way I once knew a party of buffalo hunters, who had been robbed of their horses by the Sioux, to retaliate by stealing an equal number from some perfectly peaceful Grosventres. A white or an Indian who would not himself commit any outrage will yet make no effort to prevent his fellows from organizing expeditions against men of the rival race. This is natural enough where law is weak, and where, in consequence, every man has as much as he can do to protect himself without meddling in the quarrels of his neighbors. Thus a white community will often refrain from taking active steps against men who steal horses only from the Indians, although I have known a number of instances where the ranchmen have themselves stopped such outrages.

The Indians behave in the same way. There is a peaceful tribe not very far from us which harbors two or three red horse-thieves, who steal from the whites at every chance. Recently, in our country, an expedition was raised to go against these horse-thieves, and it was only with the utmost difficulty that it was stopped: had it actually gone, accompanied as it would have been by scoundrels bent on plunder, as well as by wronged men who thought all redskins pretty much alike, the inevitable result would have been a bloody fight with all the Indians, both good and bad.

Not only do Indians differ individually, but they differ as tribes. An upper-class Cherokee is nowadays as good as a white. The Nez Percés differ from the Apaches as much as a Scotch laird does from a Calabrian bandit. A Cheyenne warrior is one of the most redoubtable foes in the whole world; a "digger" Snake one of the most despicable. The Pueblo is as thrifty, industrious, and peaceful as any European peasant, and no Arab of the Soudan is a lazier, wilder robber than is the Arapahoe.

The frontiersmen themselves differ almost as widely from one another. But in the event of an Indian outbreak all suffer alike, and so all are obliged to stand together: when the reprisals for a deed of guilt are sure to fall on the innocent, the latter have no resource save to ally themselves with the guilty. Moreover, even the best Indians are very apt to have a good deal of the wild beast in them; when they scent blood they wish their share of it, no matter from whose veins it flows. I once had a German in my employ, who, when a young child, had lost all his relations by a fate so terrible that it had weighed down his whole after-life. His family was living out on the extreme border at the time of the great Sioux outbreak towards the end of the civil war. There were many Indians around, seemingly on good terms with them; and to two of these Indians they had been able to be of much service, so that they became great friends. When the outbreak occurred, the members of this family were among the first captured. The two friendly Indians then endeavored to save their lives, doing all they could to dissuade their comrades from committing violence. Finally, after an angry discussion, the chief, who was present, suddenly ended it by braining the mother. The two former friends then, finding their efforts useless, forthwith turned round and joined with the others, first in violating the wretched daughters, and then in putting them to death with tortures that cannot even be hinted at. The boy alone was allowed to live. If he had been a native-born frontiersman, instead of a peaceful, quiet German, he probably would have turned into an inveterate Indian-slayer, resolute to kill any of the hated race wherever and whenever met—a type far from unknown on the border, of which I have myself seen at least one example.

With this incident it is only fair to contrast another that I heard related while spending the night in a small cow ranch on the Beaver, whither I had ridden on one of our many tedious hunts after lost horses. Being tired, I got into my bunk early, and while lying there listened to the conversation of two cowboys—both strangers to me—who had also ridden up to the ranch to spend the night. They were speaking of Indians, and mentioned, certainly without any marked disapprobation, a jury that had just acquitted a noted horse-thief of the charge of stealing stock from some Piegans, though he himself had openly admitted its truth. One, an unprepossessing, beetle-browed man, suddenly remarked that he had once met an Indian who was a pretty good fellow, and he proceeded to tell the story. A small party of Indians had passed the winter near the ranch at which he was employed. The chief had two particularly fine horses, which so excited his cupidity that one night he drove them off and "cached"—that is, hid—them in a safe place. The chief looked for them high and low, but without success. Soon afterwards one of the cowboy's own horses strayed. When spring came the Indians went away; but three days afterwards the chief returned, bringing with him the strayed horse, which he had happened to run across. "I could n't stand that," said the narrator, "so I just told him I reckoned I knew where his own lost horses were, and I saddled up my bronch' and piloted him to them."

Here and there on the border there is a certain amount of mixture with the Indian blood; much more than is commonly supposed. One of the most hard-working and prosperous men in our neighborhood is a Chippewa half-breed; he is married to a white wife, and ranks in every respect as a white. Two of our richest cattle-men are married to Indian women; their children are being educated in convents. In several of the most thriving North-western cities men could be pointed out, standing high in the community, who have a strong dash of Indian blood in their veins. Often, however, especially in the lower classes, they seem to feel some shame about admitting the cross, so that in a couple of generations it is forgotten.

Indians are excellent fighters, though they do not shoot well—being in this respect much inferior not only to the old hunters, but also, nowadays, to the regular soldiers, who during the past three or four years have improved wonderfully in marksmanship. They have a very effective discipline of their own, and thus a body of them may readily be an over-match for an equal number of frontiersmen if the latter have no leader whom they respect. If the cowboys have rifles—for the revolver is useless in long-range individual fighting—they feel no fear of the Indians, so long as there are but half a dozen or so on a side; but, though infinitely quicker in their movements than regular cavalry, yet, owing to their heavy saddles, they are not able to make quite so wonderful marches as the Indians do, and their unruly spirit often renders them ineffective when gathered in any number without a competent captain. Under a man like Forrest they would become the most formidable fighting horsemen in the world.

In the summer of 1886, at the time of the war-scare over the "Cutting incident," we began the organization of a troop of cavalry in our district, notifying the Secretary of War that we were at the service of the Government, and being promised every assistance by our excellent chief executive of the Territory, Governor Pierce. Of course the cowboys were all eager for war, they did not much care with whom; they were very patriotic, they were fond of adventure, and, to tell the truth, they were by no means averse to the prospect of plunder. News from the outside world came to us very irregularly, and often in distorted form, so that we began to think we might get involved in a conflict not only with Mexico, but with England also. One evening at my ranch the men began talking over the English soldiers, so I got down "Napier" and read them several extracts from his descriptions of the fighting in the Spanish peninsula, also recounting as well as I could the great deeds of the British cavalry from Waterloo to Balaklava, and finishing up by describing from memory the fine appearance, the magnificent equipment, and the superb horses of the Household cavalry and of a regiment of hussars I had once seen.

All of this produced much the same effect on my listeners that the sight of Marmion's cavalcade produced in the minds of the Scotch moss-troopers on the eve of Flodden; and at the end, one of them, who had been looking into the fire and rubbing his hands together, said with regretful emphasis, "Oh, how I would like to kill one of them!"

# Sheriff's Work on a Ranch

*Ranch Life and the Hunting Trail*

IN OUR OWN IMMEDIATE LOCALITY WE HAVE HAD MORE DIFFICULTY with white desperadoes than with the redskins. At times there has been a good deal of cattle-killing and horse-stealing, and occasionally a murder or two. But as regards the last, a man has very little more to fear in the West than in the East, in spite of all the lawless acts one reads about. Undoubtedly a long-standing quarrel sometimes ends in a shooting-match; and of course savage affrays occasionally take place in the bar-rooms; in which, be it remarked, that, inasmuch as the men are generally drunk, and, furthermore, as the revolver is at best a rather inaccurate weapon, outsiders are nearly as apt to get hurt as are the participants. But if a man minds his own business and does not go into bar-rooms, gambling saloons, and the like, he need have no fear of being molested; while a revolver is a mere foolish incumbrance for any but a trained expert, and need never be carried. Against horse-thieves, cattle-thieves, claim-jumpers, and the like, however, every ranchman has to be on his guard; and armed collisions with these gentry are sometimes inevitable. The fact of such scoundrels being able to ply their trade with impunity for any length of time can only be understood if the absolute wildness of our land is taken into account. The country is yet unsurveyed and unmapped; the course of the river itself, as put down on the various Government and railroad maps, is very much a mere piece of guesswork, its bed being in many parts—as by my ranch—ten or fifteen miles, or more, away from where these maps make it. White hunters came into the land by 1880; but the actual settlement only began in 1882, when the first cattle-men drove in their herds, all of Northern stock, the

Texans not passing north of the country around the head-waters of the river until the following year, while until 1885 the territory through which it ran for the final hundred and fifty miles before entering the Big Missouri remained as little known as ever.

Some of us had always been anxious to run down the river in a boat during the time of the spring floods, as we thought we might get good duck and goose shooting, and also kill some beaver, while the trip would, in addition, have all the charm of an exploring expedition. Twice, so far as we knew, the feat had been performed, both times by hunters, and in one instance with very good luck in shooting and trapping. A third attempt, by two men on a raft, made the spring preceding that on which we made ours, had been less successful; for, when a score or so of miles below our ranch, a bear killed one of the two adventurers, and the survivor returned.

We could only go down during a freshet; for the Little Missouri, like most plains' rivers, is usually either a dwindling streamlet, a mere slender thread of sluggish water, or else a boiling, muddy torrent, running over a bed of shifting quicksand, that neither man nor beast can cross. It rises and falls with extraordinary suddenness and intensity, an instance of which has just occurred as this very page is being written. Last evening, when the moon rose, from the ranch veranda we could see the river-bed almost dry, the stream having shrunk under the drought till it was little but a string of shallow pools, with between them a trickle of water that was not ankle deep, and hardly wet the fetlocks of the saddle-band when driven across it; yet at daybreak this morning, without any rain having fallen near us, but doubtless in consequence of some heavy cloudburst near its head, the swift, swollen current was foaming brim high between the banks, and even the fords were swimming-deep for the horses.

Accordingly we had planned to run down the river sometime towards the end of April, taking advantage of a rise; but an accident made us start three or four weeks sooner than we had intended.

In 1886 the ice went out of the upper river very early, during the first part of February; but it at times almost froze over again, the bottom ice did not break up, and a huge gorge, scores of miles in length, formed in and above the bend known as the Ox-bow, a long distance up-stream from my ranch. About the middle of March this great Ox-bow jam came down past us. It moved slowly, its front forming a high, crumbling wall, and creaming over like an immense breaker on the seashore: we could hear the dull roaring and crunching as it plowed down the river-bed long before it came in sight round the bend above us. The ice kept piling and tossing up in the middle, and not only heaped itself above the level of the banks, but also in many places spread out on each side beyond them, grinding against the cottonwood trees in front of the ranch veranda, and at one moment bidding fair to overwhelm the house itself. It did not, however, but moved slowly down past us with that look of vast, resistless, relentless force that any great body of moving ice, as a glacier, or an iceberg, always conveys to the beholder. The heaviest pressure from the water that was backed up behind being, of course, always in the middle, this part kept breaking away, and finally was pushed on clear through, leaving the river so changed that it could hardly be known. On each bank, and for a couple of hundred feet out from it into the stream, was a solid mass of ice, edging the river along most of its length, at least as far as its course lay through lands that we knew; and in the narrow channel between the sheer ice-walls the water ran like a mill-race.

At night the snowy, glittering masses, tossed up and heaped into fantastic forms, shone like crystal in the moonlight; but they soon lost their beauty, becoming fouled and blackened, and at the same time melted and settled down until it was possible to clamber out across the slippery hummocks.

We had brought out a clinker-built boat especially to ferry ourselves over the river when it was high, and were keeping our ponies on the opposite side, where there was a good range shut in by some very broken country that we knew they would not be apt to cross. This boat had already proved very useful and now came in handier than ever, as without it we could take no care of our horses. We kept it on the bank, tied to a tree, and every day would carry it or slide it across the hither ice bank, usually with not a little tumbling and scrambling on our part, lower it gently into the swift current, pole it across to the ice on the farther bank, and then drag it over that, repeating the operation when we came back. One day we crossed and walked off about ten miles to a tract of wild and rugged country, cleft in every direction by ravines and cedar cañons, in the deepest of which we had left four deer hanging a fortnight before, as game thus hung up in cold weather keeps indefinitely. The walking was very bad, especially over the clay buttes; for the sun at midday had enough strength to thaw out the soil to the depth of a few inches only, and accordingly the steep hillsides were covered by a crust of slippery mud, with the frozen ground underneath. It was hard to keep one's footing, and to avoid falling while balancing along the knife-like ridge crests, or while clinging to the stunted sage brush as we went down into the valleys. The deer had been hung in a thicket of dwarfed cedars; but when we reached the place we found nothing save scattered pieces of their carcasses, and the soft mud was tramped all over with round, deeply marked footprints, some of them but a few hours old, showing that the plunderers of our cache were a pair of cougars—"mountain lions," as they are called by the Westerners. They had evidently been at work for some time, and had eaten almost every scrap of flesh; one of the deer had been carried for some distance to the other side of a deep, narrow chasm-like gully across which the cougar must have leaped with the carcass in its mouth. We followed the fresh trail of the cougars for some time, as it was well marked, especially in the snow still remaining in the bottoms of the deeper ravines; finally it led into a tangle of rocky hills riven by dark cedar-clad gorges, in which we lost it, and we retraced our steps, intending to return on the morrow with a good track hound.

But we never carried out our intentions, for next morning one of my men who was out before breakfast came back to the house with the startling news that our boat was gone—stolen, for he brought with him the end of the rope with which it had been tied, evidently cut off with a sharp knife; and also a red woolen mitten with a leather palm, which he had picked up on the ice. We had no doubt as to who had stolen it; for whoever had done so had certainly gone down the river in it, and the only other thing in the shape of a boat on the Little Missouri was a small flat-bottomed scow in the possession of three hard characters who lived in a shack, or hut, some twenty miles above us, and whom we had shrewdly suspected for some time of wishing to get out of the country, as certain of the cattle-men had begun openly to threaten to lynch them. They belonged to a class that always holds sway during the raw youth of a frontier community, and the putting down of which is the first step towards decent government. Dakota, west of the Missouri, has been settled very recently, and every town within it has seen strange antics performed during the past six or seven years. Medora, in particular, has had more than its full share of shooting and stabbing affrays, horse-stealing, and cattle-killing. But the time for such things was passing away; and during the preceding fall the vigilantes—locally known as "stranglers," in happy allusion to their summary method of doing justice—had made a clean sweep of the cattle country along the Yellowstone and that part of the Big Missouri around and below its mouth. Be it remarked, in passing, that while the outcome of their efforts had been in the main wholesome, yet, as is always the case in an extended raid of vigilantes, several of the sixty odd victims had been perfectly innocent men who had been hung or shot in company with the real scoundrels, either through carelessness and misapprehension or on account of some personal spite.

The three men we suspected had long been accused—justly or unjustly—of being implicated both in cattle-killing and in that worst of frontier crimes, horse-stealing: it was only by an accident that they had escaped the clutches of the vigilantes the preceding fall. Their leader was a well-built fellow named Finnigan, who had long red hair reaching to his shoulders, and always wore a broad hat and a fringed buckskin shirt. He was rather a hard case, and had been chief actor in a number of shooting scrapes. The other two were a half-breed, a stout, muscular man, and an old German, whose viciousness was of the weak and shiftless type.

We knew that these three men were becoming uneasy and were anxious to leave the locality; and we also knew that traveling on horseback, in the direction in which they would wish to go, was almost impossible, as the swollen, ice-fringed rivers could not be crossed at all, and the stretches of broken ground would form nearly as impassable barriers. So we had little doubt that it was they who had taken our boat; and as they knew there was then no boat left on the river, and as the country along its banks was entirely impracticable for horses, we felt sure they would be confident that there could be no pursuit.

Accordingly we at once set to work in our turn to build a flat-bottomed scow, wherein to follow them. Our loss was very annoying, and might prove a serious one if we were long prevented from crossing over to look after the saddle-band; but the determining motive in our minds was neither chagrin nor anxiety to recover our property. In any wild country where the power of the law is little felt or heeded, and where every one has to rely upon himself for protection, men soon get to feel that it is in the highest degree unwise to submit to any wrong without making an immediate and resolute effort to avenge it upon the wrong-doers, at no matter what cost of risk or trouble. To submit tamely and meekly to theft, or to any other injury, is to invite almost certain repetition of the offense, in a place where self-reliant hardihood and the ability to hold one's own under all circumstances rank as the first of virtues.

Two of my cowboys, Seawall and Dow, were originally from Maine, and were mighty men of their hands, skilled in woodcraft and the use of the ax, paddle, and rifle. They set to work with a will, and, as by good luck there were plenty of boards, in two or three days they had turned out a first-class flat-bottom, which was roomy, drew very little water, and was dry as a bone; and though, of course, not a handy craft, was easily enough managed in going down-stream. Into this we packed flour, coffee, and bacon enough to last us a fortnight or so, plenty of warm bedding, and the mess kit; and early one cold March morning slid it into the icy current, took our seats, and shoved off down the river.

There could have been no better men for a trip of this kind than my two companions, Seawall and Dow. They were tough, hardy, resolute fellows, quick as cats, strong as bears, and able to travel like bull moose. We felt very little uneasiness as to the result of a fight with the men we were after, provided we had anything like a fair show; moreover, we intended, if possible, to get them at such a disadvantage that there would not be any fight at all. The only risk of any consequence that we ran was that of being ambushed; for the extraordinary formation of the Bad Lands, with the ground cut up into gullies, serried walls, and battlemented hill-tops, makes it the country of all others for hiding-places and ambuscades.

For several days before we started the weather had been bitterly cold, as a furious blizzard was blowing; but on the day we left there was a lull, and we hoped a thaw had set in. We all were most warmly and thickly dressed, with woolen socks and underclothes, heavy jackets and trousers, and great fur coats, so that we felt we could bid defiance to the weather. Each carried his rifle, and we had in addition a double-barreled duck gun, for water-fowl and beaver. To manage the boat, we had paddles, heavy oars, and long iron-shod poles, Seawall steering while Dow sat in the bow. Altogether we felt as if we were off on a holiday trip, and set to work to have as good a time as possible.

The river twisted in every direction, winding to and fro across the alluvial valley bottom, only to be brought up by the rows of great barren buttes that bounded it on each edge. It had worn away the sides of these till they towered up as cliffs of clay, marl, or sandstone. Across their white faces the seams of coal drew sharp black bands, and they were elsewhere blotched and varied with brown, yellow, purple, and red. This fantastic coloring, together with the jagged irregularity of their crests, channeled by the weather into spires, buttresses, and battlements, as well as their barrenness and the distinctness with which they loomed up through the high, dry air, gave them a look that was a singular mixture of the terrible and the grotesque. The bottoms were covered thickly with leafless cottonwood trees, or else with withered brown grass and stunted, sprawling sage bushes. At times the cliffs rose close to us on either hand, and again the valley would widen into a sinuous oval a mile or two long, bounded on every side, as far as our eyes could see, by a bluff line without a break, until, as we floated down close to its other end, there would suddenly appear in one corner a cleft through which the stream rushed out. As it grew dusk the shadowy outlines of the buttes lost nothing of their weirdness; the twilight only made their uncouth shapelessness more grim and forbidding. They looked like the crouching figures of great goblin beasts.

Those two hills on the right
Crouched like two bulls locked horn in horn in fight—
While to the left a tall scalped mountain....
The dying sunset kindled through a cleft:

The hills, like giants at a hunting, lay

Chin upon hand, to see the game at bay—

might well have been written after seeing the strange, desolate lands lying in western Dakota.

All through the early part of the day we drifted swiftly down between the heaped-up piles of ice, the cakes and slabs now dirty and unattractive looking. Towards evening, however, there came long reaches where the banks on either side were bare, though even here there would every now and then be necks where the jam had been crowded into too narrow a spot and had risen over the side as it had done up-stream, grinding the bark from the big cottonwoods and snapping the smaller ones short off. In such places the ice-walls were sometimes eight or ten feet high, continually undermined by the restless current; and every now and then overhanging pieces would break off and slide into the stream with a loud sullen splash, like the plunge of some great water beast. Nor did we dare to go in too close to the high cliffs, as bowlders and earth masses, freed by the thaw from the grip of the frost, kept rolling and leaping down their faces and forced us to keep a sharp lookout lest our boat should be swamped.

At nightfall we landed, and made our camp on a point of wood-covered land jutting out into the stream. We had seen very little trace of life until late in the day, for the ducks had not yet arrived; but in the afternoon a sharp-tailed prairie fowl flew across stream ahead of the boat, lighting on a low branch by the water's edge. Shooting him, we landed and picked off two others that were perched high up in leafless cottonwoods, plucking the buds. These three birds served us as supper; and shortly afterward, as the cold grew more and more biting, we rolled in under our furs and blankets and were soon asleep.

In the morning it was evident that instead of thawing it had grown decidedly colder. The anchor ice was running thick in the river, and we spent the first hour or two after sunrise in hunting over the frozen swamp bottom for white-tail deer, of which there were many tracks; but we saw nothing. Then we broke camp and again started down-stream—a simple operation, as we had no tent, and all we had to do was to cord up our bedding and gather the mess kit. It was colder than before, and for some time we went along in chilly silence, nor was it until midday that the sun warmed our blood in the least. The crooked bed of the current twisted hither and thither, but whichever way it went the icy north wind, blowing stronger all the time, drew steadily up it. One of us remarking that we bade fair to have it in our faces all day, the steersman announced that we could n't, unless it was the crookedest wind in Dakota; and half an hour afterward we overheard him muttering to himself that it *was* the crookedest wind in Dakota. We passed a group of tepees on one bottom, marking the deserted winter camp of some Grosventre Indians, which some of my men had visited a few months previously on a trading expedition. It was almost the last point on the river with which we were acquainted. At midday we landed on a sand-bar for lunch—a simple enough meal, the tea being boiled over a fire of driftwood, that also fried the bacon, while the bread only needed to be baked every other day. Then we again shoved off. As the afternoon waned the cold grew still more bitter, and the wind increased, blowing in fitful gusts against us, until it chilled us to the marrow when we sat still. But we rarely did sit still; for even the rapid current was unable to urge the light-draught scow down in the teeth of the strong blasts, and we only got her along by dint of hard work with pole and paddle. Long before the sun went down the ice had begun to freeze on the handles of the poles, and we were not sorry to haul on shore for the night. For supper we again had prairie fowl, having shot four from a great patch of bulberry bushes late in the afternoon. A man doing hard open-air work in cold weather is always hungry for meat.

During the night the thermometer went down to zero, and in the morning the anchor ice was running so thickly that we did not care to start at once, for it is most difficult to handle a boat in the deep frozen slush. Accordingly we took a couple of hours for a deer hunt, as there were evidently many white-tail on the bottom. We selected one long, isolated patch of tangled trees and brushwood, two of us beating through it while the other watched one end; but almost before we had begun four deer broke out at one side, loped easily off, evidently not much scared, and took refuge in a deep glen or gorge, densely wooded with cedars, that made a blind pocket in the steep side of one of the great plateaus bounding the bottom. After a short consultation, one of our number crept round to the head of the gorge, making a wide détour, and the other two advanced up it on each side, thus completely surrounding the doomed deer. They attempted to break out past the man at the head of the glen, who shot down a couple, a buck and a yearling doe. The other two made their escape by running off over ground so rough that it looked fitter to be crossed by their upland-loving cousins, the black-tail.

This success gladdened our souls, insuring us plenty of fresh meat. We carried pretty much all of both deer back to camp, and, after a hearty breakfast, loaded our scow and started merrily off once more. The cold still continued intense, and as the day wore away we became numbed by it, until at last an incident occurred that set our blood running freely again.

We were, of course, always on the alert, keeping a sharp lookout ahead and around us, and making as little noise as possible. Finally our watchfulness was rewarded, for in the middle of the afternoon of this, the third day we had been gone, as we came around a bend, we saw in front of us the lost boat, together with a scow, moored against the bank, while from among the bushes some little way back the smoke of a camp-fire curled up through the frosty air. We had come on the camp of the thieves. As I glanced at the faces of my two followers I was struck by the grim, eager look in their eyes. Our overcoats were off in a second, and after exchanging a few muttered words, the boat was hastily and silently shoved towards the bank. As soon as it touched the shore ice I leaped out and ran up behind a clump of bushes, so as to cover the landing of the others, who had to make the boat fast. For a moment we felt a thrill of keen excitement, and our veins tingled as we crept cautiously towards the fire, for it seemed likely that there would be a brush; but, as it turned out, this was almost the only moment of much interest, for the capture itself was as tame as possible.

The men we were after knew they had taken with them the only craft there was on the river, and so felt perfectly secure; accordingly, we took them absolutely by surprise. The only one in camp was the German, whose weapons were on the ground, and who, of course, gave up at once, his two companions being off hunting. We made him safe, delegating one of our number to look after him particularly and see that he made no noise, and then sat down and waited for the others. The camp was under the lee of a cut bank, behind which we crouched, and, after waiting an hour or over, the men we were after came in. We heard them a long way off and made ready, watching them for some minutes as they walked towards us, their rifles on their shoulders and the sunlight glinting on the steel barrels. When they were within twenty yards or so we straightened up from behind the bank, covering them with our cocked rifles, while I shouted to them to hold up their hands—an order that in such a case, in the West, a man is not apt to disregard if he thinks the giver is in earnest. The half-breed obeyed at once, his knees trembling as if they had been made of whalebone. Finnigan hesitated for a second, his eyes fairly wolfish; then, as I walked up within a few paces, covering the center of his chest so as to avoid overshooting, and repeating the command, he saw that he had no show, and, with an oath, let his rifle drop and held his hands up beside his head.

It was nearly dusk, so we camped where we were. The first thing to be done was to collect enough wood to enable us to keep a blazing fire all night long. While Seawall and Dow, thoroughly at home in the use of the ax, chopped down dead cottonwood trees and dragged the logs up into a huge pile, I kept guard over the three prisoners, who were huddled into a sullen group some twenty yards off, just the right distance for the buckshot in the double-barrel. Having captured our men, we were in a quandary how to keep them. The cold was so intense that to tie them tightly hand and foot meant, in all likelihood, freezing both hands and feet off during the night; and it was no use tying them at all unless we tied them tightly enough to stop in part the circulation. So nothing was left for us to do but to keep perpetual guard over them. Of course we had carefully searched them, and taken away not only their firearms and knives, but everything else that could possibly be used as a weapon. By this time they were pretty well cowed, as they found out very quickly that they would be well treated so long as they remained quiet, but would receive some rough handling if they attempted any disturbance.

Our next step was to cord their weapons up in some bedding, which we sat on while we took supper. Immediately afterward we made the men take off their boots—an additional safeguard, as it was a cactus country, in which a man could travel barefoot only at the risk of almost certainly laming himself for life—and go to bed, all three lying on one buffalo robe and being covered by another, in the full light of the blazing fire. We determined to watch in succession a half-night apiece, thus each getting a full rest every third night. I took first watch, my two companions, revolver under head, rolling up in their blankets on the side of the fire opposite that on which the three captives lay; while I, in fur cap, gantlets, and overcoat, took my station a little way back in the circle of firelight, in a position in which I could watch my men with the absolute certainty of being able to stop any movement, no matter how sudden. For this night-watching we always used the double-barrel with buckshot, as a rifle is uncertain in the dark; while with a shot-gun at such a distance, and with men lying down, a person who is watchful may be sure that they cannot get up, no matter how quick they are, without being riddled. The only danger lies in the extreme monotony of sitting still in the dark guarding men who make no motion, and the consequent tendency to go to sleep, especially when one has had a hard day's work and is feeling really tired. But neither on the first night nor on any subsequent one did we ever abate a jot of our watchfulness.

Next morning we started down-stream, having a well-laden flotilla, for the men we had caught had a good deal of plunder in their boats, including some saddles, as they evidently intended to get horses as soon as they reached a part of the country where there were any, and where it was possible to travel. Finnigan, who was the ringleader, and the man I was especially after, I kept by my side in our boat, the other two being put in their own scow, heavily laden and rather leaky, and with only one paddle. We kept them just in front of us, a few yards distant, the river being so broad that we knew, and they knew also, any attempt at escape to be perfectly hopeless.

For some miles we went swiftly down-stream, the cold being bitter and the slushy anchor ice choking the space between the boats; then the current grew sluggish, eddies forming along the sides. We paddled on until, coming into a long reach where the water was almost backed up, we saw there was a stoppage at the other end. Working up to this, it proved to be a small ice jam, through which we broke our way only to find ourselves, after a few hundred yards, stopped by another. We had hoped that the first was merely a jam of anchor ice, caused by the cold of the last few days; but the jam we had now come to was black and solid, and, running the boats ashore, one of us went off down the bank to find out what the matter was. On climbing a hill that commanded a view of the valley for several miles, the explanation became only too evident— as far as we could see, the river was choked with black ice. The great Ox-bow jam had stopped, and we had come down to its tail.

We had nothing to do but to pitch camp, after which we held a consultation. The Little Missouri has much too swift a current,—when it has any current at all,— with too bad a bottom, for it to be possible to take a boat up-stream; and to walk meant, of course, abandoning almost all we had. Moreover we knew that a thaw would very soon start the jam, and so made up our minds that we had best simply stay where we were, and work down-stream as fast as we could, trusting that the spell of bitter weather would pass before our food gave out.

The next eight days were as irksome and monotonous as any I ever spent: there is very little amusement in combining the functions of a sheriff with those of an arctic explorer. The weather kept as cold as ever. During the night the water in the pail would freeze solid. Ice formed all over the river, thickly along the banks; and the clear, frosty sun gave us so little warmth that the melting hardly began before noon. Each day the great jam would settle down-stream a few miles, only to wedge again, leaving behind it several smaller jams, through which we would work our way until we were as close to the tail of the large one as we dared to go. Once we came round a bend and got so near that we were in a good deal of danger of being sucked under. The current ran too fast to let us work back against it, and we could not pull the boat up over the steep banks of rotten ice, which were breaking off and falling in all the time. We could only land and snub the boats up with ropes, holding them there for two or three hours until the jam worked down once more—all the time, of course, having to keep guard over the captives, who had caused us so much trouble that we were bound to bring them in, no matter what else we lost.

We had to be additionally cautious on account of being in the Indian country, having worked down past Killdeer Mountains, where some of my cowboys had run across a band of Sioux—said to be Tetons—the year before. Very probably the Indians would not have harmed us anyhow, but as we were hampered by the prisoners, we preferred not meeting them; nor did we, though we saw plenty of fresh signs, and found, to our sorrow, that they had just made a grand hunt all down the river, and had killed or driven off almost every head of game in the country through which we were passing.

As our stock of provisions grew scantier and scantier, we tried in vain to eke it out by the chase; for we saw no game. Two of us would go out hunting at a time, while the third kept guard over the prisoners. The latter would be made to sit down together on a blanket at one side of the fire, while the guard for the time being stood or sat some fifteen or twenty yards off. The prisoners being unarmed, and kept close together, there was no possibility of their escaping, and the guard kept at such a distance that they could not overpower him by springing on him, he having a Winchester or the double-barreled shot-gun always in his hands cocked and at the ready. So long as we kept wide-awake and watchful, there was not the least danger, as our three men knew us, and understood perfectly that the slightest attempt at a break would result in their being shot down; but, although there was thus no risk, it was harassing, tedious work, and the strain, day in and day out, without any rest or let up, became very tiresome.

The days were monotonous to a degree. The endless rows of hills bounding the valley, barren and naked, stretched along without a break. When we rounded a bend, it was only to see on each hand the same lines of broken buttes dwindling off into the distance ahead of us as they had dwindled off into the distance behind. If, in hunting, we climbed to their tops, as far as our eyes could scan there was nothing but the great rolling prairie, bleak and lifeless, reaching off to the horizon. We broke camp in the morning, on a point of land covered with brown, leafless, frozen cottonwoods; and in the afternoon we pitched camp on another point in the midst of a grove of the same stiff, dreary trees. The discolored river, whose eddies boiled into yellow foam, flowed always between the same banks of frozen mud or of muddy ice. And what was, from a practical standpoint, even worse, our diet began to be as same as the scenery. Being able to kill nothing, we exhausted all our stock of provisions, and got reduced to flour, without yeast or baking-powder; and unleavened bread, made with exceedingly muddy water, is not, as a steady thing, attractive.

Finding that they were well treated and were also watched with the closest vigilance, our prisoners behaved themselves excellently and gave no trouble, though afterward, when out of our hands and shut up in jail, the half-breed got into a stabbing affray. They conversed freely with my two men on a number of indifferent subjects, and after the first evening no allusion was made to the theft, or anything connected with it; so that an outsider overhearing the conversation would never have guessed what our relations to each other really were. Once, and once only, did Finnigan broach the subject. Somebody had been speaking of a man whom we all knew, called "Calamity," who had been recently taken by the sheriff on a charge of horse-stealing. Calamity had escaped once, but was caught at a disadvantage the next time; nevertheless, when summoned to hold his hands up, he refused, and attempted to draw his own revolver, with the result of having two bullets put through him. Finnigan commented on Calamity as a fool for "not knowing when a man had the drop on him"; and then, suddenly turning to me, said, his weather-beaten face flushing darkly: "If I 'd had any show at all, you 'd have sure had to fight, Mr. Roosevelt; but there was n't any use making a break when I 'd only have got shot myself, with no chance of harming any one else." I laughed and nodded, and the subject was dropped.

Indeed, if the time was tedious to us, it must have seemed never-ending to our prisoners, who had nothing to do but to lie still and read, or chew the bitter cud of their reflections, always conscious that some pair of eyes was watching them every moment, and that at least one loaded rifle was ever ready to be used against them. They had quite a stock of books, some of a rather unexpected kind. Dime novels and the inevitable "History of the James Brothers"—a book that, together with the "Police Gazette," is to be found in the hands of every professed or putative ruffian in the West—seemed perfectly in place; but it was somewhat surprising to find that a large number of more or less drearily silly "society" novels, ranging from Ouida's to those of The Duchess and Augusta J. Evans, were most greedily devoured. As for me, I had brought with me "Anna Karénina," and my surroundings were quite gray enough to harmonize well with Tolstoï.

Our commons grew shorter and shorter; and finally even the flour was nearly gone, and we were again forced to think seriously of abandoning the boats. The Indians had driven all the deer out of the country; occasionally we shot prairie fowl, but they were not plentiful. A flock of geese passed us one morning, and afterward an old gander settled down on the river near our camp; but he was over two hundred yards off, and a rifle-shot missed him. Where he settled down, by the way, the river was covered with thick glare ice that would just bear his weight; and it was curious to see him stretch his legs out in front and slide forty or fifty feet when he struck, balancing himself with his outspread wings.

But when the day was darkest the dawn appeared. At last, having worked down some thirty miles at the tail of the ice jam, we struck an outlying cow-camp of the C Diamond (C [diamond]) ranch, and knew that our troubles were almost over. There was but one cowboy in it, but we were certain of his cordial help, for in a stock country all make common cause against either horse-thieves or cattle-thieves. He had no wagon, but told us we could get one up at a ranch near Killdeer Mountains, some fifteen miles off, and lent me a pony to go up there and see about it—which I accordingly did, after a sharp preliminary tussle when I came to mount the wiry bronco (one of my men remarking in a loud aside to our cowboy host, "the boss ain't no bronco-buster"). When I reached the solitary ranch spoken of, I was able to hire a large prairie schooner and two tough little bronco mares, driven by the settler himself, a rugged old plainsman, who evidently could hardly understand why I took so much bother with the thieves instead of hanging them off-hand. Returning to the river the next day, we walked our men up to the Killdeer Mountains. Seawall and Dow left me the following morning, went back to the boats, and had no further difficulty, for the weather set in very warm, the ice went through with a rush, and they reached Mandan in about ten days, killing four beaver and five geese on the way, but lacking time to stop to do any regular hunting.

Meanwhile I took the three thieves into Dickinson, the nearest town. The going was bad, and the little mares could only drag the wagon at a walk; so, though we drove during the daylight, it took us two days and a night to make the journey. It was a most desolate drive. The prairie had been burned the fall before, and was a mere bleak waste of blackened earth, and a cold, rainy mist lasted throughout the two days. The only variety was where the road crossed the shallow headwaters of Knife and Green rivers. Here the ice was high along the banks, and the wagon had to be taken to pieces to get it over. My three captives were unarmed, but as I was alone with them, except for the driver, of whom I knew nothing, I had to be doubly on my guard, and never let them come close to me. The little mares went so slowly, and the heavy road rendered any hope of escape by flogging up the horses so entirely out of the question, that I soon found the safest plan was to put the prisoners in the wagon and myself walk behind with the inevitable Winchester. Accordingly I trudged steadily the whole time behind the wagon through the ankle-deep mud. It was a gloomy walk. Hour after hour went by always the same, while I plodded along through the dreary landscape—hunger, cold, and fatigue struggling with a sense of dogged, weary resolution. At night, when we put up at the squalid hut of a frontier granger, the only habitation on our road, it was even worse. I did not dare to go to sleep, but making my three men get into the upper bunk, from which they could get out only with difficulty, I sat up with my back against the cabin-door and kept watch over them all night long. So, after thirty-six hours' sleeplessness, I was most heartily glad when we at last jolted into the long, straggling main street of Dickinson, and I was able to give my unwilling companions into the hands of the sheriff.

Under the laws of Dakota I received my fees as a deputy sheriff for making the three arrests, and also mileage for the three hundred odd miles gone over—a total of some fifty dollars.

*Thereafter Roosevelt always found time, no matter his job or how hard he was working, to spend time every year on hunting trips. In 1889 then President Benjamin Harrison appointed him to the Civil Service Commission and he proceeded to try to energize a moribund organization, just as he did later when he was one of the three commissioners of police in New York City and used to wander the streets of New York at night to make sure officers were on duty. He found time to finish the first two volumes of* The Winning of the West *when he was not investigating corruption in the Post Office Department, where the political spoils system traditionally operated. And he hunted grizzlies in Montana. When he was not attending to his official duties and writing books he was active in Washington social life. He was still active in the Boone & Crockett Club, of course, and in 1890 paid the visit to Yellowstone National Park that persuaded him the park should be de-commercialized and its use governed by tighter regulations.*

*The next year he went hunting again in the Rockies. The following year he was in Texas, hunting wild boar. Then he was ready to write his third hunting book:* The Wilderness Hunter. *The book is the culmination, in a way, of his years in the West. He would continue to write about hunting in the area but he was approaching a more intense involvement in his life with politics and his aspirations for office, and when he was finally out of office his thoughts turned to Africa. We offer Chapter XX, "In Cowboy Land," a chapter of campfire stories that are absolutely delightful to read.*

# In Cowboy Land

*The Wilderness Hunter*

Out on the frontier, and generally among those who spend their lives in, or on the borders of, the wilderness, life is reduced to its elemental conditions. The passions and emotions of these grim hunters of the mountains, and wild rough-riders of the plains, are simpler and stronger than those of people dwelling in more complicated states of society. As soon as the communities become settled and begin to grow with any rapidity, the American instinct for law asserts itself; but in the earlier stages each individual is obliged to be a law to himself and to guard his rights with a strong hand. Of course the transition periods are full of incongruities. Men have not yet adjusted their relations to morality and law with any niceness. They hold strongly by certain rude virtues, and on the other hand they quite fail to recognize even as shortcomings not a few traits that obtain scant mercy in older communities. Many of the desperadoes, the man-killers, and road-agents have good sides to their characters. Often they are people who, in certain stages of civilization, do, or have done, good work, but who, when these stages have passed, find themselves surrounded by conditions which accentuate their worst qualities, and make their best qualities useless. The average desperado, for instance, has, after all, much the same standard of morals that the Norman nobles had in the days of the battle of Hastings, and ethically and morally, he is decidedly in advance of the vikings, who were the ancestors of these same nobles- and to whom, by the way, he himself could doubtless trace a portion of his blood. If the transition from the wild lawlessness of life in the wilderness or on the border to a higher civilization were stretched out over a term of centuries, he and his descendants would doubtless accommodate themselves by degrees to the changing circumstances. But unfortunately in the far West the transition takes place with marvellous abruptness, and at an altogether unheard-of speed, and many a man's nature is unable to change with sufficient rapidity to allow him to harmonize with his environment. In consequence, unless he leaves for still wilder lands, he ends by getting hung instead of founding a family which would revere his name as that of a very capable, although not in all respects a conventionally moral, ancestor.

Most of the men with whom I was intimately thrown during my life on the frontier and in the wilderness were good fellows, hard-working, brave, resolute, and truthful. At times, of course, they were forced of necessity to do deeds which would seem startling to dwellers in cities and in old settled places; and though they waged a very stern and relentless warfare upon evil-doers whose midseeds had immediate and tangible bad results, they showed a wide toleration of all save the most extreme classes of wrong, and were not given to inquiring too curiously into a strong man's past, or to criticising him over-harshly for a failure to discriminate in finer ethical questions. Moreover, not a few of the men with whom I came in contact- with some of whom my relations were very close and friendly- had at different times led rather tough careers. This fact was accepted by them and by their companions as a fact, and nothing more. There were certain offences, such as rape, the robbery of a friend, or murder under circumstances of cowardice and treachery, which were never forgiven; but the fact that when the country was wild a young fellow had gone on the road- that is, become a highwayman, or had been chief of a gang of desperadoes, horse-thieves, and cattle-killers, was scarcely held to weigh against him, being treated as a regrettable, but certainly not shameful, trait of youth. He was regarded by his neighbors with the same kindly tolerance with respectable mediaeval Scotch borderers doubtless extended to their wilder young men who would persist in raiding English cattle even in time of peace.

Of course if these men were asked outright as to their stories they would have refused to tell them or else would have lied about them; but when they had grown to regard a man as a friend and companion they would often recount various incidents of their past lives with perfect frankness, and as they combined in a very curious degree both a decided sense of humor, and a failure to appreciate that there was anything especially remarkable in what they related, their tales were always entertaining.

Early one spring, now nearly ten years ago, I was out hunting some lost horses. They had strayed from the range three months before, and we had in a roundabout way heard that they were ranging near some broken country, where a man named Brophy had a ranch, nearly fifty miles from my own. When I started thither the weather was warm, but the second day out it grew colder and a heavy snowstorm came on. Fortunately I was able to reach the ranch all right, finding there one of the sons of a Little Beaver ranchman, and a young cowpuncher belonging to a Texas outfit, whom I knew very well. After putting my horse into the corral and throwing him down some hay I strode into the low hut, made partly of turf and partly of cottonwood logs, and speedily warmed myself before the fire. We had a good warm supper, of bread, potatoes, fried venison, and tea. My two companions grew very sociable and began to talk freely over their pipes. There were two bunks one above the other. I climbed into the upper, leaving my friends, who occupied the lower, sitting together on a bench recounting different incidents in the careers of themselves and their cronies during the winter that had just passed. Soon one of them asked the other what had become of a certain horse, a noted cutting pony, which I had myself noticed the preceding fall. The question aroused the other to the memory of a wrong which still rankled, and he began (I alter one or two of the proper names):

"Why, that was the pony that got stole. I had been workin' him on rough ground when I was out with the Three Bar outfit and he went tender forward, so I turned him loose by the Lazy B ranch, and when I come back to git him there was n't anybody at the ranch and I could n't find him. The sheep-man who lives about two miles west, under Red Clay butte, told me he seen a fellow in a wolf-skin coat, ridin' a pinto bronco, with white eyes, leadin' that pony of mine just two days before; and I hunted round till I hit his trail and then I followed to where I'd reckoned he was headin' for- the Short Pine Hills. When I got there a rancher told me he had seen the man pass on towards Cedartown, and sure enough when I struck Cedartown I found he lived there in a 'dobe house, just outside the town. There was a boom on the town and it looked pretty slick. There was two hotels and I went into the first, and I says, 'Where's the justice of the peace?' says I to the bartender.

" 'There ain't no justice of the peace', says he, 'the justice of the peace got shot.'

" 'Well, where's the constable?' says I.

" 'Why, it was him that shot the justice of the peace!' says he, 'he's skipped the country with a bunch of horses.'

" 'Well, ain't there no officer of the law left in this town?' says I.

" 'Why, of course', says he, 'there's a probate judge; he is over tendin' bar at the Last Chance Hotel.'

"So I went over to the Last Chance Hotel and I walked in there. 'Mornin', says I.

" 'Mornin'," says he.

" 'You're the probate judge?' says I.

" 'That's what I am,' says he. 'What do you want?' says he.

" 'I want justice,' says I.

" 'What kind of justice do you want?' says he. 'What's it for?'

" 'It's for stealin' a horse,' says I.

" 'Then by God you'll git it,' says he. 'Who stole the horse?' says he.

" 'It is a man that lives in a 'dobe house, just outside the town there,' says I.

" 'Well, where do you come from yourself?' said he.

" 'From Medory,' said I.

"With that he lost interest and settled kind o' back, and says he, 'There wont no Cedartown jury hang a Cedartown man for stealin' a Medory man's horse,' said he.

" 'Well, what am I to do about my horse?' says I.

" 'Do?' says he; 'well, you know where the man lives, don't you?' says he; 'then sit up outside his house tonight and shoot him when he comes in,' says he, 'and skip out with the horse.'

" 'All right,' says I, 'that is what I'll do,' and I walked off.

"So I went off to his house and I laid down behind some sage-brushes to wait for him. He was not at home, but I could see his wife movin' about inside now and then, and I waited and waited and waited, and it growed darker, and I begun to say to myself, 'Now here you are lyin' out to shoot this man when he comes home; and it's gettin' dark, and you don't know him, and if you do shoot the next man that comes into that house, like as not it won't be the fellow you're after at all, but some perfectly innocent man acomin' there after the other man's wife!"

"So I up and saddled the bronc' and lit out for home," concluded the narrator with the air of one justly proud of his own self-abnegating virtue.

The "town" where the judge above-mentioned dwelt was one of those squalid, pretentiously named little clusters of makeshift dwellings which on the edge of the wild country spring up with the rapid growth of mushrooms, and are often no longer lived. In their earlier stages these towns are frequently built entirely of canvas, and are subject to grotesque calamaties. When the territory purchased from the Sioux, in the Dakotas, a couple of years ago, was thrown open to settlement, there was a furious inrush of men on horseback and in wagons, and various ambitious cities sprang up overnight. The new settlers were all under the influence of that curious craze which causes every true westerner to put unlimited faith in the unknown and untried; many had left all they had in a far better farming country, because they were true to their immemorial belief that, wherever they were, their luck would be better if they went somewhere else. They were always on the move, and headed for the vague beyond. As miners see visions of all the famous mines of history in each new camp, so these would-be city founders saw future St. Pauls and Omahas in every forlorn group of tents pitched by some muddy stream in a desert of gumbo and sage-brush; and they named both the towns and the canvas buildings in accordance with their bright hopes for the morrow, rather than with reference to the mean facts of the day. One of these towns, which when twenty-four hours old boasted of six saloons, a "court-house," and an "opera house," was overwhelmed by early disaster. The third day of its life a whirlwind came along and took off the opera house and half the saloons; and the following evening lawless men nearly finished the work of the elements. The riders of a huge trail-outfit from Texas, to their glad surprise discovered the town and abandoned themselves to a night of roaring and lethal carousal. Next morning the city authorities were lamenting, with oaths of bitter rage, that "thems hell-and-twenty Flying A cowpunchers had cut the court-house up into pants." It was true. The cowboys were in need of shaps, and with an admirable mixture of adventurousness, frugality, and ready adaptability to circumstances, had made substitutes therefor in the shape of canvas overalls, cut from the roof and walls of the shaky temple of justice.

One of my valued friends in the mountains, and one of the best hunters with whom I ever travelled, was a man who had a peculiarly light-hearted way of looking at conventional social obligations. Though in some ways a true backwoods Donatello, he was a man of much shrewdness and of great courage and resolution. Moreover, he possessed what only a few men do possess, the capacity to tell the truth. He saw facts as they were, and could tell them as they were, and he never told an untruth unless for very weighty reasons. He was pre-eminently a philosopher, of a happy, sceptical turn of mind. He had no prejudices. He never looked down, as so many hard characters do, upon a person possessing a different code of ethics. His attitude was one of broad, genial tolerance. He saw nothing out of the way in the fact that he had himself been a road-agent, a professional gambler, and a desperado at different stages of his career. On the other hand, he did not in the least hold it against any one that he had always acted within the law. At the time that I knew him he had become a man of some substance, and naturally a staunch upholder of the existing order of things. But while he never boasted of his past deeds, he never apologized for them, and evidently would have been quite as incapable of understanding that they needed an apology as he would have been incapable of being guilty of mere vulgar boastfulness. He did not often allude to his past career at all. When he did, he recited its incidents perfectly naturally and simply, as event, without any reference to or regard for their ethical significance. It was this quality which made him at times a specially pleasant companion, and always an agreeable narrator. The point of his story, or what seemed to him the point, was rarely that which struck me. It was the incidental sidelights the story threw upon his own nature and the somewhat lurid surroundings amid which he had moved.

On one occasion when we were out together we killed a bear, and after skinning it, took a bath in a lake. I noticed he had a scar on the side of his foot and asked him how he got it, to which he responded, with indifference:

"Oh, that? Why a man shootin' at me to make me dance, that was all."

I expressed some curiosity in the matter, and he went on:

"Well, he way of it was this: It was when I was keeping a saloon in New Mexico, and there was a man there by the name of Fowler, and there was a reward on him of three thousand dollars-"

"Put on him by the State?"

"No, put on by his wife," said my friend; "and there was this-"

"Hold on," I interrupted; "put on by his wife did you say?"

"Yes, by his wife. Him and her had been keepin' a faro bank, you see, and they quarrelled about it, so she just put a reward on him, and so-"

"Excuse me," I said "but do you mean to say that this reward was put on publicly?" to which my friend answered, with an air of gentlemanly boredom at being interrupted to gratify my thirst for irrelevant detail:

"Oh, no, not publicly. She just mentioned it to six or eight intimate personal friends."

"Go on," I responded, somewhat overcome by this instance of the primitive simplicity with which New Mexican matrimonial disputes were managed, and he continued:

"Well, two men come ridin' in to see me to borrow my guns. My guns was Colt's self-cockers. It was a new thing then, and they was the only ones in town. These come to me, and 'Simpson,' says they, 'we want to borrow your guns; we are goin' to kill Fowler.'

" 'Hold on for a moment,' said I, 'I am willin' to lend you them guns, but I ain't goin' to know what you're goin' to do with them, no sir; but of course you can have the guns.'" Here my friend's face lightened pleasantly, and he continued:

"Well, you may easily believe I felt surprised next day when Fowler come ridin' in, and, says he, 'Simpson, here's your guns!' He had shot them two men! 'Well, Fowler,' says I, 'if I had known them men was after you, I'd never have let them have them guns nohow," says I. That was n't true, for I did know it, but there was no cause to tell him that." I murmured my approval of such prudence, and Simpson continued, his eyes gradually brightening with the light of agreeable reminiscence:

"Well, they up and they took Fowler before the justice of the peace. The justice of the peace was a Turk."

"Now, Simpson, what do you mean by that?" I interrupted:

"Well, he come from Turkey," said Simpson, and I again sank back, wondering briefly what particular variety of Mediterranean outcast had drifted down to New Mexico to be made a justice of the peace. Simpson laughed and continued.

"That Fowler was a funny fellow. The Turk, he committed Fowler, and Fowler, he riz up and knocked him down and tromped all over him and made him let him go!"

"That was an appeal to a higher law," I observed. Simpson assented cheerily, and continued:

"Well, that Turk, he got nervous for fear Fowler he was goin' to kill him, and so he comes to me and offers me twenty-five dollars a day to protect him from Fowler; and I went to Fowler, and 'Fowler,' says I, 'that Turk's offered me twenty-five dollars a day to protect him from you. Now, I ain't goin to get shot for no twenty-five dollars a day, and if you are goin' to kill the Turk, just say so and go and do it; but if you ain't goin' to kill the Turk, there's no reason why I should n't earn that twenty-five dollars a day!' and Fowler, says he, 'I ain't goin' to touch the Turk; you just go right ahead and protect him.'"

So Simpson "protected" the Turk from the imaginary danger of Fowler, for about a week, at twenty-five dollars a day. Then one evening he happened to go out and met Fowler, "and," said he, "the moment I saw him I knowed he felt mean, for he begun to shoot at my feet," which certainly did seem to offer presumptive evidence of meanness. Simpson continued:

"I didn't have no gun, so I just had to stand there and take it until something distracted his attention, and I went off home to get my gun and kill him, but I wanted to do it perfectly lawful; so I went up to the mayor (he was playin' poker with one of the judges), and says I to him, 'Mr. Mayor,' says I, 'I am goin' to shoot Fowler.' And the mayor he riz out of his chair and he took me by the hand, and says he, 'Mr. Simpson, if you do I will stand by you'; and the judge, he says, 'I'll go on your bond.'"

Fortified by this cordial approval of the executive and judicial branches of the government, Mr. Simpson started on his quest. Meanwhile, however, Fowler had cut up another prominent citizen, and they already had him in jail.

The friends of law and order feeling some little distrust as to the permanency of their own zeal for righteousness, thought it best to settle the matter before there was time for cooling, and accordingly, headed by Simpson, the mayor, the judge, the Turk, and other prominent citizens of the town, they broke into the jail and hanged Fowler. The point in the hanging which especially tickled my friend's fancy, as he lingered over the reminiscence, was one that was rather too ghastly to appeal to our own sense of humor. In the Turk's mind there still rankled the memory of Fowler's very unprofessional conduct while figuring before him a criminal. Said Simpson, with a merry twinkle of the eye: "Do you know that Turk, he was a right funny fellow too after all. Just as the boys were going to string up Fowler, says he, 'Boys, stop; one moment, gentlemen,- Mr. Fowler, good-by', and he blew a kiss to him!"

In the cow-country, and elsewhere on the wild borderland between savagery and civilization, men go quite as often by nicknames as by those to which they are lawfully entitled. Half the cowboys and hunters of my acquaintance are known by names entirely unconnected with those they inherited or received when they were christened. Occasionally some would-be desperado or make-believe mighty hunter tries to adopt what he deems a title suitable to his prowess; but such an effort is never attempted in really wild places, where it would be greeted with huge derision; for all of these names that are genuine are bestowed by outsiders, with small regard to the wishes of the person named. Ordinarily the name refers to some easily recognizable accident of origin, occupation, or aspect; as witness the innumerable Dutcheys, Frencheys, Kentucks, Texas Jacks, Bronco Bills, Bear Jones, Buckskins, Red Jims, and the like. Sometimes it is apparently meaningless; one of my cowpuncher friends is always called "Sliver" or "Splinter"- why, I have no idea. At other times some particular incident may give rise to the title: a clean-looking cowboy formerly in my employ was always known as "Muddy Bill," because he had once been bucked off his horse into mud hole.

The grewsome genesis of one such name is given in the following letter which I have just received from an old hunting-friend in the Rockies, who took a kindly interest in a frontier cabin which the Boone and Crocket Club was putting up at the Chicago World's Fair.

"Feb 16th 1893; Der Sir: I see in the newspapers that your club the Daniel Boon and Davey Crockit you Intend to erect a fruntier Cabin at the world's Far at Chicago to represent the erley Pianears of our country I would like to see you maik a success I have all my life been a fruntiersman and feel interested in your undertaking and I hoap you wile get a good assortment of relicks I want to maik one suggestion to you that is in regard to getting a good man and a genuine Mauntanner to take charg of your haus at Chicago I want to recommend a man for you to get it is Liver-eating Johnson that is the naim he is generally called he is an olde mauntneer and large and fine looking and one of the Best Story Tellers in the country and Very Polight genteel to every one he meets I wil tel you how he got that naim Liver-eating in a hard Fight with the Black Feet Indians thay Faught all day Johnson and a few Whites Faught a large Body of Indians all day after the fight Johnson cam in contact with a wounded Indian and Johnson was aut of ammunition and thay faught it out with thar Knives and Johnson got away with the Indian and in the fight cut the livver out of the Indian and said to the Boys did thay want any Liver to eat that is the way he got the naim of Liver-eating Johnson

"Yours truly" etc., etc.

Frontiersmen are often as original in their theories of life as in their names; and the originality may take the form of wild savagery, of mere uncouthness, or of an odd combination of genuine humor with simple acceptance of facts as they are. On one occasion I expressed some surprise at learning that a certain Mrs. P. had suddenly married, though her husband was alive and in jail in a neighboring town; and received for answer: "Well, you see, old man Pete he skipped the country, and left his widow behind him, and so Bob Evans he up and married her!"- which was evidently felt to be a proceeding requiring no explanation whatever.

In the cow-country there is nothing more refreshing than the light-hearted belief entertained by the average man to the effect that any animal which by main force has been saddled and ridden, or harnessed and driven a couple of times, is a "broke horse." My present foreman is firmly wedded to this idea, as well as to its complement, the belief that any animals with hoofs, before any vehicle with wheels, can be driven across any country. One summer on reaching the ranch I was entertained with the usual accounts of the adventures and misadventures which had befallen my own men and my neighbors since I had been out last. In the course of the conversation my foreman remarked: "We had a great time out here about six weeks ago. There was a professor from Ann Arbor came out with his wife to see the Bad Lands, and they asked if we could rig them up a team, and we said we guessed we could, and Foley's boy and I did; but it ran away with him and broke his leg! He was here for a month. I guess he did n't mind it though." Of this I was less certain, forlorn little Medora being a "busted" cow-town, concerning which I once heard another of my men remark, in reply to an inquisitive commercial traveller: "How many people lives here? Eleven-counting the chickens- when they're all in town!"

My foreman continued: "By George, there was something that professor said afterwards that made me feel hot. I sent word up to him by Foley's boy that seein' as how it had come out we would n't charge him nothin' for the rig; and that professor he answered that he was glad we were showing him some sign of consideration, for he'd begun to believe he'd fallen into a den of sharks, and that we gave him a runaway team a purpose. That made me hot, calling that a runaway team. Why, there was one of the horses never *could* have run away before; it had n't never been druv but twice! and the other horse maybe had run away a few times, but there was lots of times he *had n't* run away. I esteemed that team full as liable not to run away as it was to run away," concluded my foreman, evidently deeming this as good a warranty of gentleness as the most exacting could require.

The definition of good behavior on the frontier is even more elastic for a saddle-horse than for a team. Last spring one of the Three-Seven riders, a magnificent horseman, was killed on the round-up near Belfield, his horse bucking and falling on him. "It was accounted a plumb gentle horse too," said my informant, "only it sometimes sulked and acted a little mean when it was cinched up behind." The unfortunate rider did not know of this failing of the "plumb gentle horse," and as soon as he was in the saddle it threw itself over sideways with a great bound, and he fell on his head, and never spoke again.

Such accidents are too common in the wild country to attract very much attention; the men accept them with grim quiet, as inevitable in such lives as theirs- lives that are harsh and narrow in their toil and their pleasure alike, and that are ever-bounded by an iron horizon of hazard and hardship. During the last year and a half three other men from the ranches in my immediate neighborhood have met their deaths in the course of their work. One, a trail boss of the OX, was drowned while swimming his herd across a swollen river. Another, one of the fancy ropers of the W Bar, was killed while roping cattle in a corral; his saddle turned, the rope twisted round him, he was pulled off, and was trampled to death by his own horse.

The fourth man, a cowpuncher named Hamilton, lost his life during the last week of October, 1891, in the first heavy snowstorm of the season. Yet he was a skilled plainsman, on ground he knew well, and just before straying himself, he successfully instructed two men who did not know the country how to get to camp. They were all three with the round-up, and were making a circle through the Bad Lands; the wagons had camped on the eastern edge

of these Bad Lands, where they merge into the prairie, at the head of an old
disused road, which led about due east from the Little Missouri. It was a gray,
lowering day, and as darkness came on Hamilton's horse played out, and he told
his two companions not to wait, as it had begun to snow, but to keep on
towards the north, skirting some particularly rough buttes, and as soon as they
struck the road to turn to the right and follow it out to the prairie, where they
would find camp; he particularly warned them to keep a sharp look-out, so as
not to pass over the dim trail unawares in the dusk and the storm. They followed his advice, and reached camp safely; and after they had left him nobody
ever again saw him alive. Evidently he himself, plodding northwards, passed
over the road without seeing it in the gathering gloom; probably he struck it
at some point where the ground was bad, and the dim trail in consequence disappeared entirely, as is the way with these prairie roads- making them landmarks
to be used with caution. He must then have walked on and on, over rugged hills
and across deep ravines, until his horse came to a standstill; he took off its saddle and picketed it to a dwarfed ash. Its frozen carcass was found, with the saddle near by, two months later. He now evidently recognized some landmark,
and realized that he had passed the road, and was far to the north of the
round-up wagons; but he was a resolute, self-confident man, and he determined
to strike out for a line camp, which he knew lay about due east of him, two or
three miles out on the prairie, on one of the head branches of Knife River. Night
must have fallen by this time, and he missed the camp, probably passing it
within less than a mile; but he did pass it, and with it all hopes of life, and walked
wearily on to his doom, through the thick darkness and the driving snow. At
last his strength failed, and he lay down in the tall grass of a little hollow. Five
months later, in the early spring, the riders from the line camp found his
body, resting face downwards, with the forehead on folded arms.

Accidents of less degree are common. Men break their collar-bones,
arms, or legs by falling when riding at speed over dangerous ground, when
cutting cattle or trying to control a stampeded herd, or by being thrown or
rolled on by bucking or rearing horses; or their horses, and on rare occasions
even they themselves, are gored by fighting steers. Death by storm or in flood,
death in striving to master a wild and vicious horse, or in handling maddened
cattle, and too often death in brutal conflict with one of his own fellows- any
one of these is the not unnatural end of the life of the dweller on the plains
or in the mountains.

But a few years ago other risks had to be run from savage beasts, and from
the Indians. Since I have been ranching on the Little Missouri, two men have

been killed by bears in the neighborhood of my range; and in the early years of my residence there, several men living or travelling in the country were slain by small war-parties of young braves. All the old-time trappers and hunters could tell stirring tales of their encounters with Indians.

My friend, Tazewell Woody, was among the chief actors in one of the most noteworthy adventures of this kind. He was a very quiet man, and it was exceedingly difficult to get him to talk over any of his past experiences; but one day, when he was in high good-humor with me for having made three consecutive straight shots at elk, he became quite communicative, and I was able to get him to tell me one story which I had long wished to hear from his lips, having already heard of it through one of the other survivors of the incident. When he found that I already knew a good deal old Woody told me the rest.

It was in the spring of 1875, and Woody and two friends were trapping on the Yellowstone. The Sioux were very bad at the time and had killed many prospectors, hunters, cowboys, and settlers; the whites retaliated whenever they got a chance, but, as always in Indian warfare, the sly, lurking, bloodthirsty savages inflicted much more loss than they suffered.

The three men, having a dozen horses with them, were camped by the river-side in a triangular patch of brush, shaped a good deal like a common flat-iron. On reaching camp they started to put out their traps; and when he came back in the evening Woody informed his companions that he had seen a great deal of Indian sign, and that he believed there were Sioux in the neighborhood. His companions both laughed at him, assuring him that they were not Sioux at all but friendly Crows, and that they would be in camp next morning; "and sure enough," said Woody, meditatively, "they *were* in camp next morning." By dawn one of the men went down the river to look at some of the traps, while Woody started out to where the horses were, the third man remaining in camp to get breakfast. Suddenly two shots were heard down the river, and in another moment a mounted Indian swept towards the horses. Woody fired, but missed him, and he drove off five while Woody, running forward, succeeded in herding the other seven into camp. Hardly had this been accomplished before the man who had gone down the river appeared, out of breath with his desperate run, having been surprised by several Indians, and just succeeding in making his escape by dodging from bush to bush, threatening his pursuers with his rifle.

These proved to be but the forerunners of a great war party, for when the sun rose the hills around seemed black with Sioux. Had they chosen to dash right in on the camp, running the risk of losing several of their men in the charge, they could of course have eaten up the three hunters in a minute; but such a charge is rarely practiced by Indians, who, although they are admirable in defensive warfare, and even in certain kinds of offensive movements, and although from their skill in hiding they usually inflict much more loss than they suffer when matched against white troops, are yet very reluctant to make any movement where the advantage gained must be offset by considerable loss of life. The three men thought they were surely doomed, but being veteran frontiersmen and long inured to every kind of hardship and danger, they set to work with cool resolution to make as effective a defence as possible, to beat off their antagonists if they might, and if this proved impracticable, to sell their lives as dearly as they could. Having tethered the horses in a slight hollow, the only one which offered any protection, each man crept out to a point of the triangular brush patch and lay down to await events.

In a very short while the Indians began closing in on them, taking every advantage of cover, and then, both from their side of the river and from the opposite bank, opened a perfect fusillade, wasting their cartridges with a recklessness which Indians are apt to show when excited. The hunters could hear the hoarse commands of the chiefs, the war-whoops, and the taunts in broken English which some of the warriors hurled at them. Very soon all of their horses were killed, and the brush was fairly riddled by the incessant volleys; but the three men themselves, lying flat on the ground and well concealed, were not harmed. The more daring young warriors then began to creep toward the hunters, going stealthily from one piece of cover to the next; and now the whites in turn opened fire. They did not shoot recklessly, as did their foes, but coolly and quietly, endeavoring to make each shot tell. Said Woody: "I only fired seven times all day; I reckoned on getting meat every time I pulled trigger." They had an immense advantage over their enemies, in that whereas they lay still and entirely concealed, the Indians of course had to move from cover to cover in order to approach, and so had at times to expose themselves. When the whites fired at all they fired at a man, whether moving or motionless, whom they could clearly see, while the Indians could only shoot at the smoke, which imperfectly marked the position of their unseen foes. In consequence the assailants speedily found that it was a task of hopeless danger to try in such a manner to close in on three plains veterans, men of iron nerve and skilled in the use of the rifle. Yet some of the more daring crept up very close to the patch of brush, and one actually got inside it, and was killed among the bedding that lay by the smouldering camp-fire. The wounded and such of the dead as did not lie in too exposed positions were promptly taken away by their comrades; but seven bodies fell into the hands of the three hunters. I asked Woody how many he himself had killed. He said he could only be sure of two that he got; one he shot in the head as he peeped over a bush, and the other he shot through the smoke as he attempted to rush in. "My, how that Indian did yell," said Woody, retrospectively; "*he* was no great of a Stoic." After two or three hours of this deadly skirmishing, which resulted in nothing more serious to the whites than in two of them being slightly wounded, the Sioux became disheartened by the loss they were suffering and withdrew, confining themselves thereafter to a long range and harmless fusillade. When it was dark the three men crept out to the river bed, and taking advantage of the pitchy night broke through the circle of their foes; they managed to reach the settlements without further molestation, having lost everything except their rifles.

For many years one of the most important of the wilderness dwellers was the West Point officer, and no man has played a greater part than he in the wild warfare which opened the regions beyond the Mississippi to white settlement. Since 1879, there has been but littler regular Indian fighting in the North, though there have been one or two very tedious and wearisome campaigns waged against the Apaches in the South. Even in the North, however, there have been occasional uprisings which had to be quelled by the regular troops.

After my elk hunt in September, 1891, I came out through the Yellowstone Park, as I have elsewhere related, riding in company with a surveyor of the Burlington and Quincy railroad, who was just coming in from his summer's work. It was the first of October. There had been a heavy snow-storm and the snow was still falling. Riding a stout pony each, and leading another packed with our bedding, etc., we broke our way from the upper to the middle geyser basin. Here we found a troop of the 1st Cavalry camped, under the command of old friends of mine, Captain Frank Edwards and Lieutenant (now Captain) John Pitcher. They gave us hay for our horses and insisted upon our stopping to lunch, with the ready hospitality always shown by army officers. After lunch we began exchanging stories. My travelling companion, the surveyor, had that spring performed a feat of note, going through one of the canyons of the Big Horn for the first time. He went with an old mining inspector, the two of them dragging a cottonwood sledge over the ice. The walls of the canyon are so sheer and the water so rough that it can be descended only when the stream is frozen. However, after six days' labor and hardship the descent was accomplished; and the surveyor, in concluding, described his experience in going through the Crow Reservation.

This turned the conversation upon Indians, and it appeared that both of our hosts had been actors in Indian scrapes which had attracted my attention at the time they occurred, as they took place among tribes that I knew and in a country which I had sometimes visited, either when hunting or when purchasing horses for the ranch. The first, which occurred to Captain Edwards, happened late in 1886, at the time when the Crow Medicine Chief, Sword-Bearer, announced himself as the Messiah of the Indian race, during one of the usual epidemics of ghostdancing. Sword-Bearer derived his name from always wearing a medicine sword- that is, a sabre painted red. He claimed to possess magic power, and, thanks to the performance of many dextrous feats of juggling, and the lucky outcome of certain prophecies, he deeply stirred the Indians, arousing the young warriors in particular to the highest pitch of excitement. They became sullen, began to paint, and armed themselves; and the agent and the settlers near by grew so apprehensive that the troops were ordered to go to the reservation. A body of cavalry, including Captain Edwards' troop, was accordingly marched thither, and found the Crow warriors, mounted on their war ponies and dressed in their striking battle-garb, waiting on a hill.

The position of troops at the beginning of such an affair is always peculiarly difficult. The settlers round-about are sure to clamor bitterly against them, no matter what they do, on the ground that they are not thorough enough and are showing favor to the savages, while on the other hand, even if they fight purely in self-defence, a large number of worthy but weak-minded senti-mentalists in the East are sure to shriek about their having brutally attacked the Indians. The war authorities always insist that they must not fire the first shot under any circumstances, and such were the orders at this time. The Crows on the hill-top showed a sullen and threatening front, and the troops advanced slowly towards them and then halted for a parley. Meanwhile a mass of black thunder-clouds gathering on the horizon threatened one of those cloudbursts of extreme severity and suddenness so characteristic of the plains country. While still trying to make arrangements for a parley, a horse-man started out of the Crow ranks and galloped headlong down towards the troops. It was the medicine chief, Sword-Bearer. He was painted and in his bat-tle-dress, wearing his war-bonnet of floating, trailing eagle feathers, while the plumes of the same bird were braided in the mane and tail of his fiery little horse. On he came at a gallop almost up to the troops and then began to cir-cle around them, calling and singing and throwing his crimson sword into the air, catching it by the hilt as it fell. Twice he rode completely around the sol-diers, who stood in uncertainty, not knowing what to make of his performance, and expressly forbidden to shoot at him. Then paying no further heed to them he rode back towards the Crows. It appears that he had told them that he would ride twice around the hostile force, and by his incantations would call down rain from heaven, which would make the hearts of the white men like water, so that they should go back to their homes. Sure enough, while the arrangements for the parley were still going forward, down came the cloud-burst, drenching the command and making the ground on the hills in front nearly impassable; and before it dried a courier arrived with orders to the troops to go back to camp.

This fulfilment of Sword-Bearer's prophecy of course raised his reputation to the zenith and the young men of the tribe prepared for war, while the older chiefs, who more fully realized the power of the whites, still hung back. When the troops next appeared they came upon the entire Crow force, the women and children with their tepees being off to one side beyond a little stream while almost all the warriors of the tribe were gathered in front. Sword-Bearer started to repeat his former ride, to the intense irritation of the soldiers. Luckily, however, this time some of his young men could not be restrained. They too began to ride near the troops, and one of them was unable to refrain from firing on Captain Edwards' troop, which was in the van. This gave the soldiers their chance. They instantly responded with a volley, and Captain Edwards' troop charged. The fight lasted but a minute or two, for Sword-Bearer was struck by a bullet and fell, and as he had boasted himself invulnerable, and promised that his warriors should be invulnerable also if they would follow him, the hearts of the latter became as water and they broke in every direction. One of the amus-ing, though irritating, incidents of the affair was to see the plumed and painted warriors race headlong for the camp, plunge into the stream, wash off their war paint, and remover their feathers; in another moment they would be stolidly sitting on the ground, with their blankets over their shoulders, rising to greet the pursuing cavalry with unmoved composure and calm assurances that they had always been friendly and had much disapproved the conduct of the young bucks who had just been scattered on the field outside. It was much to the credit of the discipline of the army that no bloodshed followed the fight proper. The loss to the whites was small.

The other incident, related by Lieutenant Pitcher, took place in 1890, near Tongue River, in northern Wyoming. The command with which he was serving was camped near the Cheyenne Reservation. One day two young Cheyenne bucks, met one of the government herders, and promptly killed him- in a sudden fit, half of ungovernable blood lust, half of mere ferocious light-heartedness. They then dragged his body into the brush and left it. The disappearance of the herder of course attracted attention, and a search was organized by the cavalry. At first the Indians stoutly denied all knowledge of the missing man; but when it became evident that the search party would shortly find him, two or three of the chiefs joined them, and piloted them to where the body lay; and acknowledged that he had been murdered by two of their band, though at first they refused to give their names. The commander of the post demanded that the murderers be given up. The chiefs said that they were very sorry, that this could not be done, but that they were willing to pay over any reasonable number of ponies to make amends for the death. This offer was of course promptly refused, and the commander notified them that if they did not surrender the murderers by a certain time he would hold the whole tribe responsible and would promptly move out and attack them. Upon this the chiefs, after holding full counsel with the tribe, told the commander that they had no power to surrender the murderers, but that the latter had said the sooner than see their tribe involved in a hopeless struggle they would of their own accord come in and meet the troops anywhere the latter chose to appoint, and die fighting. To this the commander responded: "All right; let them come into the agency in half an hour." The chief acquiesced, and withdrew.

Immediately the Indians sent mounted messengers at speed from camp to camp, summoning all their people to witness the act of fierce self-doom; and soon the entire tribe of Cheyennes, many of them having their faces blackened in token of mourning, moved down and took up a position on the hill-side close to the agency. At the appointed hour both young men appeared in their handsome war dress, galloped to the top of the hill near the encampment, and deliberately opened fire on the troops. The latter merely fired a few shots to keep the young desperadoes off, while Lieutenant Pitcher and a score of cavalrymen left camp to make a circle and drive them in; they did not wish to hurt them, but to capture and give them over to the Indians, so that the latter might be forced themselves to inflict the punishment. However, they were unable to accomplish their purpose; one of the young braves went straight at them, firing his rifle and wounding the horse of one of the cavalrymen, so that, simply in self-defence, the latter had to fire a volley, which laid low the assailant; the other, his horse having been shot, was killed in the brush, fighting to the last. All the while, from the moment the two doomed braves appeared until they fell, the Cheyennes on the hill-side had been steadily singing the death chant. When the young men had both died, and had thus averted the fate which their misdeeds would else have brought upon the tribe, the warriors took their bodies and bore them away for burial honors, the soldiers looking on in silence. Where the slain men were buried the whites never knew; but all that night they listened to the dismal wailing of the dirges with which the tribes-men celebrated their gloomy funeral rights.

Frontiersmen are not, as a rule, apt to be very superstitious. They lead lives too hard and practical, and have too little imagination in things spiritual and supernatural. I have heard but few ghost stories while living on the frontier, and these few were of a perfectly commonplace and conventional type.

But I once listened to a goblin story which rather impressed me. It was told by a grisled, weather-beaten old mountain hunter, named Bauman, who was born and had passed all his life on the frontier. He must have believed what he said, for he could hardly repress a shudder at certain points of the tale; but he was of German ancestry, and in childhood had doubtless been saturated with all kinds of ghost and goblin lore, so that many fearsome superstitions were latent in his mind; besides, he knew well the stories told by the Indian medicine men in their winter camps, of the snow-walkers, and the spectres, and the formless evil beings that haunt the forest depths, and dog and waylay the lonely wanderer who after nightfall passes through the regions where they lurk; and it may be that when overcome by the horror of the fate that befell his friend, and when oppressed by the awful dread of the unknown, he grew to attribute, both at the time and still more in remembrance, weird and elfin traits to what was merely some abnormally wicked and cunning wild beast; but whether this was so or not, no man can say.

When the even occurred Bauman was still a young man, and was trapping with a partner among the mountain dividing the forks of the Salmon from the head of Wisdom River. Not having had much luck, he and his partner determined to go up into a particularly wild and lonely pass through which ran a small stream said to contain many beaver. The pass had an evil reputation because the year before a solitary hunter who had wandered into it was there slain, seemingly by a wild beast, the half-eaten remains being afterwards found by some mining prospectors who had passed his camp only the night before.

The memory of this event, however, weighed very lightly with the two trappers, who were as adventurous and hardy as others of their kind. They took their two lean mountain ponies to the foot of the pass, where they left them in an open beaver meadow, the rocky timber-clad ground being from thence onwards impracticable for horses. They then struck out on foot through the vast, gloomy forest, and in about four hours reached a little open glade where they concluded to camp, as signs of game were plenty.

There was still an hour or two of daylight left, and after building a brush lean-to and throwing down and opening their packs, they started up stream. The country was very dense and hard to travel through, as there was much down timber, although here and there the sombre woodland was broken by small glades of mountain grass.

At dusk they again reached camp. The glade in which it was pitched was not many yards wide, the tall, close-set pines and firs rising round it like a wall. On one side was a little stream, beyond which rose the steep mountain-slopes, covered with the unbroken growth of the evergreen forest.

They were surprised to find that during their short absence something, apparently a bear, had visited camp, and had rummaged about their things, scattering the contents of their packs, and in sheer wantonness destroying their lean-to. The footprints of the beast were quite plain, but at first they had no particular heed to them, busying themselves with rebuilding the lean-to, laying out their beds and stores, and lighting the fire.

While Bauman was making ready supper, it being already dark, his companion began to examine the tracks more closely, and soon took a brand from the fire to follow them up, where the intruder had walked along a game trail after leaving camp. When the brand flickered out, he returned and took another, repeating his inspection of the footprints very closely. Coming back to the fire, he stood by in a minute or two, peering out into the darkness, and suddenly remarked: "Bauman, that bear has been walking on two legs." Bauman laughed at this, but his partner insisted that he was right, and upon again examining the tracks with a torch, they certainly did seem to be made by but two paws, or feet. However, it was too dark to make sure. After discussing whether the footprints could possibly be those of a human being, and coming to the conclusion that they could not be, the two men rolled up in their blankets, and went to sleep under the lean-to.

At midnight Bauman was awakened by some noise, and sat up in his blankets. As he did so his nostrils were struck by a strong, wild-beast odor, and he caught the loom of a great body in the darkness at the mouth of the lean-to. Grasping his rifle, he fired at the vague, threatening shadow, but must have missed, for immediately afterwards he heard the smashing of the underwood as the thing, whatever it was, rushed off into the impenetrable blackness of the forest and the night.

After this the two men slept but little, sitting up by the rekindled fire, but they heard nothing more. In the morning they started out to look at the few traps they had set the previous evening and to put out new ones. By an unspoken agreement they kept together all day, and returned to camp towards evening.

On nearing it they saw, hardly to their astonishment, that the lean-to had been again torn down. The visitor of the preceding day had returned, and in wanton malice had tossed about their camp kit and bedding, and destroyed the shanty. The ground was marked up by its tracks, and on leaving the camp it had gone along the soft earth by the brook, where the footprints were as plain as if on snow, and, after a careful scrutiny of the trail, it certainly did seem as if, whatever the thing was, it had walked off on but two legs.

The men, thoroughly uneasy, gathered a great heap of dead logs, and kept up a roaring fire throughout the night, one or the other sitting on guard most of the time. About midnight the thing came down through the forest opposite, across the brook, and stayed there on the hill-side for nearly an hour. They could hear the branches crackle as it moved about, and several times it uttered a harsh, grating, long-drawn moan, a peculiarly sinister sound. Yet it did not venture near the fire.

In the morning the two trappers, after discussing the strange events of the last thirty-six hours, decided that they would shoulder their packs and leave the valley that afternoon. They were the more ready to do this because in spite of seeing a good deal of game sign they had caught very little fur. However, it was necessary first to go along the line of their traps and gather them, and this they started out to do.

All the morning they kept together, picking up trap after trap, each one empty. On first leaving camp they had the disagreeable sensation of being followed. In the dense spruce thickets they occasionally heard a branch snap after they had passed; and now and then there were slight rustling noises among the small pines to one side of them.

At noon they were back within a couple of miles of camp. In the high, bright sunlight their fears seemed absurd to the two armed men, accustomed as they were, through long years of lonely wandering in the wilderness to face every kind of danger from man, brute, or element. There were still three beaver traps to collect from a little pond in a wide ravine near by. Bauman volunteered to gather these and bring them in, while his companion went ahead to camp and made ready the packs.

On reaching the pond Bauman found three beaver in the traps, one of which had been pulled loose and carried into a beaver house. He took several hours in securing and preparing the beaver, and when he started homewards he marked with some uneasiness how low the sun was getting. As he hurried towards camp, under the tall trees, the silence and desolation of the forest weighed on him. His feet made no sound on the pine needles, and the slanting sun rays, striking through among the straight trunks, made a gray twilight in which objects at a distance glimmered indistinctly.

There was nothing to break the ghostly stillness which, when there is no breeze, always broods over these sombre primeval forests.

At last he came to the edge of the little glade where the camp lay, and shouted as he approached it, but got no answer. The camp fire had gone out, though the thin blue some was still curling upwards. Near it lay the packs, wrapped and arranged. At first Bauman could see nobody; nor did he receive an answer to his call. Stepping forward he again shouted, and as he did so his eye fell on the body of his friend, stretched beside the trunk of a great fallen spruce. Rushing towards it the horrified trapper found that the body was still warm, but that the neck was broken, while there were four great fang marks in the throat.

The footprints of the unknown beast-creature, printed deep in the soft soil, told the whole story.

The unfortunate man, having finished his packing, had sat down on the spruce log with his face to the fire, and his back to the dense woods, to wait for his companion. While thus waiting, his monstrous assailant, which must have been lurking nearby in the woods, waiting for a chance to catch one of the adventurers unprepared, came silently up from behind, walking with long, noiseless steps, and seemingly still on two legs. Evidently unheard, it reached the man, and broke his neck by wrenching his head back with its forepaws, while it buried its teeth in his throat. It had not eaten the body, but apparently had romped and gambolled round it in uncouth, ferocious glee, occasionally rolling over and over it; and had then fled back into the soundless depths of the woods.

Bauman, utterly unnerved, and believing that the creature with which he had to deal was something either half human or half devil, some great goblin-beast, abandoned everything but his rifle and struck off at speed down the pass, not halting until he reached the beaver meadows where the hobbled ponies were still grazing. Mounting, he rode onwards through the night, until far beyond the reach of pursuit.

*These are stories about other people, the people of the West he had so much respect for. I cannot leave this section without repeating a story Roosevelt tells in his Autobiography about himself—the story of his bar fight. This was the Wild West, after all, and these things didn't just happen in the minds of Hollywood script writers. He was looking for lost horses, he says, and had stopped at a "primitive" hotel, he does not say where, that consisted of a bar-room, attached dining room, the kitchen in a shed, and upstairs a loft for sleeping.*

It was late in the evening when I reached the place. I heard one or two shots in the bar-room as I came up, and I disliked going in. But there was nowhere else to go, and it was a cold night. Inside the room were several men, who, including the bartender, were wearing the kind of smile worn by men who are making believe to like what they don't like. A shabby individual in a broad hat with a cocked gun in each hand was walking up and down the floor talking with strident profanity. He had evidently been shooting at the clock, which had two or three holes in its face.

He was not a "bad man" of the really dangerous type, the true man-killer type, but he was an objectionable creature, a would-be bad man, a bully who for the moment was having things all his own way. As soon as he saw me he hailed me as "Four eyes," in reference to my spectacles, and said, "Four eyes is going to treat." I joined in the laugh and got behind the stove and sat down, thinking to escape notice. He followed me, however, and though I tried to pass it off as a jest this merely made him more offensive, and he stood leaning over me, a gun in each hand, using very foul language. He was foolish to stand so near, and, moreover, his heels were close together, so that his position was unstable. Accordingly, in response to his reiterated command that I should set up the drinks, I said, "Well, if I've got to, I've got to," and rose, looking past him.

As I rose, I struck quick and hard with my right just to one side of the point of his jaw, hitting with my left as I straightened out, and then again with my right. He fired the guns, but I do not know whether this was merely a convulsive action of his hands or whether he was trying to shoot at me. When he went down he struck the corner of the bar with his head. It was not a case in which one could afford to take chances, and if he had moved I was about to drop on his ribs with my knees; but he was senseless. I took away his guns, and the other people in the room, who were now loud in their denunciation of him, hustled him out and put him in a shed. I got dinner as soon as possible, sitting in a corner of the dining-room away from the windows, and then went upstairs to bed where it was dark so that there would be no chance of any one shooting at me from the outside. However, nothing happened. When my assailant came to, he went down to the station and left on a freight.

*Speak softly, carry a big stick. Roosevelt lost the boxing championship in his weight class at Harvard, but he made it clear throughout his life that one should not mess with him. He was a tough man. At the same time he was cautious—cautious after decking his man here, cautious in all dangerous situations. He was much too intelligent to be merely belligerent. Yet when the rage for battle came on him, as we shall see in the next section, he could be a magnificent warrior and leader.*

✴

PART TWO

# Into the Thick of it

✴

# Into the Thick of It

By 1893, WHEN HE PUBLISHED The Wilderness Hunter, ROOSEVELT HAD served for four years on the Civil Service Commission in Washington. He had done his best to bring reform to the Post Office, and he had campaigned for and won a Congressional investigation into the actions of the Postmaster General, John Wanamaker. When a Democrat, Grover Cleveland, won the Presidency in 1892, he asked Roosevelt, a lifelong Republican, to stay on. No one doubted Theodore Roosevelt's rectitude. He was slowly acquiring a national reputation as a reformer and as a writer. He had not held an elective office since his days in the New York State Assembly, but he was still relatively young. In 1894, New York City elected a reform mayor, William Strong, and he asked Roosevelt to return to New York and serve as Police Commissioner. At the time the police department had four commissioners. Roosevelt was not someone who could blend in and easily become a member of a group, but he took the job anyway. Within a few months he had completely overshadowed the other three commissioners. In any pack, Roosevelt was soon the alpha male.

His first major act was to force out the chief of police, Thomas Byrnes, who was known to be corrupt. Graft was so rife in the police department that guide books to the city published figures estimating what the department received on an annual basis from it. Byrnes left the department worth $350,000; convert the buying power of that amount into today's money, and he would be a millionaire many times over. Roosevelt could not make all the graft go away, but he worked hard to clean the place up. He got everyone's attention by taking walking tours of the city late at night, after midnight, to check up on police officers who were supposed to be walking their beats. He took a reporter along on these trips, none other than Jacob Riis, whose book, How the Other Half Lives, had called the whole country's attention to the desperate lives of the urban poor. Roosevelt was a master of publicity. He actively courted reporters, invited them into inner councils, made clear rules about what they could quote and what they couldn't, and then explained to them exactly how the world worked. The effect on the police department, needless to add, was profound. Officers never knew whether those two men looming out of the dark might not be Roosevelt and Riis, come to check up on them. If he caught them taking a bribe from the local saloon keeper or pimp, or asleep on the job, or otherwise derelict in their duties, he at once brought them up on charges. The police department began to shape up.

Roosevelt kept the job for two years, but it was frustrating work. He could never get entirely around the other commissioners, one of whom strongly resented Roosevelt's assumption of control. In 1896 he spent the fall campaigning for William McKinley for President. He gave speeches in New York, then traveled all over the upper Midwest on McKinley's behalf. His work in New York had made a wider name for himself and he was already known in the West as an easterner who was also one of them. He spoke to huge crowds, he was an excellent speaker, and the campaign only increased his growing reputation. The country knew him as "Teddy Roosevelt," not Theodore, and his enthusiasm was catching. Roosevelt had much to do with McKinley's election. His reward? A job he had wanted for years: Assistant Secretary of the Navy.

It wasn't easy to obtain. McKinley was afraid that Roosevelt, once in office, would start lobbying immediately to get the United States involved in a war. What war, nobody had any doubts about. It would be with Spain, mostly over Cuba, where rebels had been fighting for years to free the island from the Spanish yoke. The Navy had a secretary, a man named John D. Long, but Long was not the firebrand Roosevelt was and he was fond of long vacations. It was clear even to Long that anyone who would become assistant secretary could take the job and run with it if he liked. It was also clear that Roosevelt was that kind of man.

He was indeed, and when he did get the job, in the spring of 1897, he moved rapidly to pursue the policy he had believed in ever since he wrote The Naval War of 1812, which now, incidentally, his publishers reissued. That policy was a strong navy. "Speak softly, and carry a big stick"—Roosevelt believed the U. S. Navy was at much too low a strength to suit a country that was rapidly becoming one of the world's major powers. Roosevelt knew Alfred T. Mahan—they were, indeed, friends— and had influenced Mahan's great and influential book, The Influence of Sea Power Upon History, which had come out in 1890. Mahan in turn influenced Roosevelt. With John Long having pretty much stepped aside, Roosevelt set in motion the process that would make the U. S. Navy dominant on the seas. He also did precisely what William McKinley had feared he would do. He promoted a war with Spain. Roosevelt was nothing if not expansionist. It wasn't just Cuba that Spain controlled, it was the Philippines. The naval war plan that appeared in late June,

1897, was a plan that assumed that the next war would be with Spain. That summer Roosevelt was able to secure an appointment for a friend as commander of the Navy's Asiatic Squadron. The friend was Commodore George Dewey. With Dewey in command, the Asiatic Squadron was in place—that is, it was in the Philippines—when war at last broke out the following April.

It began, of course, with the blowing up of the U.S.S Maine in Havana harbor on February 15, 1898. To this day it remains unclear how it happened, but no one questions that American expansionists like Roosevelt used it as an excuse to go to war. When war was declared in April, Roosevelt's first act was to resign from the Navy Department and participate with his friend Leonard Wood in the formation of a volunteer regiment, the First U. S. Volunteer Cavalry, which started training in Texas on May 15. It quickly became known as the Rough Riders and it took men very much like the men Roosevelt had worked with out West. It took cowboys. Roosevelt had always thought they would make a first-rate fighting force, and he actively recruited them. The regiment had its share of upper-class Easterners as well, many of them Roosevelt's friends. Training lasted less than a month. The regiment shipped out to Cuba in mid-June and fought its first battle about a week later. On July 1 it fought the battle that made Roosevelt one of the most famous men in the country—the battle for San Juan Hill, a ridgeline just south of Santiago, Cuba. Our selection is from the fourth chapter of The Rough Riders, Roosevelt's account of the war. This was a cavalry regiment, by the way, but the reader will see that they fought on foot.

# The Cavalry at Santiago

*The Rough Riders*

On June 30th we received orders to hold ourselves in readiness to march against Santiago, and all the men were greatly overjoyed, for the inaction was trying. The one narrow road, a mere muddy track along which the army was encamped, was choked with the marching columns. As always happened when we had to change camp, everything that the men could not carry, including, of course, the officers' baggage, was left behind.

About noon the Rough Riders struck camp and drew up in column beside the road in the rear of the First Cavalry. Then we sat down and waited for hours before the order came to march, while regiment after regiment passed by, varied by bands of tatterdemalion Cuban insurgents, and by mule-trains with ammunition. Every man carried three days' provisions. We had succeeded in borrowing mules sufficient to carry along the dynamite gun and the automatic Colts.

At last, toward mid-afternoon, the First and Tenth Cavalry, ahead of us, marched, and we followed. The First was under the command of Lieutenant-Colonel Veile, the Tenth under Lieutenant-Colonel Baldwin. Every few minutes there would be a stoppage in front, and at the halt I would make the men sit or lie down beside the track, loosening their packs. The heat was intense as we passed through the still, close jungle, which formed a wall on either hand. Occasionally we came to gaps or open spaces, where some regiment was camped, and now and then one of these regiments, which apparently had been left out of its proper place, would file into the road, breaking up our line of march. As a result, we finally found ourselves following merely the tail of the regiment ahead of us, an infantry regiment being thrust into the interval. Once or twice we had to wade streams. Darkness came on, but we still continued to march. It was about eight o'clock when we turned to the left and climbed El Poso hill, on whose summit there was a ruined ranch and sugar factory, now, of course, deserted. Here I found General Wood, who was arranging for the camping of the brigade. Our own arrangements for the night were simple. I extended each troop across the road into the jungle, and then the men threw down their belongings where they stood and slept on their arms. Fortunately, there was no rain. Wood and I curled up under our rain-coats on the saddle-blankets, while his two aides, Captain A. L. Mills and Lieutenant W. E. Shipp, slept near us. We were up before dawn and getting breakfast. Mills and Shipp had nothing to eat, and they breakfasted with Wood and myself, as we had been able to get some handfuls of beans, and some coffee and sugar, as well as the ordinary bacon and hardtack.

We did not talk much, for though we were in ignorance as to precisely what the day would bring forth, we knew that we should see fighting. We had slept soundly enough, although, of course, both Wood and I during the night had made a round of the sentries; he of the brigade, and I of the regiment; and I suppose that, excepting among hardened veterans, there is always a certain feeling of uneasy excitement the night before the battle.

Mills and Shipp were both tall, fine-looking men, of tried courage, and thoroughly trained in every detail of their profession; I remember being struck by the quiet, soldierly way they were going about their work early that morning. Before noon one was killed and the other dangerously wounded.

General Wheeler was sick, but with his usual indomitable pluck and entire indifference to his own personal comfort, he kept to the front. He was unable to retain command of the cavalry division, which accordingly devolved upon General Samuel Sumner, who commanded it until mid-afternoon, when the bulk of the fighting was over. General Sumner's own brigade fell to Colonel Henry Carroll. General Sumner led the advance with the cavalry, and the battle was fought by him and by General Kent, who commanded the infantry division, and whose foremost brigade was led by General Hawkins.

As the sun rose the men fell in, and at the same time a battery of field-guns was brought up on the hill-crest just beyond, between us and toward Santiago. It was a fine sight to see the great horses straining under the lash as they whirled the guns up the hill and into position.

Our brigade was drawn up on the hither side of a kind of half basin, a big band of Cubans being off to the left. As yet we had received no orders, except that we were told that the main fighting was to be done by Lawton's infantry division, which was to take El Caney, several miles to our right, while we were simply to make a diversion. This diversion was to be made mainly with the artillery, and the battery which had taken position immediately in front of us was to begin when Lawton began.

It was about six o'clock that the first report of the cannon from El Caney came booming to us across the miles of still jungle. It was a very lovely morning, the sky of cloudless blue, while the level, shimmering rays from the just-risen sun brought into fine relief the splendid palms which here and there towered above the lower growth. The lofty and beautiful mountains hemmed in the Santiago plain, making it an amphitheatre for the battle.

Immediately our guns opened, and at the report great clouds of white smoke hung on the ridge crest. For a minute or two there was no response. Wood and I were sitting together, and Wood remarked to me that he wished our brigade could be moved somewhere else, for we were directly in line of any return fire aimed by the Spaniards at the battery. Hardly had he spoken when there was a peculiar whistling, singing sound in the air, and immediately afterward the noise of something exploding over our heads. It was shrapnel from the Spanish batteries. We sprung to our feet and leaped on our horses. Immediately afterward a second shot came which burst directly above us; and then a third. From the second shell one of the shrapnel bullets dropped on my wrist, hardly breaking the skin, but raising a bump about as big as a hickory-nut. The same shell wounded four of my regiment, one of them being Mason Mitchell, and two or three of the regulars were also hit, one losing his leg by a great fragment of shell. Another shell exploded right in the middle of the Cubans, killing and wounding a good many, while the remainder scattered like guinea-hens. Wood's lead horse was also shot through the lungs. I at once hustled my regiment over the crest of the hill into the thick underbrush, where I had no little difficulty in getting them together again into column.

Meanwhile the firing continued for fifteen or twenty minutes, until it gradually died away. As the Spaniards used smokeless powder, their artillery had an enormous advantage over ours, and, moreover, we did not have the best type of modern guns, our fire being slow.

As soon as the firing ceased, Wood formed his brigade, with my regiment in front, and gave me orders to follow behind the First Brigade, which was just moving off the ground. In column of fours we marched down the trail toward the ford of the San Juan River. We passed two or three regiments of infantry, and were several times halted before we came to the ford. The First Brigade, which was under Colonel Carroll—Lieutenant-Colonel Hamilton commanding the Ninth Regiment, Major Wessels the Third, and Captain Kerr the Sixth—had already crossed and was marching to the right, parallel to, but a little distance from, the river. The Spaniards in the trenches and block-houses on top of the hills in front were already firing at the brigade in desultory fashion. The extreme advance of the Ninth Cavalry was under Lieutenants McNamee and Hartwick. They were joined by General Hawkins, with his staff, who was looking over the ground and deciding on the route he should take his infantry brigade.

Our orders had been of the vaguest kind, being simply to march to the right and connect with Lawton—with whom, of course, there was no chance of our connecting. No reconnoissance had been made, and the exact position and strength of the Spaniards was not known. A captive balloon was up in the air at this moment, but it was worse than useless. A previous proper reconnoissance and proper look-out from the hills would have given us exact information. As it was, Generals Kent, Sumner, and Hawkins had to be their own reconnoissance, and they fought their troops so well that we won anyhow.

I was now ordered to cross the ford, march half a mile or so to the right, and then halt and await further orders; and I promptly hurried my men across, for the fire was getting hot, and the captive balloon, to the horror of everybody, was coming down to the ford. Of course, it was a special target for the enemy's fire. I got my men across before it reached the ford. There it partly collapsed and remained, causing severe loss of life, as it indicated the exact position where the Tenth and the First Cavalry, and the infantry, were crossing.

As I led my column slowly along, under the intense heat, through the high grass of the open jungle, the First Brigade was to our left, and the firing between it and the Spaniards on the hills grew steadily hotter and hotter. After awhile I came to a sunken lane, and as by this time the First Brigade had stopped and was engaged in a stand-up fight, I halted my men and sent back word for orders. As we faced toward the Spanish hills my regiment was on the right with next to it and a little in advance the First Cavalry, and behind them the Tenth. In our front the Ninth held the right, the Sixth the centre, and the Third the left; but in the jungle the lines were already overlapping in places. Kent's infantry were coming up, farther to the left.

Captain Mills was with me. The sunken lane, which had a wire fence on either side, led straight up toward, and between, the two hills in our front, the hill on the left, which contained heavy block-houses, being farther away from us than the hill on our right, which we afterward grew to call Kettle Hill, and which was surmounted merely by some large ranch buildings or haciendas, with sunken brick-lined walls and cellars. I got the men as well-sheltered as I could. Many of them lay close under the bank of the lane, others slipped into the San

Juan River and crouched under its hither bank, while the rest lay down behind the patches of bushy jungle in the tall grass. The heat was intense, and many of the men were already showing signs of exhaustion. The sides of the hills in front were bare; but the country up to them was, for the most part, covered with such dense jungle that in charging through it no accuracy of formation could possibly be preserved.

The fight was now on in good earnest, and the Spaniards on the hills were engaged in heavy volley firing. The Mauser bullets drove in sheets through the trees and the tall jungle grass, making a peculiar whirring or rustling sound; some of the bullets seemed to pop in the air, so that we thought they were explosive; and, indeed, many of those which were coated with brass did explode, in the sense that the brass coat was ripped off, making a thin plate of hard metal with a jagged edge, which inflicted a ghastly wound. These bullets were shot from a .45-calibre rifle carrying smokeless powder, which was much used by the guerillas and irregular Spanish troops. The Mauser bullets themselves made a small clean hole, with the result that the wound healed in a most astonishing manner. One or two of our men who were shot in the head had the skull blown open, but elsewhere the wounds from the minute steelcoated bullet, with its very high velocity, were certainly nothing like as serious as those made by the old large-calibre, low-power rifle. If a man was shot through the heart, spine, or brain he was, of course, killed instantly; but very few of the wounded died—even under the appalling conditions which prevailed, owing to the lack of attendance and supplies in the field-hospitals with the army.

While we were lying in reserve we were suffering nearly as much as afterward when we charged. I think that the bulk of the Spanish fire was practically unaimed, or at least not aimed at any particular man, and only occasionally at a particular body of men; but they swept the whole field of battle up to the edge of the river, and man after man in our ranks fell dead or wounded, although I had the troopers scattered out far apart, taking advantage of every scrap of cover.

Devereux was dangerously shot while he lay with his men on the edge of the river. A young West Point cadet, Ernest Haskell, who had taken his holiday with us as an acting second lieutenant, was shot through the stomach. He had shown great coolness and gallantry, which he displayed to an even more marked degree after being wounded, shaking my hand and saying: "All right, Colonel, I'm going to get well. Don't bother about me, and don't let any man come away with me." When I shook hands with him, I thought he would surely die; yet he recovered.

The most serious loss that I and the regiment could have suffered befell just before we charged. Bucky O'Neill was strolling up and down in front of his men, smoking his cigarette, for he was inveterately addicted to the habit. He had a theory that an officer ought never to take cover—a theory which was, of course, wrong, though in a volunteer organization the officers should certainly expose themselves very fully, simply for the effect on the men; our regimental toast on the transport running, "The officers; may the war last until each is killed, wounded, or promoted." As O'Neill moved to and fro, his men begged him to lie down, and one of the sergeants said, "Captain, a bullet is sure to hit you." O'Neill took his cigarette out of his mouth, and blowing out a cloud of smoke laughed and said, "Sergeant, the Spanish bullet isn't made that will kill me." A little later he discussed for a moment with one of the regular officers the direction from which the Spanish fire was coming. As he turned on his heel a bullet struck him in the mouth and came out at the back of his head; so that even before he fell his wild and gallant soul had gone out into the darkness.

My orderly was a brave young Harvard boy, Sanders, from the quaint old Massachusetts town of Salem. The work of an orderly on foot, under the blazing sun, through the hot and matted jungle, was very severe, and finally the heat overcame him. He dropped; nor did he ever recover fully, and later he died from fever. In his place I summoned a trooper whose name I did not know. Shortly afterward, while sitting beside the bank, I directed him to go back and ask whatever general he came across if I could not advance, as my men were being much cut up. He stood up to salute and then pitched forward across my knees, a bullet having gone through his throat, cutting the carotid.

When O'Neill was shot, his troop, who were devoted to him, were for the moment at a loss whom to follow. One of their number, Henry Bardshar, a huge Arizona miner, immediately attached himself to me as my orderly, and from that moment he was closer to me, not only in the fight, but throughout the rest of the campaign, than any other man, not even excepting the color-sergeant, Wright.

Captain Mills was with me; gallant Ship had already been killed. Mills was an invaluable aide, absolutely cool, absolutely unmoved or flurried in any way.

I sent messenger after messenger to try to find General Sumner or General Wood and get permission to advance, and was just about making up my mind that in the absence of orders I had better "march toward the guns," when Lieutenant-Colonel Dorst came riding up through the storm of bullets with the welcome command "to move forward and support the regulars in the assault on the hills in front." General Sumner had obtained authority to advance from Lieutenant Miley, who was representing General Shafter at the front, and was in the thick of the fire. The General at once ordered the first brigade to advance on the hills, and the second to support it. He himself was riding his horse along the lines, superintending the fight. Later I overheard a couple of my men talking together about him. What they said illustrates the value of a display of courage among the officers in hardening their soldiers; for their theme was how, as they were lying down under a fire which they could not return, and were in consequence feeling rather nervous, General Sumner suddenly appeared on horseback, sauntering by quite unmoved; and, said one of the men, "That made us feel all right. If the General could stand it, we could."

The instant I received the order I sprang on my horse and then my "crowded hour" began. The guerillas had been shooting at us from the edges of the jungle and from their perches in the leafy trees, and as they used smokeless powder, it was almost impossible to see them, though a few of my men had from time to time responded. We had also suffered from the hill on our right front, which was held chiefly by guerillas, although there were also some Spanish regulars with them, for we found their dead. I formed my men in column of troops, each troop extended in open skirmishing order, the right resting on the wire fences which bordered the sunken lane. Captain Jenkins led the first squadron, his eyes literally dancing with joyous excitement.

I started in the rear of the regiment, the position in which the colonel should theoretically stay. Captain Mills and Captain McCormick were both with me as aides; but I speedily had to send them off on special duty in getting the different bodies of men forward. I had intended to go into action on foot as at Las Guasimas, but the heat was so oppressive that I found I should be quite unable to run up and down the line and superintend matters unless I was mounted; and, moreover, when on horseback, I could see the men better and they could see me better.

A curious incident happened as I was getting the men started forward. Always when men have been lying down under cover for some time, and are required to advance, there is a little hesitation, each looking to see whether the others are going forward. As I rode down the line, calling to the troopers to go forward, and rasping brief directions to the captains and lieutenants, I came upon a man lying behind a little bush, and I ordered him to jump up. I do not think he understood that we were making a forward move, and he looked up at me for a moment with hesitation, and I again bade him rise, jeering him and saying: "Are you afraid to stand up when I am on horseback?" As I spoke, he suddenly fell forward on his face, a bullet having struck him and gone through him lengthwise. I suppose the bullet had been aimed at me; at any rate, I, who was on horseback in the open, was unhurt, and the man lying flat on the ground in the cover beside me was killed. There were several pairs of brothers with us; of the two Nortons one was killed; of the two McCurdys one was wounded.

I soon found that I could get that line, behind which I personally was, faster forward than the one immediately in front of it, with the result that the two rearmost lines of the regiment began to crowd together; so I rode through them both, the better to move on the one in front. This happened with every line in succession, until I found myself at the head of the regiment.

Both lieutenants of B Troop from Arizona had been exerting themselves greatly, and both were overcome by the heat; but Sergeants Campbell and Davidson took it forward in splendid shape. Some of the men from this troop and from the other Arizona troop (Bucky O'Neill's) joined me as a kind of fighting tail.

The Ninth Regiment was immediately in front of me, and the First on my left, and these went up Kettle Hill with my regiment. The Third, Sixth, and Tenth went partly up Kettle Hill (following the Rough Riders and the Ninth and First), and partly between that and the block-house hill, which the infantry were assailing. General Sumner in person gave the Tenth the order to charge the hills; and it went forward at a rapid gait. The three regiments went forward more or less intermingled, advancing steadily and keeping up a heavy fire. Up Kettle Hill Sergeant George Berry, of the Tenth, bore not only his own regimental colors but those of the Third, the color-sergeant of the Third having been shot down; he kept shouting, "Dress on the colors, boys, dress on the colors!" as he followed Captain Ayres, who was running in advance of his men, shouting and waving his hat. The Tenth Cavalry lost a greater proportion of its officers than any other regiment in the battle—eleven out of twenty-two.

By the time I had come to the head of the regiment we ran into the left wing of the Ninth Regulars, and some of the First Regulars, who were lying down; that is, the troopers were lying down, while the officers were walking to and fro. The officers of the white and colored regiments alike took the greatest pride in seeing that the men more than did their duty; and the mortality among them was great.

I spoke to the captain in command of the rear platoons, saying that I had been ordered to support the regulars in the attack upon the hills, and that in my judgment we could not take these hills by firing at them, and that we must rush them. He answered that his orders were to keep his men lying where they were, and that he could not charge without orders. I asked where the Colonel was, and as he was not in sight, said, "Then I am the ranking officer here and I give the order to charge"—for I did not want to keep the men longer in the open suffering under a fire which they could not effectively return. Naturally the captain hesitated to obey this order when no word had been received from his own Colonel. So I said, "Then let my men through, sir," and rode on through the lines, followed by the grinning Rough Riders, whose attention had been completely taken off the Spanish bullets, partly by my dialogue with the regulars, and partly by the language I had been using to themselves as I got the lines forward, for I had been joking with some and swearing at others, as the exigencies of the case seemed to demand. When we started to go through, however, it proved too much for the regulars, and they jumped up and came along, their officers and troops mingling with mine, all being delighted at the chance. When I got to where the head of the left wing of the Ninth was lying, through the courtesy of Lieutenant Hartwick, two of whose colored troopers threw down the fence, I was enabled to get back into the lane, at the same time waving my hat, and giving the order to charge the hill on our right front. Out of my sight, over on the right, Captains McBlain and Taylor, of the Ninth, made up their minds independently to charge at just about this time; and at almost the same moment Colonels Carroll and Hamilton, who were off, I believe, to my left, where we could see neither them nor their men, gave the order to advance. But of all this I knew nothing at the time. The whole line, tired of waiting, and eager to close with the enemy, was straining to go forward; and it seems that different parts slipped the leash at almost the same moment. The First Cavalry came up the hill just behind, and partly mixed with my regiment and the Ninth. As already said, portions of the Third, Sixth, and Tenth followed, while the rest of the members of these three regiments kept more in touch with the infantry on our left.

By this time we were all in the spirit of the thing and greatly excited by the charge, the men cheering and running forward between shots, while the delighted faces of the foremost officers, like Captain C. J. Stevens, of the Ninth, as they ran at the head of their troops, will always stay in my mind. As soon as I was in the line I galloped forward a few yards until I saw that the men were well started, and then galloped back to help Goodrich, who was in command of his troop, get his men across the road so as to attack the hill from that side. Captain Mills had already thrown three of the other troops of the regiment across this road for the same purpose. Wheeling around, I then again galloped toward the hill, passing the shouting, cheering, firing men, and went up the lane, splashing through a small stream; when I got abreast of the ranch buildings on the top of Kettle Hill, I turned and went up the slope. Being on horseback I was, of course, able to get ahead of the men on foot, excepting my orderly, Henry Bardshar, who had run ahead very fast in order to get better shots at the Spaniards, who were now running out of the ranch buildings. Sergeant Campbell and a number of the Arizona men, and Dudley Dean, among others, were very close behind. Stevens, with his platoon of the Ninth, was abreast of us; so were McNamee and Hartwick. Some forty yards from the top I ran into a wire fence and jumped off Little Texas, turning him loose. He had been scraped by a couple of bullets, one of which nicked my elbow, and I never expected to see him again. As I ran up to the hill, Bardshar stopped to shoot, and two Spaniards fell as he emptied his magazine. These were the only Spaniards I actually saw fall to aimed shots by any one of my men, with the exception of two guerillas in trees.

Almost immediately afterward the hill was covered by the troops, both Rough Riders and the colored troopers of the Ninth, and some men of the First. There was the usual confusion, and afterward there was much discussion as to exactly who had been on the hill first. The first guidons planted there were those of the three New Mexican troops, G, E, and F, of my regiment, under their Captains, Llewellen, Luna, and Muller, but on the extreme right of the hill, at the opposite end from where we struck it, Captains Taylor and McBlain and their men of the Ninth were first up. Each of the five captains was firm in the belief that his troop was first up. As for the individual men, each of whom honestly thought he was first on the summit, their name was legion. One Spaniard was captured in the buildings, another was shot as he tried to hide himself, and a few others were killed as they ran.

Among the many deeds of conspicuous gallantry here performed, two, both to the credit of the First Cavalry, may be mentioned as examples of the others, not as exceptions. Sergeant Charles Karsten, while close beside Captain Tutherly, the squadron commander, was hit by a shrapnel bullet. He continued on the line, firing until his arm grew numb; and he then refused to go to the rear, and devoted himself to taking care of the wounded, utterly unmoved by the heavy fire. Trooper Hugo Brittain, when wounded, brought the regimental standard forward, waving it to and fro, to cheer the men.

No sooner were we on the crest than the Spaniards from the line of hills in our front, where they were strongly intrenched, opened a very heavy fire upon us with their rifles. They also opened upon us with one or two pieces of artillery, using time fuses which burned very accurately, the shells exploding right over our heads.

On the top of the hill was a huge iron kettle, or something of the kind, probably used for sugar refining. Several of our men took shelter behind this. We had a splendid view of the charge on the San Juan block-house to our left, where the infantry of Kent, led by Hawkins, were climbing the hill. Obviously the proper thing to do was to help them, and I got the men together and started them volley-firing against the Spaniards in the San Juan block-house and in the trenches around it. We could only see their heads; of course this was all we ever could see when we were firing at them in their trenches. Stevens was directing not only his own colored troopers, but a number of Rough Riders; for in a mêlée good soldiers are always prompt to recognize a good officer, and are eager to follow him.

We kept up a brisk fire for some five or ten minutes; meanwhile we were much cut up ourselves. Gallant Colonel Hamilton, than whom there was never a braver man, was killed, and equally gallant Colonel Carroll wounded. When near the summit Captain Mills had been shot through the head, the bullet destroying the sight of one eye permanently and of the other temporarily. He would not go back or let any man assist him, sitting down where he was and waiting until one of the men brought him word that the hill was stormed. Colonel Veile planted the standard of the First Cavalry on the hill, and General Sumner rode up. He was fighting his division in great form, and was always himself in the thick of the fire. As the men were much excited by the firing, they seemed to pay very little heed to their own losses.

Suddenly, above the cracking of the carbines, rose a peculiar drumming sound, and some of the men cried, "The Spanish machine-guns!" Listening, I made out that it came from the flat ground to the left, and jumped to my feet, smiting my hand on my thigh, and shouting aloud with exultation, "It's the Gatlings, men, our Gatlings!" Lieutenant Parker was bringing his four gatlings into action, and shoving them nearer and nearer the front. Now and then the drumming ceased for a moment; then it would resound again, always closer to San Juan hill, which Parker, like ourselves, was hammering to assist the infantry attack. Our men cheered lustily. We saw much of Parker after that, and there was never a more welcome sound than his Gatlings as they opened. It was the only sound which I ever heard my men cheer in battle.

The infantry got nearer and nearer the crest of the hill. At last we could see the Spaniards running from the rifle-pits as the Americans came on in their final rush. Then I stopped my men for fear they should injure their comrades, and called to them to charge the next line of trenches, on the hills in our front, from which we had been undergoing a good deal of punishment. Thinking that the men would all come, I jumped over the wire fence in front of us and started at the double; but, as a matter of fact, the troopers were so excited, what with shooting and being shot, and shouting and cheering, that they did not hear, or did not heed me; and after running about a hundred yards I found I had only five men along with me. Bullets were ripping the grass all around us, and one of the men, Clay Green, was mortally wounded; another, Winslow Clark, a Harvard man, was shot first in the leg and then through the body. He made not the slightest murmur, only asking me to put his water canteen where he could get at it, which I did; he ultimately recovered. There was no use going on with the remaining three men, and I bade them stay where they were while I went back and brought up the rest of the brigade. This was a decidedly cool request, for there was really no possible point in letting them stay there while I went back; but at the moment it seemed perfectly natural to me, and apparently so to them, for they cheerfully nodded, and sat down in the grass, firing back at the line of trenches from which the Spaniards were shooting at them. Meanwhile, I ran back, jumped over the wire fence, and went over the crest of the hill, filled with anger against the troopers, and especially those of my own regiment, for not having accompanied me. They, of course, were quite innocent of wrong-doing; and even while I taunted them bitterly for not having followed me, it was all I could do not to smile at the look of injury and surprise that came over their faces, while they cried out, "We didn't hear you, we didn't see you go, Colonel; lead on now, we'll sure follow you." I wanted the other regiments to come too, so I ran down to where General Sumner was and asked him if I might make the charge; and he told me to go and that he would see that the men followed. By this time everybody had his attention attracted, and when I leaped over the fence again, with Major Jenkins beside me, the men of the various regiments which were already on the hill came with a rush, and we started across the wide valley which lay between us and the Spanish intrenchments. Captain Dimmick, now in command of the Ninth, was bringing it forward; Captain McBlain had a number of Rough Riders mixed in with his troop, and led them all together; Captain Taylor had been severely wounded. The long-legged men like Greenway, Goodrich, sharp-shooter Proffit, and others, outstripped the rest of us, as we had a considerable distance to go. Long before we got near them the Spaniards ran, save a few here and there, who either surrendered or were shot down. When we reached the trenches we found them filled with dead bodies in the light blue and white uniform of the Spanish regular army. There were very few wounded. Most of the fallen had little holes in their heads from which their brains were oozing; for they were covered from the neck down by the trenches.

It was at this place that Major Wessels, of the Third Cavalry, was shot in the back of the head. It was a severe wound, but after having it bound up he again came to the front in command of his regiment. Among the men who were foremost was Lieutenant Milton F. Davis, of the First Cavalry. He had been joined by three men of the Seventy-first New York, who ran up, and, saluting, said, "Lieutenant, we want to go with you, our officers won't lead us." One of the brave fellows was soon afterward shot in the face. Lieutenant Davis's first sergeant, Clarence Gould, killed a Spanish soldier with his revolver, just as the Spaniard was aiming at one of my Rough Riders. At about the same time I also shot one. I was with Henry Bardshar, running up at the double, and two Spaniards leaped from the trenches and fired at us, not ten yards away. As they turned to run I closed in and fired twice, missing the first and killing the second. My revolver was from the sunken battle-ship Maine, and had been given me by my brother-in-law, Captain W. S. Cowles, of the Navy. At the time I did not know of Gould's exploit, and supposed my feat to be unique; and although Gould had killed his Spaniard in the trenches, not very far from me, I never learned of it until weeks after. It is astonishing what a limited area of vision and experience one has in the hurly-burly of a battle.

There was very great confusion at this time, the different regiments being completely intermingled—white regulars, colored regulars, and Rough Riders. General Sumner had kept a considerable force in reserve on Kettle Hill, under Major Jackson, of the Third Cavalry. We were still under a heavy fire and I got together a mixed lot of men and pushed on from the trenches and ranch-houses which we had just taken, driving the Spaniards through a line of palm-trees, and over the crest of a chain of hills. When we reached these crests we found ourselves overlooking Santiago. Some of the men, including Jenkins, Greenway, and Goodrich, pushed on almost by themselves far ahead. Lieutenant Hugh Berkely, of the First, with a sergeant and two troopers, reached the extreme front. He was, at the time, ahead of everyone; the sergeant was killed and one trooper wounded; but the lieutenant and the remaining trooper stuck to their post for the rest of the afternoon until our line was gradually extended to include them.

While I was re-forming the troops on the chain of hills, one of General Sumner's aides, Captain Robert Howze—as dashing and gallant an officer as there was in the whole gallant cavalry division, by the way—came up with orders to me to halt where I was, not advancing farther, but to hold the hill at all hazards. Howze had his horse, and I had some difficulty in making him take proper shelter; he stayed with us for quite a time, unable to make up his mind to leave the extreme front, and meanwhile jumping at the chance to render any service, of risk or otherwise, which the moment developed.

I now had under me all the fragments of the six cavalry regiments which were at the extreme front, being the highest officer left there, and I was in immediate command of them for the remainder of the afternoon and that night. The Ninth was over to the right, and the Thirteenth Infantry afterward came up beside it. The rest of Kent's infantry was to our left. Of the Tenth, Lieutenants Anderson, Muller, and Fleming reported to me; Anderson was slightly wounded, but he paid no heed to this. All three, like every other officer, had troopers of various regiments under them; such mixing was inevitable in making repeated charges through thick jungle; it was essentially a troop commanders', indeed, almost a squad leaders', fight. The Spaniards who had been holding the trenches and the line of hills, had fallen back upon their supports and we were under a very heavy fire both from rifles and great guns. At the point where we were, the grass-covered hill-crest was gently rounded, giving poor cover, and I made my men lie down on the hither slope.

On the extreme left Captain Beck, of the Tenth, with his own troop, and small bodies of the men of other regiments, was exercising a practically independent command, driving back the Spaniards whenever they showed any symptoms of advancing. He had received his orders to hold the line at all hazards from Lieutenant Andrews, one of General Sumner's aides, just as I had received mine from Captain Howze. Finally, he was relieved by some infantry, and then rejoined the rest of the Tenth, which was engaged heavily until dark, Major Wint being among the severely wounded. Lieutenant W. N. Smith was killed, Captain Bigelow had been wounded three times.

Our artillery made one or two efforts to come into action on the firing-line of the infantry, but the black powder rendered each attempt fruitless. The Spanish guns used smokeless powder, so that it was difficult to place them. In this respect they were on a par with their own infantry and with our regular infantry and dismounted cavalry; but our only two volunteer infantry regiments, the Second Massachusetts and the Seventy-first New York, and our artillery, all had black powder. This rendered the two volunteer regiments, which were armed with the antiquated Springfield, almost useless in the battle, and did practically the same thing for the artillery wherever it was formed within rifle range. When one of the guns was discharged a thick cloud of smoke shot out and hung over the place, making an ideal target, and in a half minute every Spanish gun and rifle within range was directed at the particular spot thus indicated; the consequence was that after a more or less lengthy stand the gun was silenced or driven off. We got no appreciable help from our guns on July 1st. Our men were quick to realize the defects of our artillery, but they were entirely philosophic about it, not showing the least concern at its failure. On the contrary, whenever they heard our artillery open they would grin as they looked at one another and remark, "There go the guns again; wonder how soon they'll be shut up," and shut up they were sure to be. The light battery of Hotchkiss one-pounders, under Lieutenant J. B. Hughes, of the Tenth Cavalry, was handled with conspicuous gallantry.

On the hill-slope immediately around me I had a mixed force composed of members of most of the cavalry regiments, and a few infantrymen. There were about fifty of my Rough Riders with Lieutenants Goodrich and Carr. Among the rest were perhaps a score of colored infantrymen, but, as it happened, at this particular point without any of their officers. No troops could have behaved better than the colored soldiers had behaved so far; but they are, of course, peculiarly dependent upon their white officers. Occasionally they produce non-commissioned officers who can take the initiative and accept responsibility precisely like the best class of whites; but this cannot be expected normally, nor is it fair to expect it. With the colored troops there should always be some of their own officers; whereas, with the white regulars, as with my own Rough Riders, experience showed that the non-commissioned officers could usually carry on the fight by themselves if they were once started, no matter whether their officers were killed or not.

At this particular time it was trying for the men, as they were lying flat on their faces, very rarely responding to the bullets, shells, and shrapnel which swept over the hill-top, and which occasionally killed or wounded one of their number. Major Albert G. Forse, of the First Cavalry, a noted Indian fighter, was killed about this time. One of my best men, Sergeant Greenly, of Arizona, who was lying beside me, suddenly said, "Beg pardon, Colonel; but I've been hit in the leg." I asked, "Badly?" He said, "Yes, Colonel; quite badly." After one of his comrades had helped him fix up his leg with a first-aid-to-the-injured bandage, he limped off to the rear.

None of the white regulars or Rough Riders showed the slightest sign of weakening; but under the strain the colored infantrymen (who had none of their officers) began to get a little uneasy and to drift to the rear, either helping wounded men, or saying that they wished to find their own regiments. This I could not allow, as it was depleting my line; so I jumped up, and walking a few yards to the rear, drew my revolver, halted the retreating soldiers, and called out to them that I appreciated the gallantry with which they had fought and would be sorry to hurt them, but that I should shoot the first man who, on any pretence whatever, went to the rear. My own men had all sat up and were watching my movements with utmost interest; so was Captain Howze. I ended my statement to the colored soldiers by saying: "Now, I shall be very sorry to hurt you, and you don't know whether or not I will keep my word, but my men can tell you that I always do;" whereupon my cow-punchers, hunters, and miners solemnly nodded their heads and commented in chorus, exactly as if in a comic opera, "He always does; he always does!"

This was the end of the trouble, for the "smoked Yankees"—as the Spaniards called the colored soldiers—flashed their white teeth at one another, as they broke into broad grins, and I had no more trouble with them, they seeming to accept me as one of their own officers. The colored cavalry men had already so accepted me; in return, the Rough Riders, although for the most part Southwesterners, who have a strong color prejudice, grew to accept them with hearty good-will as comrades, and were entirely willing, in their own phrase, "to drink out of the same canteen." Where all the regular officers did so well, it is hard to draw any distinction; but in the cavalry division a peculiar meed of praise should be given to the officers of the Ninth and Tenth for their work, and under their leadership the colored troops did as well as any soldiers could possibly do.

In the course of the afternoon the Spaniards in our front made the only offensive movement which I saw them make during the entire campaign; for what were ordinarily called "attacks" upon our lines consisted merely of heavy firing from their trenches and from their skirmishers. In this case they did actually begin to make a forward movement, their cavalry coming up as well as the marines and reserve infantry, while their skirmishers, who were always bold, redoubled their activity. It could not be called a charge, and not only was it not pushed home, but it was stopped almost as soon as it began, our men immediately running forward to the crest of the hill with shouts of delight at seeing their enemies at last come into the open. A few seconds' firing stopped their advance and drove them into the cover of the trenches.

They kept up a very heavy fire for some time longer, and our men again lay down, only replying occasionally. Suddenly we heard on our right the peculiar drumming sound which had been so welcome in the morning, when the infantry were assailing the San Juan block-house. The Gatlings were up again! I started over to inquire, and found that Lieutenant Parker, not content with using his guns in support of the attacking forces, had thrust them forward to the extreme front of the fighting line, where he was handling them with great effect. From this time on, throughout the fighting, Parker's Gatlings were on the right of my regiment, and his men and mine fraternized in every way. He kept his pieces at the extreme front, using them on every occasion until the last Spanish shot was fired. Indeed, the dash and efficiency with which the Gatlings were handled by Parker was one of the most striking features of the campaign; he showed that a first-rate officer could use machine-guns, on wheels, in battle and skirmish, in attacking and defending trenches, alongside of the best troops, and to their great advantage.

As night came on, the firing gradually died away. Before this happened, however, Captains Morton and Boughton, of the Third Cavalry, came over to tell me that a rumor had reached them to the effect that there had been some talk of retiring and that they wished to protest in the strongest manner. I had been watching them both, as they handled their troops with the cool confidence of the veteran regular officer, and had been congratulating myself that they were off toward the right flank, for as long as they were there, I knew I was perfectly safe in that direction. I had heard no rumor about retiring, and I cordially agreed with them that it would be far worse than a blunder to abandon our position.

To attack the Spaniards by rushing across open ground, or through wire entanglements and low, almost impassable jungle, without the help of artillery, and to force unbroken infantry, fighting behind earthworks and armed with the best repeating weapons, supported by cannon, was one thing; to repel such an attack ourselves, or to fight our foes on anything like even terms in the open, was quite another thing. No possible number of Spaniards coming at us from in front could have driven us from our position, and there was not a man on the crest who did not eagerly and devoutly hope that our opponents would make the attempt, for it would surely have been followed, not merely by a repulse, but by our immediately taking the city. There was not an officer or a man on the firing-line, so far as I saw them, who did not feel this way.

As night fell, some of my men went back to the buildings in our rear and foraged through them, for we had now been fourteen hours charging and fighting without food. They came across what was evidently the Spanish officers' mess, where their dinner was still cooking, and they brought it to the front in high glee. It was evident that the Spanish officers were living well, however the Spanish rank and file were faring. There were three big iron pots, one filled with beef-stew, one with boiled rice, and one with boiled peas; there was a big demijohn of rum (all along the trenches which the Spaniards held were empty wine and liquor bottles); there were a number of loaves of rice-bread; and there were even some small cans of preserves and a few salt fish. Of course, among so many men, the food, which was equally divided, did not give very much to each, but it freshened us all.

Soon after dark, General Wheeler, who in the afternoon had resumed command of the cavalry division, came to the front. A very few words with General Wheeler reassured us about retiring. He had been through too much heavy fighting in the Civil War to regard the present fight as very serious, and he told us not to be under any apprehension, for he had sent word that there was no need whatever of retiring, and was sure we would stay where we were until the chance came to advance. He was second in command; and to him more than to any other one man was due the prompt abandonment of the proposal to fall back—a proposal which, if adopted, would have meant shame and disaster.

Shortly afterward General Wheeler sent us orders to intrench. The men of the different regiments were now getting in place again and sifting themselves out. All of our troops who had been kept at Kettle Hill came forward and rejoined us after nightfall. During the afternoon Greenway, apparently not having enough to do in the fighting, had taken advantage of a lull to explore the buildings himself, and had found a number of Spanish intrenching tools, picks, and shovels, and these we used in digging trenches along our line. The men were very tired indeed, but they went cheerfully to work, all the officers doing their part.

Crockett, the ex-Revenue officer from Georgia, was a slight man, not physically very strong. He came to me and told me he didn't think he would be much use in digging, but that he had found a lot of Spanish coffee and would spend his time making coffee for the men, if I approved. I did approve very heartily, and Crockett officiated as cook for the next three or four hours until the trench was dug, his coffee being much appreciated by all of us.

So many acts of gallantry were performed during the day that it is quite impossible to notice them all, and it seems unjust to single out any; yet I shall mention a few, which it must always be remembered are to stand, not as exceptions, but as instances of what very many men did. It happened that I saw these myself. There were innumerable others, which either were not seen at all, or were seen only by officers who happened not to mention them; and, of course, I know chiefly those that happened in my own regiment.

Captain Llewellen was a large, heavy man, who had a grown-up son in the ranks. On the march he had frequently carried the load of some man who weakened, and he was not feeling well on the morning of the fight. Nevertheless, he kept at the head of his troop all day. In the charging and rushing, he not only became very much exhausted, but finally fell, wrenching himself terribly, and though he remained with us all night, he was so sick by morning that we had to take him behind the hill into an improvised hospital. Lieutenant Day, after handling his troop with equal gallantry and efficiency, was shot, on the summit of Kettle Hill.

He was hit in the arm and was forced to go to the rear, but he would not return to the States, and rejoined us at the front long before his wound was healed. Lieutenant Leahy was also wounded, not far from him. Thirteen of the men were wounded and yet kept on fighting until the end of the day, and in some cases never went to the rear at all, even to have their wounds dressed. They were Corporals Waller and Fortescue and Trooper McKinley of Troop E; Corporal Roades of Troop D; Troopers Albertson, Winter, McGregor, and Ray Clark of Troop F; Troopers Bugbee, Jackson, and Waller of Troop A; Trumpeter McDonald of Troop L; Sergeant Hughes of Troop B; and Trooper Gievers of Troop G. One of the Wallers was a cow-puncher from New Mexico, the other the champion Yale high-jumper. The first was shot through the left arm so as to paralyze the fingers, but he continued in battle, pointing his rifle over the wounded arm as though it had been a rest. The other Waller, and Bugbee, were hit in the head, the bullets merely inflicting scalp wounds. Neither of them paid any heed to the wounds except that after nightfall each had his head done up in a bandage. Fortescue I was at times using as an extra orderly. I noticed he limped, but supposed that his foot was skinned. It proved, however, that he had been struck in the foot, though not very seriously, by a bullet, and I never knew what was the matter until the next day I saw him making wry faces as he drew off his bloody boot, which was stuck fast to the foot. Trooper Rowland again distinguished himself by his fearlessness.

For gallantry on the field of action Sergeants Dame, Ferguson, Tiffany, Greenwald, and, later on, McIlhenny, were promoted to second lieutenancies, as Sergeant Hayes had already been. Lieutenant Carr, who commanded his troop, and behaved with great gallantry throughout the day, was shot and severely wounded at nightfall. He was the son of a Confederate officer; his was the fifth generation which, from father to son, had fought in every war of the United States. Among the men whom I noticed as leading in the charges and always being nearest the enemy, were the Pawnee, Pollock, Simpson of Texas, and Dudley Dean. Jenkins was made major, Woodbury Kane, Day, and Frantz captains, and Greenway and Goodrich first lieutenants, for gallantry in action, and for the efficiency with which the first had handled his squadron, and the other five their troops—for each of them, owing to some accident to his superior, found himself in command of his troop.

Dr. Church had worked quite as hard as any man at the front in caring for the wounded; as had Chaplain Brown. Lieutenant Keyes, who acted as adjutant, did so well that he was given the position permanently. Lieutenant Coleman similarly won the position of quartermaster.

We finished digging the trench soon after midnight, and then the worn-out men laid down in rows on their rifles and dropped heavily to sleep. About one in ten of them had blankets taken from the Spaniards. Henry Bardshar, my orderly, had procured one for me. He, Goodrich, and I slept together. If the men without blankets had not been so tired that they fell asleep anyhow, they would have been very cold, for, of course, we were all drenched with sweat, and above the waist had on nothing but our flannel shirts, while the night was cool, with a heavy dew. Before anyone had time to wake from the cold, however, we were all awakened by the Spaniards, whose skirmishers suddenly opened fire on us. Of course, we could not tell whether or not this was the forerunner of a heavy attack, for our Cossack posts were responding briskly. It was about three o'clock in the morning, at which time men's courage is said to be at the lowest ebb; but the cavalry division was certainly free from any weakness in that direction. At the alarm everybody jumped to his feet and the stiff, shivering, haggard men, their eyes only half-opened, all clutched their rifles and ran forward to the trench on the crest of the hill.

The sputtering shots died away and we went to sleep again. But in another hour dawn broke and the Spaniards opened fire in good earnest. There was a little tree only a few feet away, under which I made my head-quarters, and while I was lying there, with Goodrich and Keyes, a shrapnel burst among us, not hurting us in the least, but with the sweep of its bullets killing or wounding five men in our rear, one of whom was a singularly gallant young Harvard fellow, Stanley Hollister. An equally gallant young fellow from Yale, Theodore Miller, had already been mortally wounded. Hollister also died.

The Second Brigade lost more heavily than the First; but neither its brigade commander nor any of its regimental commanders were touched, while the commander of the First Brigade and two of its three regimental commanders had been killed or wounded.

In this fight our regiment had numbered 490 men, as, in addition to the killed and wounded of the first fight, some had had to go to the hospital for sickness and some had been left behind with the baggage, or were detailed on other duty. Eighty-nine were killed and wounded: the heaviest loss suffered by any regiment in the cavalry division. The Spaniards made a stiff fight, standing firm until we charged home. They fought much more stubbornly than at Las Guasimas. We ought to have expected this, for they have always done well in holding intrenchments. On this day they showed themselves to be brave foes, worthy of honor for their gallantry.

In the attack on the San Juan hills our forces numbered about 6,600. There were about 4,500 Spaniards against us. Our total loss in killed and wounded was 1,071. Of the cavalry division there were, all told, some 2,300 officers and men, of whom 375 were killed and wounded. In the division over a fourth of the officers were killed or wounded, their loss being relatively half as great again as that of the enlisted men—which was as it should be.

I think we suffered more heavily than the Spaniards did in killed and wounded (though we also captured some scores of prisoners). It would have been very extraordinary if the reverse was the case, for we did the charging; and to carry earthworks on foot with dismounted cavalry, when these earthworks are held by unbroken infantry armed with the best modern rifles, is a serious task.

*Roosevelt biographer Edmund Morris thinks something in Roosevelt came to a climax on that charge up San Juan Hill—his lust for war. He had satisfied it, and it came to an end. It was an amazingly swift little war, declared in April, over in a few weeks in July, the peace treaty signed in December. Admiral Dewey's decimation of the Spanish fleet in the Philippines destroyed Spain as a world power. The United States took over Puerto Rico and the little island of Guam in the far Pacific, and the Philippines themselves. Rebels almost at once began to fight the U. S. occupying forces, a nasty little war that Roosevelt would have to deal with as President. But Roosevelt was never again so eager to go to war. He still believed in being ready for it, but he seems to have lost his taste for it.*

*He returned home to parades and acclaim, all that America offers its heroes. He ran for and won the governorship of New York that fall. New York governors then served two-year terms. He used his one and only term to begin at the state level programs that would become his legacy at the national level. He proposed, and was able to get through the legislature, legislation to improve sweatshop conditions and to impose taxes on corporate utility companies. By administrative fiat he created state forest and wildlife reserves. He managed to do all this in spite of the machinations of U. S. Senator Thomas Platt, boss of the Republican Party in New York, who fought him every step of the way. The reason Roosevelt was named to William McKinley's ticket as his vice-presidential candidate in 1900 was largely because Platt wanted to get him out of New York. Roosevelt was doing too much damage to the party's traditional alliance with big business. The moguls all hated him.*

*During the presidential campaign in the fall of 1900 Roosevelt did the campaigning while McKinley stayed at home, campaigning, as it were, from his front porch. Traveling* all over the country, Roosevelt made 673 speeches in all. That year he published his book of essays called The Strenuous Life. Strenuous indeed. But it must have been effective. McKinley won a second term, and Theodore Roosevelt was now the Vice-President of the United States. He held the office for six months. On Friday, September 6, an anarchist named Leon Czolgosz shot William McKinley at an exposition in Buffalo. Roosevelt rushed to his side. At first the President seemed to rally, and it was thought he would recover. Roosevelt left for the Adirondacks for a short vacation with his family. On September 13 he was sitting on a rock toward the top of a mountain when the telegram came. McKinley was dying. A few days later Theodore Roosevelt was the President of the United States.

This is not the venue in which to discuss his Presidency. His accomplishments are well-known: the construction of the Panama Canal; the trust-busting; the peace he negotiated between the Russians and the Japanese. He should be remembered most of all, perhaps, for his conservation efforts. He continued to hunt during his years in office, taking vacations in the West and South for that purpose. In 1905 he published yet another book, Outdoor Pastimes of an American Hunter, from which we take our next two selections. One he wrote in 1893 for inclusion in one of the books published by the Boone & Crockett Club. It contains a straightforward tale of a hunt for bighorn sheep, but its real importance is its emphasis on the radical depletion of game in the country. By 1893 his conservationist views were fairly well fixed, and many of his pieces are like this, full of awareness that the losses were large, and we needed to do something about it. The second describes a trip he took ten years later while he was President, to Yellowstone, with John Burroughs, the naturalist. The piece is essentially an argument for more wildlife preserves like Yellowstone. It also identifies some of the problems with tourists and with the surrounding population of ranchers that still plague Yellowstone a hundred years later.

# A Shot at a Mountain Sheep

*Outdoor Pastimes of an American Hunter*

In the fall of 1893 I was camped on the Little Missouri, some ten miles below my ranch. The bottoms were broad and grassy, and were walled in by curving rows of high, steep bluffs. Back of them lay a mass of broken country, in many places almost impassable for horses. The wagon was drawn up on the edge of the fringe of tall cottonwoods which stretched along the brink of the shrunken river. The weather had grown cold, and at night the frost gathered thickly on our sleeping-bags. Great flocks of sandhill cranes passed overhead from time to time, the air resounding with their strange, musical, guttural clangor.

For several days we had hunted perseveringly, but without success, through broken country. We had come across tracks of mountain sheep, but not the animals themselves, and the few blacktail which we had seen had seen us first and escaped before we could get within shot. The only thing killed had been a young whitetail, which Lambert, who was with me, had knocked over by a very pretty shot as we were riding through a long, heavily-timbered bottom. Four men in stalwart health and taking much out-door exercise have large appetites, and the flesh of the whitetail was almost gone.

One evening Lambert and I hunted nearly to the head of one of the creeks which opened close to our camp, and, in turning to descend what we thought was one of the side coulees leading into it, we contrived to get over the divide into the coulees of an entirely different creek system, and did not discover our error until it was too late to remedy it. We struck the river about nightfall, and were not quite sure where, and had six miles' tramp in the dark along the sandy river bed and through the dense timber bottoms, wading the stream a dozen times before we finally struck camp, tired and hungry, and able to appreciate to the full the stew of hot venison and potatoes, and afterward the comfort of our buffalo and caribou and hide sleeping-bags. The next morning the Sheriff's remark of "Look alive, you fellows, if you want any breakfast," awoke the other members of the party shortly after dawn. It was bitterly cold as we scrambled out of our bedding, and, after a hasty wash, huddled around the fire, where the venison was sizzling and the coffee-pot boiling, while the bread was kept warm in the Dutch oven. About a third of a mile away to the west the bluffs, which rose abruptly from the river bottom, were crowned by a high plateau, where the grass was so good that overnight the horses had been led up and pick-eted on it, and the man who had led them up had stated the previous evening that he had seen what he took to be fresh footprints of a mountain sheep cross-ing the surface of a bluff fronting our camp. From the footprints it appeared that the animal had been there since the camp was pitched. The face of the bluff on this side was very sheer, the path by which the horses scrambled to the top being around a shoulder and out of sight of camp.

While sitting close around the fire finishing breakfast, and just as the first level sunbeams struck the top of the plateau, we saw on this cliff crest something mov-ing, and at first supposed it to be one of the horses which had broken loose from its picket pin. Soon the thing, whatever it was, raised its head, and we were all on our feet in a moment, exclaiming that it was a deer or a sheep. It was feeding in plain sight of us only about a third of a mile distant, and the horses, as I afterward found, were but a few rods beyond it on the plateau. The instant I realized that it was game of some kind I seized my rifle, buckled on my cartridge-belt, and slunk off toward the river bed. As soon as I was under the protection of the line of cot-tonwoods, I trotted briskly toward the cliff, and when I got up to where it impinged on the river I ran a little to the left, and, selecting what I deemed to be a favorable place, began to make the ascent. The animal was on a grassy bench, some eight or ten feet below the crest, when I last saw it; but it was evidently mov-ing hither and thither, sometimes on this bench and sometimes on the crest itself, cropping the short grass and browsing on the young shrubs. The cliff was divided by several shoulders or ridges, there being hollows like vertical gullies between them, and up one of these I scrambled, using the utmost caution not to dislodge earth or stones. Finally I reached the bench just below the skyline, and then, turn-ing to the left, wriggled cautiously along it, hat in hand. The cliff was so steep and bulged so in the middle, and moreover, the shoulders or projecting ridges in the surface spoken of above were so pronounced, that I knew it was out of the ques-tion for the animal to have seen me, but I was afraid it might have heard me. The air was absolutely still, and so I had no fear of its sharp nose. Twice in succession I peered with the utmost caution around shoulders on the cliff, merely to see nothing beyond save another shoulder some forty or fifty yards distant. Then I crept up to the edge and looked over the level plateau. Nothing was in sight excepting the horses, and these were close up to me, and, of course, they all raised their heads to look. I nervously turned half round, sure that if the animal, whatever it was, was in sight, it would promptly take the alarm. However, by good luck, it appeared that at this time it was below the crest on the terrace or bench already mentioned, and, on creeping to the next shoulder, I at last saw it- a yearling mountain sheep- walking slowly away from me, and evidently utterly unsuspicious of any danger. I straightened up, bringing my rifle to my shoulder, and as it wheeled I fired, and the sheep made two or three blind jumps in my direction. So close was I to the camp, and so still was the cold morning, that I distinctly heard one of the three men, who had remained clustered about the fire eagerly watching my movements, call, "By George, he's missed! I saw the bullet strike the cliff." I had fired behind the shoulders, and the bullet, going through, had buried itself in the bluff beyond. The wound was almost instantaneously fatal, and the sheep, after striving in vain to keep its balance, fell heels over head down a crevice, where it jammed. I descended, released the carcass, and pitched it on ahead of me, only to have it jam again near the foot of the cliff. Before I got it loose I was joined by my three companions, who had been running headlong toward me through the brush ever since the time they had seen the animal fall.

I never obtained another sheep under circumstances which seemed to me quite so remarkable as these; for sheep are, on the whole, the wariest of game. Nevertheless, with all game there is an immense amount of chance in the chase, and it is perhaps not wholly uncharacteristic of a hunter's luck that, after having hunted faithfully in vain and with much hard labor for several days through a good sheep country, we should at last have obtained one within sight and earshot of camp. Incidentally I may mention that I have never tasted better mutton, or meat of any kind, than that furnished by this tender yearling.

The nomenclature and exact specific relationships of American sheep, deer and antelope offer difficulties not only to the hunter but to the naturalist. As regards the nomenclature, we share the trouble encountered by all peoples of European descent who have gone into strange lands. The incomers are almost invariably men who are not accustomed to scientific precision of expression. Like other people, they do not like to invent names if they can by any possibility make use of those already in existence, and so in a large number of cases they call the new birds and animals by names applied to entirely different birds and animals of the Old World to which, in the eyes of the settlers, they bear some resemblance. In South America the Spaniards, for instance, christened "lion" and "tiger" the great cats which are properly known as cougar and jaguar. In South Africa the Dutch settlers, who came from a land where all big game had long been exterminated, gave fairly grotesque names to the great antelopes, calling them after the European elk, stag, and chamois. The French did but little better in Canada. Even in Ceylon the English, although belonging for the most part to the educated classes, did no better than the ordinary pioneer settlers, miscalling the sambur stag an elk, and the leopard a cheetah. Our own pioneers behaved in the same way. Hence it is that we have no distinctive name at all for the group of peculiarly American game birds of which the bobwhite it the typical representative; and that, when we could not use the words quail, partridge, or pheasant, we went for our terminology to the barn-yard, and called our fine grouse, fool-hens, sage-hens, and prairie-chickens. The bear and wolf our people recognized at once. The bison they called a buffalo, which was no worse than the way in which in Europe the Old World bison was called an aurochs. The American true elk and reindeer were rechristened moose and caribou- excellent names, by the way, derived from the Indian. The huge stag was called an elk. The extraordinary antelope of the high Western peaks was christened the white goat; not unnaturally, as it has a most goatlike look. The prongbuck of the plains, an animal standing entirely alone among ruminants, was simply called antelope. Even when we invented names for ourselves, we applied them loosely. The ordinary deer is sometimes known as the red deer, sometimes as the Virginia deer, and sometimes as the white-tail deer- the last being by far the best and most distinctive term.

In the present condition of zoological research it is not possible to state accurately how many "species" of deer and sheep there are in North America, both because mammalogists have not at hand a sufficient amount of material in the way of large series of specimens from different localities, and because they are not agreed among themselves as to the value of "species," or indeed as to exactly what is denoted by the term. Of course, if we had a complete series of specimens of extinct and fossil deer before us, there would be a perfect intergradation among all the existing forms through their long-vanished ancestral types, as the existing gaps have been created by the extinction and transformation of those former types. Where the gap is very broad and well marked no difficulty exists in using terms which shall express the difference. Thus the gap separating the moose, the caribou, and the wapiti from one another, and from the smaller American deer, is so wide, and there is so complete a lack of transitional forms, that the differences among them are expressed by naturalists by the use of the different generic terms. The gap between the whitetail and the different forms of blacktail, though much less, is also clearly marked. But when we come to consider the blacktail among themselves, we find two very distinct types which yet show a certain tendency to intergrade; and with the whitetail very wide differences exist, even in the United States, both individually among the deer of certain localities, and also as between all the deer of one locality when compared with all the deer of another. Our present knowledge of the various forms hardly justifies us in dogmatizing as to their exact relative worth; and even if our knowledge was more complete, naturalists are as yet wholly at variance as to the laws which should govern specific nomenclature. However, the hunter, the mere field naturalist, and the lover of out-door life, are only secondarily interested in the niceness of these distinctions.

In addition to being a true sportsman and not a game butcher, in addition to being a humane man as well as keen-eyed, strong-limbed, and stout-hearted, the big game hunter should be a field naturalist. If possible, he should be an adept with the camera; and hunting with the camera will tax his skill far more than hunting with the rifle, while the results in the long run give much greater satisfaction. Wherever possible he should keep a note-book, and should carefully study and record the habits of the wild creatures, especially when in some remote regions to which trained scientific observers but rarely have access. If we could only produce a hunter who would do for American big game what John Burroughs has done for the smaller wild life of hedgerow and orchard, farm and garden and grove, we should indeed be fortunate. Yet even though a man does not possess the literary faculty and the powers of trained observation necessary for such a task, he can do his part toward adding to our information by keeping careful notes of all the important facts which he comes across. Such note-books would show the changed habits of game with the changed seasons, their abundance at different times and different places, the melancholy data of their disappearance, the pleasanter facts as to their change of habits which enable them to continue to exist in the land, and, in short, all their traits. A real and lasting service would thereby be rendered not only to naturalists, but to all who care for nature.

Along the Little Missouri there have been several curious changes in the fauna within my own knowledge. Thus magpies have greatly decreased in numbers. This is, I believe, owing to the wolf hunters, for magpies often come around carcasses and pick up poisoned baits. I have seen as many as seven lying dead around a bait. They are much less plentiful than they formerly were. In 1894

I was rather surprised at meeting a porcupine, usually a beast of the timber, at least twenty miles from trees. He was grubbing after sage-brush roots on the edge of a cut bank by a half-dried creek. I was stalking an antelope at the time, and stopped to watch him for about five minutes. He paid no heed to me, though I was within three or four paces of him. Porcupines are easily exterminated; and they have diminished in numbers in this neighborhood. Both the lucivee, or northern lynx, and the wolverene have been found on the Little Missouri, near the Kildeer Mountains, but I do not know of a specimen of either that has been killed there for some years past. Bobcats are still not uncommon. The blackfooted ferret was always rare, and is rare now. But few beaver are left; they were very abundant in 1880, but were speedily trapped out when the Indians vanished and the Northern Pacific Railroad was built. While this railroad was building, the beaver frequently caused much trouble by industriously damming the culverts.

With us the first animal to disappear was the buffalo. In the old days, say from 1870 to 1880, the buffalo were probably the most abundant of all animals along the Little Missouri in the region that I know, ranging, say, from Pretty Buttes to the Kildeer Mountains. They were migratory, and at times almost all of them might leave; but, on the whole, they were the most abundant of the game animals. In 1881 they were still almost as numerous as ever. In 1883 all were killed but a few stragglers, and the last of these stragglers that I heard of as seen in our immediate neighborhood was in 1885. The second game animal in point of abundance was the blacktail. It did not go out on the prairies, but in the broken country adjoining the river it was far more plentiful than any other kind of game. Blacktail were not much slaughtered until the buffalo began to give out, say in 1882; but by 1896 thy were not a twentieth- probably not a fiftieth- as plentiful as they had been in 1882. A few are still found in out-of-the-way places, where the ground is very rough. Elk were plentiful in 1880, though never anything like as abundant as the buffalo and the blacktail. Only straggling parties or individuals have been seen since 1883. The last I shot near my ranch was in 1886; but two or three have been shot since, and a cow and calf were seen, chased and almost roped by the riders on the round-up in the fall of 1893. Whitetail were never as numerous as the other game, but they held their own better, and a few can be shot yet. In 1883 probably twenty blacktail were killed for every one whitetail; in 1896 the numbers were about equal. Antelope were plentiful in the old days, though not nearly so much so as the buffalo and blacktail. The hunters did not molest them while the buffalo and elk lasted, and they then turned their attention to the blacktail. For some years after 1889 I think the pronghorn in our neighborhood positively increased in numbers. In 1886 I thought them more plentiful than I had ever known them before. Then they decreased; after 1894 the decrease was rapid. A few still remain. Mountain sheep were never very plentiful, and decreased proportionately with less rapidity than any other game; but they are now almost exterminated. Bears likewise were never plentiful, and cougars were always scarce.

There were two stages of hunting in this country, as in almost all other countries similarly situated. In 1880 the Northern Pacific Railroad was built nearly to the edge of the Bad Lands, and the danger of Indian war was totally eliminated. A great inrush of hunters followed. In 1881, 1882 and 1883 buffalo, elk and blacktail were slaughtered in enormous numbers, and a good many whitetail and prongbuck were killed too. By 1884 the game had been so thinned out that hide-hunting and meat-hunting ceased to pay. A few professional hunters remained, but most of them moved elsewhere, or were obliged to go into other business. From that time the hunting has chiefly been done by ranchers and occasional small grangers. In consequence, for six or eight years the game about held its own- the antelope, as I have said above, at one time increasing; but the gradual growth in the number of actual settlers then began to tell, and the game became scarce. Nowadays settlers along the Little Missouri can kill an occasional deer or antelope; but it can hardly be called a game country.

# Wilderness Preserves

*Outdoor Pastimes of an American Hunter*

THE MOST STRIKING AND MELANCHOLY FEATURE IN CONNECTION WITH American big game is the rapidity with which it has vanished. When, just before the outbreak of the Revolutionary War, the rifle-bearing hunters of the backwoods first penetrated the great forests west of the Alleghanies, deer, elk, black bear, and even buffalo, swarmed in what are now the States of Kentucky and Tennessee, and the country north of the Ohio was a great and almost virgin hunting-ground. From that day to this the shrink-age has gone on, only partially checked here and there, and never arrested as a whole. As a matter of historical accuracy, however, it is well to bear in mind that many writers, in lamenting this extinction of game, have from time to time anticipated or overstated the fact. Thus as good an author as Colonel Richard Irving Dodge spoke of the buffalo as practically extinct, while the great Northern herd still existed in countless thousands. As early as 1880 sporting authorities spoke not only of the buffalo, but of the elk, deer, and antelope as no longer to be found in plenty; and recently one of the greatest of living hunters has stated that it is no longer possible to find any American wapiti bearing heads comparable with the red deer of Hungary. As a matter of fact, in the early eighties there were still large regions where every species of game that had ever been known within historic times on our continent was still to be found as plentifully as ever. In the early nineties there were still big tracts of wilderness in which this was true of the elk in portions of northwestern Wyoming, of the blacktail in the northwestern Colorado, of the whitetail here and there in the Indian Territory, and of the antelope in parts of New Mexico. Even at the present day there are smaller, but still considerable, regions where those four animals are yet found in abundance; and I have seen antlers of wapiti shot since 1900 far surpassing any of which there is record from Hungary. In New England and New York, as well as New Brunswick and Nova Scotia, the whitetail deer is more plentiful than it was thirty years ago, and in Maine (and to an even greater extent in New Brunswick) the moose, and here and there the caribou, have, on the whole, increased during the same period. There is yet ample opportunity for the big game hunter in the United States, Canada and Alaska.

While it is necessary to give this word of warning to those who, in praising time past, always forget the opportunities of the present, it is a thousandfold more necessary to remember that these opportunities are, nevertheless, vanishing; and if we are a sensible people, we will make it our business to see that the process of extinction is arrested. At the present moment the great herds of caribou are being butchered, as in the past the great herds of bison and wapiti have been butchered. Every believer in manliness, and therefore in manly sport, and every love of nature, every man who appreciates the majesty and beauty of the wilderness and of wild life, should strike hands with the far-sighted men who wish to preserve natural resources, in the effort to keep our forests and our game beasts, game birds, and game fish- indeed, all the living creatures of the prairie, and woodland, and seashore- from wanton destruction.

Above all, we should realize that the effort toward this end is essentially a democratic movement. It is entirely in our power as a nation to preserve large tracts of wilderness, which are valueless for agricultural purposes and unfit for settlement, as playgrounds for rich and poor alike, and to preserve the game so that it shall continue to exist for the benefit of all lovers of nature, and to give reasonable opportunities for the exercise of the skill of the hunter, whether he is or is not a man of means. But this end can only be achieved by wise laws and by a resolute enforcement of the laws. Lack of such legislation and administration will result in harm to all of us, but most of all in harm to the nature lover who does not possess vast wealth. Already there have sprung up here and there through the country, as in New Hampshire and the Adirondacks, large private preserves. These preserves often serve a useful purpose, and should be encouraged within reasonable limits; but it would be a misfortune if they increased beyond a certain extent or if they took the place of great tracts of wild land, which continue as such either because of their very nature, or because of the protection of the State exerted in the form of making them State or national parks or reserves. It is foolish to regard proper game laws as undemocratic, unrepublican. On the contrary, they are essentially in the interests of the people as a whole, because it is only through their enactment and enforcement that the people as a whole can preserve the game and can prevent its becoming purely the property of the rich, who are able to create and maintain extensive private preserves. The wealthy man can get hunting anyhow, but the man of small means is dependent solely upon wise and well-executed game laws for his enjoyment of the sturdy pleasure of the chase. In Maine, in Vermont, in the Adirondacks, even in parts of Massachusetts and on Long Island, people have waked up to this fact, particularly so far as the common whitetail deer is concerned, and in Maine also as regards the moose and caribou. The effect is shown in the increase in these animals. Such game protection results, in the first place, in securing to the people who live in the neighborhood permanent opportunities for hunting; and in the next place, it provides no small source of wealth to the locality because of the visitors which it attracts. A deer wild in the woods is worth to the people of the neighborhood many times the value of its carcass, because of the way it attracts sportsmen, who give employment and leave money behind them.

True sportsmen, worthy of the name, men who shoot only in season and in moderation, do no harm whatever to game. The most objectionable of all game destroyers is, of course, the kind of game butcher who simply kills for the sake of the record of slaughter, who leaves deer and ducks and prairie-chickens to rot after he has slain them. Such a man is wholly obnoxious; and, indeed, so is any man who shoots for the purpose of establishing a record of the amount of game killed. To my mind this is one very unfortunate feature of what is otherwise the admirably sportsmanlike English spirit in these matters. The custom of shooting great bags of deer, grouse, partridges, and pheasants, the keen rivalry in making such bags, and their publication in sporting journals, are symptoms of a spirit which is most unhealthy from every standpoint. It is to be earnestly hoped that every American hunting or fishing club will strive to inculcate among its own members, and in the minds of the general public, that anything like an excessive bag, any destruction for the sake of making a record, is to be severely reprobated.

But after all, this kind of perverted sportsman, unworthy though he be, is not the chief actor in the destruction of our game. The professional skin or market hunter is the real offender. Yet he is of all others the man who would ultimately be most benefited by the preservation of the game. The frontier settler, in a thoroughly wild country, is certain to kill game for his own use. As long as he does no more than this, it is hard to blame him; although if he is awake to his own interests he will soon realize that to him, too, the live deer is worth far more than the dead deer, because of the way in which it brings money into the wilderness. The professional market hunter who kills game for the hide, or for the feathers, or for the meat, or to sell antlers and other trophies; the market men who put game in cold storage; and the rich people, who are content to buy what they have not the skill to get by their own exertions- these are the men who are the real enemies of the game. Where there is no law which checks the market hunters, the inevitable result of their butchery is that the game is completely destroyed, and with it their own means of livelihood. If, on the other hand, they were willing to preserve it, they could make much more money by acting as guides. In northwestern Colorado, at the present moment, there are still blacktail deer in abundance, and some elk are left. Colorado has fairly good game laws, but they are indifferently enforced. The country in which the game is found can probably never support any but a very sparse population, and a large portion of the summer range is practically useless for settlement. If the people of Colorado generally, and above all the people of the counties in which the game is located, would resolutely cooperate with those of their own number who are already alive to the importance of preserving the game, it could, without difficulty, be kept always as abundant as it now is, and this beautiful region would be a permanent health resort and playground for the people of a large part of the Union. Such action would be a benefit to every one, but it would be a benefit most of all to the people of the immediate locality.

The practical common sense of the American people has been in no way made more evident during the last few years than by the creation and use of a series of large land reserves- situated for the most part on the great plains and among the mountains of the West- intended to keep the forests from destruction, and therefore to conserve the water supply. These reserves are, and should be, created primarily for economic purposes. The semi-arid regions can only support a reasonable population under conditions of the strictest economy and wisdom in the use of the water supply, and in addition to their other economic uses the forests are indispensably necessary for the preservation of the water supply and for rendering possible its useful distribution throughout the proper seasons. In addition, however, to this economic use of the wilderness, selected portions of it have been kept here and there in a state of nature, not merely for the sake of preserving the forests and the water, but for the sake of preserving all its beauties and wonders unspoiled by greedy and short-sighted vandalism. What has been actually accomplished in the Yellowstone Park affords the best possible object-lesson as to the desirability and practicability of establishing such wilderness reserves. This reserve is a natural breeding-ground and nursery for those stately and beautiful haunters of the wilds which have now vanished from so many of the great forests, the vast and lonely plains, and the high mountain ranges, where they once abounded.

On April 8, 1903, John Burroughs and I reached the Yellowstone Park, and were met by Major John Pitcher of the Regular Army, the Superintendent of the Park. The Major and I forthwith took horses; he telling me that he could show me a good deal of game while riding up to his house at the Mammoth Hot Springs. Hardly had we left the little town of Gardiner and gotten within the limits of the Park before we saw prongbuck. There was a band of at least a hundred feeding some distance from the road. We rode leisurely toward them. They were tame compared to their kindred in unprotected places; that is, it was easy to ride within fair rifle range of them; and though they were not familiar in the sense that we afterwards found the bighorn and the deer to be familiar, it was extraordinary to find them showing such familiarity almost literally in the streets of a frontier town. It spoke volumes for the good sense and law-abiding spirit of the people of the town. During the two hours following my entry into the Park we rode around the plains and lower slopes of the foothills in the neighborhood of the mouth of the Gardiner and we saw several hundred- probably a thousand all told- of these antelopes. Major Pitcher informed me that all the pronghorns in the Park wintered in this neighborhood. Toward the end of April on the first of May they migrate back to their summering homes in the open valleys along the Yellowstone and in the plains south of the Golden Gate. While migrating they go over the mountains and through forests if occasion demands. Although there are plenty of coyotes in the Park, there are no big wolves, and save for very infrequent poachers the only enemy of the antelope, as indeed the only enemy of all the game, is the cougar.

Cougars, known in the Park, as elsewhere through the West, as "mountain lions," are plentiful, having increased in numbers of recent years. Except in the neighborhood of the Gardiner River, that is within a few miles of Mammoth Hot Springs, I found them feeding on elk, which in the Park far outnumber all other game put together, being so numerous that the ravages of the cougars are of no real damage to the herds. But in the neighborhood of the Mammoth Hot Springs the cougars are noxious because of the antelope, mountain sheep, and deer which they kill; and the Superintendent has imported some hounds with which to hunt them. These hounds are managed by Buffalo Jones, a famous old plainsman, who is now in the Park taking care of the buffalo. On this first day of my visit to the Park I came across the carcasses of a deer and of an antelope which the cougars had killed. On the great plains cougars rarely get antelope, but here the country is broken so that the big cats can make their stalks under favorable circumstances. To deer and mountain sheep the cougar is a most dangerous enemy- much more so than the wolf.

The antelope we saw were usually in bands of from twenty to one hundred and fifty, and they travelled strung out almost in single file, though those in the rear would sometimes bunch up. I did not try to stalk them, but got as near them as I could on horseback. The closest approach I was able to make was to within about eighty yards of two which were by themselves- I think a doe and a last year's fawn. As I was riding up to them, although they looked suspiciously at me, one actually lay down. When I was passing them at about eighty yards' distance the big one became nervous, gave a sudden jump, and away the two went at full speed.

Why the prongbucks were so comparatively shy I do not know, for right on the ground with them we came upon deer, and, in the immediate neighborhood, mountain sheep, which were absurdly tame. The mountain sheep were nineteen in number, for the most part does and yearlings with a couple of three-year-old rams, but not a single big fellow- for the big fellows at this season are off by themselves, singly or in little bunches, high up in the mountains. The band I saw was tame to a degree matched by but a few domestic animals.

They were feeding on the brink of a steep washout at the upper edge of one of the benches on the mountain-side just below where the abrupt slope began. They were alongside a little gully with sheer walls. I rode my horse to within forty yards of them, one of them occasionally looking up and at once continuing to feed. Then they moved slowly off and leisurely crossed the gully to the other side. I dismounted, walked around the head of the gully, and moving cautiously, but in plain sight, came closer and closer until I was within twenty yards, when I sat down on a stone and spent certainly twenty minutes looking at them. They paid hardly any attention to my presence- certainly no more than well-treated domestic creatures would pay. One of the rams rose on his hind legs, leaning his fore-hoofs against a little pine tree, and browsed the ends of the budding branches. The others grazed on the short grass and herbage or lay down and rested- two of the yearlings several times playfully butting at one another. Now and then one would glance in my direction without the slightest feign of fear- barely even of curiosity. I have no question whatever but that with a little patience this particular band could be made to feed out of a man's hand. Major Pitcher intends during the coming winter to feed them alfalfa- for game animals of several kinds have become so plentiful in the neighborhood of the Hot Springs, and the Major has grown so interested in them, that he wishes to do something toward feeding them during the severe weather. After I had looked at the sheep to my heart's content, I walked back to my horse, my departure arousing as little interest as my advent.

Soon after leaving them we began to come across blacktail deer, singly, in twos and threes, and in small bunches of a dozen or so. They were almost as tame as the mountain sheep, but not quite. That is, they always looked alertly at me, and though if I stayed still they would graze, they kept a watch over my movements and usually moved slowly off when I got within less than forty yards of them. Up to that distance, whether on foot or on horseback, they paid but little heed to me, and on several occasions they allowed me to come much closer. Like the bighorn, the blacktails at this time were grazing, not browsing; but I occasionally saw them nibble some willow buds. During the winter they had been browsing. As we got close to the Hot Springs we came across several white-tail in an open, marshy meadow. They were not quite as tame as the blacktail, although without any difficulty I walked up to within fifty yards of them. Handsome though the blacktail is, the whitetail is the most beautiful of all deer when in motion, because of the springy, bounding grace of its trot and canter, and the way it carries its head and white flag aloft.

Before reaching the Mammoth Hot Springs we also saw a number of ducks in the little pools and on the Gardiner. Some of them were rather shy. Others- probably those which, as Major Pitcher informed me, had spent the winter there- were as tame as barn-yard fowls.

Just before reaching the post the Major took me into the big field where Buffalo Jones had some Texas and Flathead Lake buffalo- bulls and cows- which he was tending with solicitous care. The original stock of buffalo in the Park have now been reduced to fifteen or twenty individuals, and their blood is being recruited by the addition of buffalo purchased out of the Flathead Lake and Texas Panhandle herds. The buffalo were at first put within a wire fence, which, when it was built, was found to have included both blacktail and whitetail deer. A bull elk was also put in with them at one time, he having met with some accident which made the Major and Buffalo Jones bring him in to doctor him. When he recovered his health he became very cross. Not only would he attack men, but also buffalo, even the old and surly master bull, thumping them savagely with his antlers if they did anything to which he objected. The buffalo are now breeding well.

When I reached the post and dismounted at the Major's house, I supposed my experiences with wild beasts were ended for the day; but this was an error. The quarters of the officers and men and the various hotel buildings, stables, residences of the civilian officials, etc., almost completely surround the big parade-ground at the post, near the middle of which stands the flag-pole, while the gun used for morning and evening salutes is well off to one side. There are large gaps between some of the buildings, and Major Pitcher informed me that through-

out the winter he had been leaving alfalfa on the parade-grounds, and that numbers of blacktail deer had been in the habit of visiting it every day, sometimes
as many as seventy being on the parade-ground at once. As spring-time came on
the numbers diminished. However, in mid-afternoon, while I was writing in my
room in Major Pitcher's house, on looking out of the window I saw five deer on
the parade-ground. They were as tame as so many Alderney cows, and when I
walked out I got within twenty yards of them without any difficulty. It was most
amusing to see them as the time approached for the sunset gun to be fired. The
notes of the trumpeter attracted their attention at once. They all looked at him
eagerly. One of them resumed feeding, and paid no attention whatever either
to the bugle, the gun or the flag. The other four, however, watched the prepara-
tions for firing the gun with an intent gaze, and at the sound of the report gave
two or three jumps; then instantly wheeling, looked up at the flag as it came down.
This they seemed to regard as something rather more suspicious than the gun,
and they remained very much on the alert until the ceremony was over. Once
it was finished, they resumed feeding as if nothing had happened. Before it was
dark they trotted away from the parade-ground back to the mountains.

The next day we rode off to the Yellowstone River, camping some miles
below Cottonwood Creek. It was a very pleasant camp. Major Pitcher, an old friend,
had a first-class pack-train, so that we were as comfortable as possible, and on such
a trip there could be no pleasanter or more interesting companion than John
Burroughs- "Oom John," as we soon grew to call him. Where our tents were
pitched the bottom of the valley was narrow, the mountains rising steep and cliff-
broken on either side. There were quite a number of blacktail in the valley,
which were tame and unsuspicious, although not nearly as much so as those in
the immediate neighborhood of the Mammoth Hot Springs. One mid-afternoon
three of them swam across the river a hundred yards above our camp. But the
characteristic animals of the region were the elk- the wapiti. They were certainly
more numerous than when I was last through the Park twelve years before.

In the summer the elk spread all over the interior of the Park. As winter
approaches they divide, some going north and others south. The southern bands,
which, at a guess, may possibly include ten thousand individuals, winter out of
the Park, for the most part in Jackson's Hole- though of course here and there within
the limits of the Park a few elk may spend both winter and summer in an unusually favorable location. It was the members of the northern band that I met. During
the winter time they are nearly stationary, each band staying within a very few
miles of the same place, and from their size and the open nature of their habitat it
is almost as easy to count them as if they were cattle. From a spur of Bison Peak one

day, Major Pitcher, the guide Elwood Hofer, John Burroughs and I spent about four hours with the glasses counting and estimating the different herds within sight. After most careful work and cautious reduction of estimates in each case to the minimum the truth would permit, we reckoned three thousand herd of elk, all lying or feeding and all in sight at the same time. An estimate of some fifteen thousand for the number of elk in these Northern bands cannot be far wrong. These bands do not go out of the Park at all, but winter just within its northern boundary. At the time when we saw them, the snow had vanished from the bottoms of the valleys and the lower slopes of the mountains, but remained as continuous sheets farther up their sides. The elk were for the most part found up on the snow slopes, occasionally singly or in small gangs- more often in bands of from fifty to a couple of hundred. The larger bulls were highest up the mountains and generally in small troops by themselves, although occasionally one or two would be found associating with a big herd of cows, yearlings, and two-year-olds. Many of the bulls had shed their antlers; many had not. During the winter the elk had evidently done much browsing, but at this time they were grazing almost exclusively, and seemed by preference to seek out the patches of old grass which were last left bare by the retreating snow. The bands moved about very little, and if one were seen one day it was generally possible to find it within a few hundred yards of the same spot the next day, and certainly not more than a mile or two off. There were severe frosts at night, and occasionally light flurries of snow; but the hardy beasts evidently cared nothing for any but heavy storms, and seemed to prefer to lie in the snow rather than upon the open ground. They fed at irregular hours throughout the day, just like cattle; one band might be lying down while another was feeding. While travelling they usually went almost in single file. Evidently the winter had weakened them, and they were not in condition for running; for on the one or two occasions when I wanted to see them close up I ran right into them on horseback, both on level plains and going up hill along the sides of rather steep mountains. One band in particular I practically rounded up for John Burroughs, finally getting them to stand in a huddle while he and I sat on our horses less than fifty yards off. After they had run a little distance they opened their mouths wide and showed evident signs of distress.

We came across a good many carcasses. Two, a bull and a cow, had died from scab. Over half the remainder had evidently perished from the cold or starvation. The others, including a bull, three cows and a score of yearlings, had been killed by cougars. In the Park the cougar is at present their only animal foe. The cougars were preying on nothing but elk in the Yellowstone Valley, and kept hanging about the neighborhood of the big bands. Evidently they usually selected some outlying yearling, stalked it as it lay or as it fed, and seized

it by the head and throat. The bull which they killed was in a little open valley by himself, many miles from any other elk. The cougar which killed it, judging from its tracks, was a big male. As the elk were evidently rather too
numerous for the feed, I do not think the cougars were doing any damage.

Coyotes are plentiful, but the elk evidently have no dread of them. One day
I crawled up to within fifty yards of a band of elk lying down. A coyote was walking about among them, and beyond an occasional look they paid no heed to him.
He did not venture to go within fifteen to twenty paces of any one of them. In
fact, except the cougar, I saw but one living thing attempt to molest the elk. This
was a golden eagle. We saw several of these great birds. On one occasion we had
ridden out to the foot of a sloping mountain side, dotted over with bands and
strings of elk amounting in the aggregate probably to a thousand head. Most of
the bands were above the snow-line- some appearing away back toward the
ridge crests, and looking as small as mice. There was one band well below the snow-
line, and toward this we rode. While the elk were not shy or wary, in the sense
that a hunter would use the words, they were by no means as familiar as the deer;
and this particular band of elk, some twenty or thirty in all, watched us with interest as we approached. When we were still half a mile off they suddenly started
to run towards us, evidently frightened by something. They ran quartering,
and when about four hundred yards away we saw that an eagle was after them.
Soon it swooped, and a yearling in the rear, weakly, and probably frightened by
the swoop, turned a complete somersault, and when it recovered its feet stood
still. The great bird followed the rest of the band across a little ridge, beyond which
they disappeared. Then it returned, soaring high in the heavens, and after two
or three wide circles, swooped down at the solitary yearling, its legs hanging down.
We halted at two hundred yards to see the end. But the eagle could not quite make
up its mind to attack. Twice it hovered within a foot or two of the yearling's head,
again flew off and again returned. Finally the yearling trotted off after the rest
of the band, and the eagle returned to the upper air. Later we found the carcass
of a yearling, with two eagles, not to mention ravens and magpies, feeding on it;
but I could not tell whether they had themselves killed the yearling or not.

Here and there in the region where the elk were abundant we came upon
horses, which for some reason had been left out through the winter. They were
much wilder than the elk. Evidently the Yellowstone Park is a natural nursery
and breeding-ground of the elk, which here, as said above, far outnumber all
the other game put together. In the winter, if they cannot get to open water,
they eat snow; but in several places where there had been springs which kept
open all winter, we could see by the tracks that they had been regularly used

by bands of elk. The men working at the new road along the face of the cliffs beside the Yellowstone River near Tower Falls informed me that in October enormous droves of elk coming from the interior of the Park and travelling northward to the lower lands had crossed the Yellowstone just above Tower Falls. Judging by their description, the elk had crossed by thousands in an uninter- rupted stream, the passage taking many hours. In fact nowadays these Yellowstone elk are, with the exception of the Arctic caribou, the only American game which at times travel in immense droves like the buffalo of old days.

A couple of days after leaving Cottonwood Creek—where we had spent sev- eral days—we camped at the Yellowstone Canyon below Tower Falls. here we saw a second band of mountain sheep, numbering only eight—none of them old rams. We were camped on the west side of the canyon; the sheep had their abode on the opposite side, where they had spent the winter. It has recently been cus- tomary among some authorities, especially the English hunters and naturalists who have written of the Asiatic sheep, to speak as if sheep were naturally crea- tures of the plains rather than mountain climbers. I know nothing of the Old World sheep, but the Rocky Mountain bighorn is to the full as characteristic a moun- tain animal, in every sense of the word, as the chamois, and I think, as the ibex. These sheep were well known to the road builders, who had spent the winter in the locality. They told me they never went back on the plains, but throughout the winter had spent theor days and nights on the top of the cliff and along its face. This cliff was an alternation of sheer precipices and vedry steep inclines. When coated with ice it would be difficult to imagine an uglier bit of climbing; but throughout the iwnter, and even in the wildest storms, the sheep had habitually gone down it to drink at the water below. When we first saw them they were lying sunning themselves on the edge of the canyon where the rolling grassy country behind it broke off into the sheer descent. It was mid-afternoon and they were under some pines. After a while they got up and began to graze, and soon hopped unconcernedly down the side of the cliff until they were half-way to the bottom. They then grazed along the sides, and spent some time licking at a place where there was evidently a mineral deposit. Before dark they all lay down again on a steeply inclined jutting spur midway between the top and bottom of the canyon.

Next morning I thought I would like to see them close up, so I walked down three or four miles below where the canyon ended, crossed the stream, and came up the other side until I got on what was literally the stamping-ground of the sheep. Their tracks showed that they had spent their time for many weeks, and probably for all the winter, within a very narrow radius. For perhaps a mile and a half, or two miles at the very outside, they had wandered to and fro on the summit of the canyon, making what was almost a well-beaten path; always very near and usually on the edge of the cliff, and hardly ever going more than a few yards back into the grassy plain-and-hill country. Their tracks and dung covered the ground. They had also evidently descended into the depths of the canyon wherever there was the slightest break or even lowering in the upper line of the basalt cliffs. Although mountain sheep often browse in winter, I saw but few traces of browsing here; probably on the sheer cliff side they always get some grazing.

When I spied the band they were lying not far from the spot in which they had lain the day before, and in the same position on the brink of the canyon. They saw me and watched me with interest when I was two hundred yards off, but they let me getup within forty yards and sit down on a large stone to look at them, without running off. Most of them were lying down, but a couple were feeding steadily throughout the time I watched them. Suddenly one took the alarm and dashed straight over the cliff, the others all following at once. I ran after them to the edge in time to see the last yearling drop off the edge of the basalt cliff and stop short on the sheer slope below, while the stones dislodged by his hoofs rattled down the canyon. They all looked up at me with great interest, and then strolled off to the edge of a jutting spur and lay down almost directly underneath me and some fifty yards off. That evening on my return to camp we watched the band make its way right down to the river bed, going over places where it did not seem possible a four-footed creature could pass. They halted to graze here and there, and down the worst places they went very fast with great bounds. It was a marvellous exhibition of climbing.

After we had finished this horseback trip we went on sleds and skis to the upper Geyser Basin and the Falls of the Yellowstone. Although it was the third week in April, the snow was still several feet deep, and only thoroughly trained snow horses could have taken the sleighs along, while around the Yellowstone Falls it was possible to move only on snowshoes. There was little life in those woods. In the upper basin I caught a meadow mouse on the snow; I afterwards sent it to Hart Merriam, who told me it was of a species he had described from Idaho, *Microtus nanus;* it had not been previously found in the Yellowstone region. We saw an occasional pine squirrel, snowshoe rabbit or marten; and in the open meadows around the hot waters there were Canada geese and ducks of several species, and now and then a coyote. Around camp Clark's crows and Stellar's jays, and occasionally magpies, came to pick at the refuse; and of course they were accompanied by the whiskey jacks, which behaved with their usual astounding familiarity. At Norris Geyser Basin there was a perfect chorus of bird music from robins, western purple finches, juncos and mountain bluebirds. In the woods there were mountain chickadees and pygmy nuthatches, together with an occasional woodpecker. In the northern country we had come across a very few blue grouse and ruffed grouse, both as tame as possible. We had seen a pygmy owl no larger than a robin sitting on the top of a pine in broad daylight, and uttering at short intervals a queer un-owl like cry.

The birds that interested us most were there solitaires, and especially the dippers or water-ousels. We were fortunate enough to hear the solitaires sing not only when perched on trees, but on the wing, soaring over a great canyon. They are striking birds in every way, and their habit of singing while soaring, and their song, are alike noteworthy. Once I heard a solitaire singing at the top of a canyon; and an ousel also singing about a thousand feet below him; and in this case I thought the ousel sang better than his unconscious rival. The ousels are to my mind wellnigh the most attractive of all our birds, because of their song, their extraordinary habits, their whole personality. They stay through the winter in the Yellowstone because the waters are in many places open. We heard them singing cheerfully, their ringing melody having a certain suggestion of the winter wren's. Usually they sang while perched on some rock on the edge or in the middle of the stream; but sometimes on the wing; and often just before dipping under the torrent, or just after slipping out from it onto some ledge of rock or ice. In the open places the Western meadow lark was uttering its beautiful song; a real song as compared to the plaintive notes of its Eastern brother, and though short, yet with continuity and tune as well as melody. I love to hear the Eastern meadow lark in the early spring; but I love still more the song of the Western meadow lark. No bird escaped John Burrough's eye; no bird note escaped his ear.

I cannot understand why the Old World ousel should have received such comparatively scant attention in the books, whether from nature writers or poets; whereas our ousel has greatly impressed all who know him. John Muir's description comes nearest doing him justice. To me he seems a more striking bird than for instance the skylark; though of course I not only admire but am very fond of the skylark. There are various pipits and larks in our own country which sing in highest air, as does the skylark, and their songs, though not as loud, are almost as sustained; and though they lack the finer kind of melody, so does his. The ousel, on the contrary, is a really brilliant singer, and in his habits he is even farther removed from the commonplace and the uninteresting than the lark himself. Some birds, such as the ousel, the mocking-bird, the solitaire, show marked originality, marked distinction; other do not; the chipping sparrow, for instance, while in no way objectionable (like the imported house sparrow), is yet a hopelessly commonplace little bird alike in looks, habits and voice.

On the last day of my stay it was arranged that I should ride down from Mammoth Hot Springs to the town of Gardiner, just outside the Park limits, and there make an address at the laying of the corner-stone of the arch by which the main road is to enter the Park. Some three thousand people had gathered to attend the ceremonies. A little over a mile from Gardiner we came down out of the hills to the flat plain; from the hills we could see the crowd gathered around the arch waiting for me to come. We put spurs to our horses and cantered rapidly toward the appointed place, and on the way we passed within forty yards of a score of blacktails, which merely moved to one side and looked at us, and within almost as short a distance of half a dozen antelope. To any lover of nature it could not help being a delightful thing to see the wild and timid creatures of the wilderness rendered so tame; and their tameness in the immediate neighborhood of Gardiner, on the very edge of the Park, spoke volumes for the patriotic good sense of the citizens of Montana. At times the antelope actually cross the Park line to Gardiner, which is just outside, and feed unmolested in the very streets of the town; a fact which shows how very far advanced the citizens of Gardiner are in right feeling on this subject; for of course the Federal laws cease to protect the antelope as soon as they are out of the Park. Major Pitcher informed me that both the Montana and Wyoming people were cooperating with him in zealous fashion to preserve the game and put a stop to poaching. For their attitude in this regard they deserve the cordial thanks of all Americans interested in these great popular playgrounds, where bits of the old wilderness scenery and the old wilderness life are to be kept unspoiled for the benefit of our children's children. Eastern people, and especially Eastern sportsmen, need to keep steadily in mind the fact that the westerners who live in the neighborhood of the forest preserves are the men who in the last resort will determine whether or not these preserves are to be permanent. They cannot in the long run be kept as forest and game reservations unless the settlers roundabout believe in them and heartily support them; and the rights of these settlers must be carefully safeguarded, and they must be shown that the movement is really in their interest. The Eastern sportsman who fails to recognize these facts can do little but harm by advocacy of forest reserves.

It was in the interior of the Park, at the hotels beside the lake, the falls, and the various geyser basins, that we would have seen the bears had the season been late enough; but unfortunately the bears were still for the most part hibernating. We saw two or three tracks, but the animals themselves had not yet begun to come about the hotels. Nor were the hotels open. No visitors had previously entered the Park in the winter or early spring, the scouts and other employees being the only ones who occasionally traverse it. I was sorry not to see the bears, for the effect of protection upon bear life in the Yellowstone has been one of the phenomena of natural history. Not only have they grown to realize that they are safe, but, being natural scavengers and foul feeders, they have come to recognize the garbage heaps of the hotels as their special sources of food supply. Throughout the summer months they come to all the hotels in numbers, usually appearing in the late afternoon or evening, and they have become as indifferent to the presence of men as the deer themselves- some of them very much more indifferent. They have now taken their place among the recognized sights of the Park, and the tourists are nearly as much interested in them as in the geysers. In mussing over the garbage heaps they sometimes get tin cans stuck on their paws, and the result is painful. Buffalo Jones and some of the other scouts in extreme cases, rope the bear, tie him up, cut the tin can off his paw, and let him go again. It is not an easy feat, but the astonishing thing is that it should be performed at all.

It was amusing to read the proclamation addressed to the tourists by the Park management, in which they were solemnly warned that the bears were really wild animals, and that they must on no account be either fed or teased. It is curious to think that the descendants of the great grizzlies which were the dread of the early explorers and hunters should now be semi-domesticated creatures, boldly hanging around crowded hotels for the sake of what they can pick up, and quite harmless so long as any reasonable precaution is exercised. They are much safer, for instance, than any ordinary bull or stallion, or even ram, and, in fact, there is no danger from them at all unless they are encouraged to grow too familiar or are in some way molested. Of course among the thousands of tourist there is a percentage of fools; and when fools go out in the afternoon to look at the bears feeding they occasionally bring themselves into jeopardy by some senseless act. The black bears and the cubs of the bigger bears can readily be driven up trees, and some of the tourists occasionally do this. Most of the animals never think of resenting it; but now and then one is run across which has its feelings ruffled by the performance. In the summer of 1902 the result proved disastrous to a too inquisitive tourist. He was travelling with his wife, and at one of the hotels they went out toward the garbage pile to see the feeding. The only bear in sight was a large she, which, as it turned out, was in a bad temper because another party of tourists a few minutes before had been chasing her cubs up a tree. The man left his wife and walked toward the bear to see how close he could get. When he was some distance off she charged him, whereupon he bolted back toward his wife. The bear overtook him, knocked him down and bit him severely. But the man's wife, without hesitation, attacked the bear with that thoroughly feminine weapon, an umbrella, and frightened her off. The man spent several weeks in the Park hospital before he recovered. Perhaps the following telegram sent by the manager of the Lake Hotel to Major Pitcher illustrates with sufficient clearness the mutual relations of the bears, the tourists, and the guardians of the public weal in the Park. The original was sent me by Major Pitcher. It runs:

"Lake. 7-27-'03. Major Pitcher, Yellowstone: As many as seventeen bears in an evening appear on my garbage dump. To-night eight to ten. Campers and people not of my hotel throw things at them to make them run away. I cannot, unless there personally, control this. Do you think you could detail a trooper to be there every evening from six o'clock until dark and make people remain behind danger line laid out by Warden Jones? Otherwise I fear some accident. The arrest of one or two of these campers might help. My own guests do pretty well as they are told. James Barton Key. 9 A.M."

Major Pitcher issued the order as requested.

At times the bears get so bold that they take to making inroads on the kitchen. One completely terrorized a Chinese cook. It would drive him off and then feast upon whatever was left behind. When a bear begins to act in this way or shows surliness it is sometimes necessary to shoot it. Other bears are tamed until they will feed out of the hand, and will come at once if called. Not only have some of the soldiers and scouts tamed bears in this fashion, but occasionally a chambermaid or waiter girl at one of the hotels has thus developed a bear as a pet.

The accompanying photographs not only show bears very close up, with men standing by within a few yards of them, but they also show one bear being fed from the piazza by a cook, and another standing beside a particular friend, a chambermaid in one of the hotels. In these photographs it will be seen that some are grizzlies and some black bears.

This whole episode of bear life in the Yellowstone is so extraordinary that it will be well worth while for any man who has the right powers and enough time, to make a complete study of the life and history of the Yellowstone bears. Indeed, nothing better could be done by some of our out-door faunal naturalists than to spend at least a year in the Yellowstone, and to study the life habits of all the wild creatures therein. A man able to do this, and to write down accurately and interestingly what he had seen, would make a contribution of permanent value to our nature literature.

In May after leaving the Yellowstone, I visited the Grand Canyon of the Colorado, and then went through the Yosemite Park with John Muir- the companion above all others for such a trip. It is hard to make comparisons among different kinds of scenery, all of them very grand and very beautiful; but nothing that I have ever seen has impressed me quite as much as the desolate and awful sublimity of the Grand Canyon of the Colorado. I earnestly wish that Congress would make it a national park, and I am sure that such course would meet the approbation of the people of Arizona. The people of California with wise and generous forethought have given the Yosemite Valley to the National Government to be kept as a national park, just as the surrounding country, including some of the groves of giant trees, has been kept. The flower-clad slopes of the Sierras- golden with the blazing poppy, brilliant with lilies and tulips and red-stemmed Manzinita bush- are unlike anything else in this country. As for the giant trees, no words can describe their majesty and beauty.

John Muir and I, with two packers and three pack mules, spent a delightful three days in Yosemite. The first night was clear, and we lay in the open, on beds of soft fir boughs, among the huge, cinnamon-colored trunks of the sequoias. It was like lying in a great solemn cathedral, far vaster and more beautiful than any built by the hand of man. Just at nightfall I heard among other birds, thrushes which I think were Rocky Mountain hermits- the appropriate choir for such a place of worship. Next day we went by trail through the woods, seeing some deer- which were not wild- as well as mountain quail and blue grouse. Among the birds which we saw was a white-headed woodpecker; the interesting carpenter woodpeckers were less numerous than lower down. In the afternoon we struck snow, and had considerable difficulty in breaking our trails. A snow-storm came on toward evening, but we kept warm and comfortable in a grove of splendid silver firs- rightly named "magnificent"- near the brink of the wonderful Yosemite Valley. Next day we clambered down into it and at nightfall camped in its bottom, facing the giant cliffs over which the waterfalls thundered.

Surely our people do not understand even yet the rich heritage that is theirs. There can be nothing in the world more beautiful than the Yosemite, the groves of giant sequoias and redwoods, the Canyon of the Colorado, the Canyon of the Yellowstone, the Three Tetons; and our people should see to it that they are preserved for their children and their children's children forever, with their majestic beauty all unmarred.

★

PART THREE

# The Expeditions

★

# The Expeditions

It was at a dinner party that Roosevelt decided to go to Africa after his second term in office came to an end. He was an extremely popular President and might have run for a third term, but he had promised on the eve of his election in 1904 not to run again if he should win, and he meant to stick to that promise. What he did instead was to hand pick the Republican candidate in 1908, William Howard Taft, and extract a pledge that Taft would continue his policies. Taft would rather have become a justice of the Supreme Court, but he went along. Roosevelt knew himself well enough to know that once Taft took over he should get out of the country. The urge to interfere in Taft's administration would be too strong. He met Carl Akeley, the African explorer, at dinner sometime early in 1908 and decided then and there that Africa would be his next stop. He would go on safari. He would collect specimens for the Smithsonian. He would take a group of naturalists. It would be a scientific trip. Just incidentally, he might bag a lion or two.

It proved to be an unusually protracted trip. Taft was inaugurated on March 4, 1909. Roosevelt left for Africa on March 23, taking his son Kermit with him. By April 24 they were on safari with four naturalists from the Smithsonian and a small army of native porters. Roosevelt did not return to the United States for well over a year. Most of the time was spent in Africa; he hunted in Kenya, Uganda, and the Belgian Congo, then ran down the Nile to Khartoum, where his wife and youngest daughter joined him. He then continued to Cairo and from there to Europe, where he accepted the Nobel Peace Prize in Norway in May. It is an indication of his popularity that when his ship docked in New York in June 1910, 100,000 people were on hand to greet him.

The hunting, meanwhile, had been good. Roosevelt often went out alone, accompanied only by several porters, who carried his guns and whatever small supplies he might need. Over time he acquired a nickname from these porters, Bwana Makuba, or "great master," while Kermit, then 20 years old, acquired the name of "young master." Kermit had inherited his father's love of the outdoors. We print, from Roosevelt's account of the trip, African Game Trails, two chapters: Chapter Three, "Lion Hunting on the Kapiti Plains"; and Chapter Seven, "Trekking Through the Thirst to the Sotik."

# A Lion Hunt

*African Game Trails*

THE DANGEROUS GAME OF AFRICA ARE THE LION, BUFFALO, ELEPHANT, rhinoceros, and leopard. The hunter who follows any of these animals always does so at a certain risk to life or limb; a risk which it is his business to minimize by coolness, caution, good judgment, and straight shooting. The leopard is in point of pluck and ferocity more than the equal of the other four; but his small size always renders it likely that he will merely maul, and not kill, a man. My friend, Carl Akeley, of Chicago, actually killed bare-handed a leopard which sprang on him. He had already wounded the beast twice, crippling it in one front and one hind paw; whereupon it charged, followed him as he tried to dodge the charge, and struck him full just as he turned. It bit him in one arm, biting again and again as it worked up the arm from the wrist to the elbow; but Akeley threw it, holding its throat with the other hand, and flinging its body to one side. It luckily fell on its side with its two wounded legs uppermost, so that it could not tear him. He fell forward with it and crushed in its chest with his knees until he distinctly felt one of its ribs crack; this, said Akeley, was the first moment when he felt he might conquer. Redoubling his efforts, with knees and hand, he actually choked and crushed the life out of it, although his arm was badly bitten. A leopard will charge at least as readily as one of the big beasts and is rather more apt to get his charge home, but the risk is less to life than to limb.

There are other animals often or occasionally dangerous to human life which are, nevertheless, not dangerous to the hunter. Crocodiles are far greater pests, and far more often man-eaters, than lions or leopards; but their shooting is not accompanied by the smallest element of risk. Poisonous snakes are fruitful sources of accident, but they are actuated only by fear, and the anger born of fear. The hippopotamus sometimes destroys boats and kills those in them; but again there is no risk in hunting him. Finally, the hyena, too cowardly ever to be a source of danger to the hunter, is sometimes a dreadful curse to the weak and helpless. The hyena is a beast of unusual strength, and of enormous power in his jaws and teeth, and thrice over would he be dreaded were fang and sinew driven by a heart of the leopard's cruel courage. But though the creature's foul and evil ferocity has no such backing as that yielded by the angry daring of the spotted cat, it is yet fraught with a terror all its own; for on occasion the hyena takes to man-eating after its own fashion. Carrion-feeder though it is, in certain places it will enter native huts and carry away children or even sleeping adults; and where famine or disease has worked havoc among a people, the hideous spotted beasts become bolder and prey on the survivors. For some years past Uganda has been scourged by the sleeping sickness, which has ravaged it as in the Middle Ages the Black Death ravaged Europe. Hundreds of thousands of natives have died. Every effort has been made by the government officials to cope with the disease; and among other things sleeping-sickness camps have been established, where those stricken by the dread malady can be isolated and cease to be possible sources of infection to their fellows. Recovery among those stricken is so rare as to be almost unknown, but the disease is often slow, and months may elapse during which the diseased man is still able to live his life much as usual. In the big camps of doomed men and women thus established there were, therefore, many persons carrying on their avocations much as in an ordinary native village. But the hyenas speedily found that in many of the huts the inmates were a helpless prey. In 1908 and throughout the early part of 1909 they grew constantly bolder, haunting these sleeping-sickness camps, and each night entering them, bursting into the huts and carrying off and eating the dying people. To guard against them each little group of huts was inclosed by a thick hedge; but after a while the hyenas learned to break through the hedges, and continued their ravages; so that every night armed sentries had to patrol the camps, and every night they could be heard firing at the marauders.

The men thus preyed on were sick to death, and for the most part helpless. But occasionally men in full vigor are attacked. One of Pease's native hunters was seized by a hyena as he slept beside the camp-fire, and part of his face torn off. Selous informed me that a friend of his, Major R.T. Coryndon, then administrator of Northwestern Rhodesia, was attacked by a hyena but two or three years ago. At the time Major Coryndon was lying, wrapped in a blanket, beside his wagon. A hyena, stealthily approaching through the night, seized him by the hand, and dragged him out of bed; but as he struggled and called out, the beast left him and

ran off into the darkness. In spite of his torn hand the major was determined
to get his assailant, which he felt sure would soon return. Accordingly, he went
back to his bed, drew his cocked rifle beside him, pointing toward his feet, and
feigned sleep. When all was still once more, a dim form loomed up through the
uncertain light, toward the foot of the bed; it was the ravenous beast returning
for his prey; and the major shot and killed it where it stood.

A few months ago a hyena entered the outskirts of Nairobi, crept into a hut,
and seized and killed a native man. At Nairobi the wild creatures are always at the
threshold of the town, and often cross it. At Governor Jackson's table, at Government
House, I met Mr. and Mrs. Sandiford. Mr. Sandiford is managing the railroad. A
few months previously, while he was sitting, with his family, in his own house in
Nairobi, he happened to ask his daughter to look for something in one of the bed-
rooms. She returned in a minute, quietly remarking, "Father, there's a leopard
under the bed." So there was; and it was then remembered that the house-cat had
been showing a marked and alert distrust of the room in question- very probably
the leopard had gotten into the house while trying to catch her or one of the dogs.
A neighbor with a rifle was summoned, and shot the leopard.

Hyenas not infrequently kill mules and donkeys, tearing open their bellies, and
eating them while they are still alive. Yet when themselves assailed they usually
behave with abject cowardice. The Hills had a large Airedale terrier, an energetic
dog of much courage. Not long before our visit this dog put up a hyena from a bushy
ravine, in broad daylight, ran after it, overtook it, and flew at it. The hyena made
no effective fight, although the dog- not a third its weight- bit it severely, and delayed
its flight so that it was killed. During the first few weeks of our trip I not infrequently
heard hyenas after nightfall, but saw none. Kermit, however, put one out of a ravine
or dry creek-bed- a donga, as it is locally called- and though the brute had a long
start he galloped after it and succeeded in running it down. The chase was a long
one, for twice the hyena got in such rocky country that he almost distanced his
pursuer; but at last, after covering nearly ten miles, Kermit ran into it in the open,
shooting it from the saddle as it shambled along at a canter growling with rage and
terror. I would not have recognized the cry of the hyenas from what I had read,
and it was long before I heard them laugh. Pease said that he had only once heard
them really laugh. On that occasion he was watching for lions outside a Somali
zareba. Suddenly a leopard leaped clear over the zarba, close beside him, and in a
few seconds came flying back again, over the high thorn fence, with a sheep in its
mouth; but no sooner had it landed than the hyenas rushed at it and took away
the sheep; and then their crackling and shrieking sounded exactly like the most
unpleasant kind of laughter. The normal death of very old lions, as they grow starved

and feeble- unless they are previously killed in an encounter with dangerous game like buffalo- is to be killed and eaten by hyenas; but of course a lion in full vigor pays no heed to hyenas, unless it is to kill one if it gets in the way.

During the last few decades, in Africa, hundreds of white hunters, and thousands of native hunters, have been killed or wounded by lions, buffaloes, elephants, and rhinos. All are dangerous game; each species has to its grewsome credit a long list of mighty hunters slain or disabled. Among those competent to express judgment there is the widest difference of opinion as to the comparative danger in hunting the several kinds of animals. Probably no other hunter who has ever lived has combined Selous's experience with his skill as a hunter and his power of accurate observation and narration. He has killed between three and four hundred lions, elephants, buffaloes, and rhinos, and he ranks the lion as much the most dangerous, and the rhino as much the least, while he puts the buffalo and elephant in between, and practically on par. Governor Jackson has killed between eighty and ninety of the four animals; and he puts the buffalo unquestionably first in point of formidable capacity as a foe, the elephant equally unquestionably second, the lion third, and the rhino last. Stigand puts them in the following order: lion, elephant, rhino, leopard, and buffalo. Drummond, who wrote a capital book on South African game, who was for years a professional hunter like Selous, and who had fine opportunities for observation, but who was a much less accurate observer than Selous, put the rhino as unquestionably the most dangerous, with the lion as second, and the buffalo and elephant nearly on a level. Samuel Baker, a mighty hunter and good observer, but with less experience of African game than any one of the above, put the elephant first, the rhino second, the buffalo seemingly third, and the lion last. The experts of the greatest experience thus absolutely disagree among themselves; and there is the same wide divergence of view among good hunters and trained observers whose opportunities have been less. Mr. Abel Chapman, for instance, regards both the elephant and the rhino as more dangerous than the lion; and many of the hunters I met in East Africa seemed inclined to rank the buffalo as more dangerous than any other animal. A man who has shot but a dozen or a score of these various animals, all put together, is not entitled to express any but the most tentative opinion as to their relative prowess and ferocity; yet on the whole it seems to me that the weight of opinion among those best fitted to judge is that the lion is the most formidable opponent of the hunter, under ordinary conditions. This is my own view. But we must ever keep in mind the fact that the surrounding conditions, the geographical locality, and the wide individual variation of temper within the ranks of each species, must all be taken into account. Under certain circumstances a lion may be easily killed, whereas a rhino would be a dangerous foe. Under other conditions the rhino could be attacked with impunity, and the lion only with the utmost hazard; and one bull buffalo might flee and one bull elephant charge, and yet the next couple met with might show an exact reversal of behavior.

At any rate, during the last three or four years, in German and British East Africa and Uganda, over fifty white men have been killed or mauled by lions, buffaloes, elephants, and rhinos; and the lions have much the larges list of victims to their credit. In Nairobi church-yard I was shown the graves of seven men who had been killed by lions, and of one who had been killed by a rhino. The first man to meet us on the African shore was Mr. Campbell, Governor Jackson's A.D.C., and only a year previously he had been badly mauled by a lion. We met one gentleman who had been crippled for life by a lioness. He had marked her into some patches of brush, and coming up, tried to put her out of one thick clump. Failing, he thought she might have gone into another thicket, and walked toward it; instantly that his back was turned, the lioness, who had really been in the first clump of brush, raced out after him, threw him down, and bit him again and again before she was driven off. One night we camped at the very spot where, a score of years before, a strange tragedy had happened. It was in the early days of the opening of the country, and an expedition was going toward Uganda; one of the officials in charge was sleeping in a tent with the flap open. There was an askari on duty; yet a lion crept up, entered the tent, and seized and dragged forth the man. He struggled and made outcry; there was a rush of people, and the lion dropped his prey and bounded off. The man's wounds were dressed, and he was put back to bed in his own tent; but an hour or two after the camp again grew still, the lion returned, bent on the victim of whom he had been robbed; he re-entered the tent, seized the unfortunate wounded man with his great fangs, and this time made off with him into the surrounding darkness, killed and ate him. Not far from the scene of this tragedy, another had occurred. An English officer named Stewart, while endeavoring to kill his first lion, was himself set on and slain. As yet another place we were shown where two settlers, Messrs. Lucas and Goldfinch, had been one killed and one crippled by a lion they had been hunting. They had been following the chase on horseback, and being men of bold nature, and having killed several lions, had become too daring. They hunted the lion into a small piece of brush and rode too near it. It came out at a run and was on them before their horses could get under way. Goldfinch was knocked over and badly bitten and clawed; Lucas went to his assistance, and was in his turn knocked over, and the lion then lay on him and bit him to death. Goldfinch, in spite of his own sever wounds, crawled over and shot the great beast as it lay on his friend.

Most of the settlers with whom I was hunting had met with various adventures in connection with lions. Sir Alfred had shot many in different parts of Africa; some had charged fiercely, but he always stopped them. Captain Slatter had killed a big male with a mane a few months previously. He was hunting it in company with Mr. Humphery, the district commissioner of whom I have already spoken, and it gave them some exciting moments, for when hit it charged savagely. Humphery had a shot-gun loaded with buckshot, Slatter his rifle. When wounded, the lion charged straight home, hit Slatter, knocking him flat and rolling him over and over in the sand, and then went after the native gun-bearer, who was running away- the worst possible course to follow with a charging lion. The mechanism of Slatter's rifle was chocked by the sand, and as he rose to his feet he saw the lion overtake the fleeing man, rise on his hind legs like a rearing horse- not springing- and strike down the fugitive. Humphery fired into him with buckshot, which merely went through the skin; and some minutes elapsed before Slatter was able to get his rifle in shape to kill the lion, which, fortunately, had begun to feel the effect of his wounds, and was too sick to resume hostilities of its own accord. The gun-bearer was badly but not fatally injured. Before this, Slatter, while on a lion hunt, had been set afoot by one of the animals he was after, which had killed his horse. It was at night and the horse was tethered within six yards of his sleeping master. The latter was aroused by the horse galloping off, and he heard it staggering on for some sixty yards before it fell. He and his friend followed it with lanterns and drove off the lion, but the horse was dead. The tracks and the marks on the horse showed what had happened. The lion has sprung clean on the horse's back, his fore claws dug into the horse's shoulders, his hind claws cutting into its haunches, while the great fangs bit at the neck. The horse struggled off at a heavy run, carrying its fearsome burden. After going some sixty yards the lion's teeth went through the spinal cord, and the ride was over. Neither animal had made a sound and the lion's feet did not touch the earth until the horse fell.

While a magistrate in the Transvaal, Pease had under him as game officer a white hunter, a fine fellow, who underwent an extraordinary experience. He had been off some distance with his Kaffir boys, to hunt a lion. On his way home the hunter was hunted. It was after nightfall. He had reached a region where lions had not been seen for a long time, and where an attack by them was unknown. He was riding along a trail in the darkness, his big boarhound trotting ahead, his native "boys" some distance behind. He heard a rustle in the bushes alongside the path, but paid no heed, thinking it was a reedbuck. Immediately afterward two lions came out in the path behind him and raced after him. One sprang on him, tore him out of the saddle, and trotted off holding him in its mouth, while the other continued after the frightened horse. The lion had him by the right shoulder, and yet with his left hand he wrenched his knife out of his belt and twice stabbed it. The second stab went to the heart and the beast let go of him, stood a moment, and fell dead. Meanwhile, the dog had followed the other lion, which now, having abandoned the chase of the horse, and with the dog still at his heels, came trotting back to look for the man. Crippled though he was, the hunter managed to climb a small tree; and though the lion might have gotten him out of it, the dog interfered. Whenever the lion came toward the tree the dog worried him, and kept him off until, at the shouts and torches of the approaching Kaffir boys, he sullenly retired, and the hunter was rescued.

Percival had a narrow escape from a lion, which nearly got him, though probably under a misunderstanding. He was riding through a wet spot of ground, where the grass was four feet high, when his horse suddenly burst into a run and the next moment a lion had galloped almost alongside of him. Probably the lion thought it was a zebra, for when Percival, leaning over, yelled in his face, the lion stopped short. But he at once came on again, and nearly caught the horse. However, they were now out of the tall grass, and the lion gradually drew up when they reached the open country.

The two Hills, Clifford and Harold, were running an ostrich-farm. The lions sometimes killed their ostriches and stock; and the Hills in return had killed several lions. The Hills were fine fellows; Africanders, as their forefathers for three generations had been, and frontiersmen of the best kind. From the first moment they and I became fast friends, for we instinctively understood one another, and found that we felt alike on all the big questions, and looked at life, and especially the life of effort led by the pioneer settler, from the same stand-point. They reminded me, at ever moment, of those Western ranchmen and homemakers with whom I have always felt a special sense of companionship and with whose ideals and aspirations I have always felt a special sympathy. A couple of months before my visit, Harold Hill had met with a rather unpleasant adventure. He was walking home across the lonely plains, in the broad daylight, never dreaming that lions might be abroad, and was unarmed. When still some miles from his house, while plodding along, he glanced up and saw three lions in the trail only fifty yards off, staring fixedly at him. It happened to be a place where the grass was rather tall, and lions are always bold where there is the slightest cover; whereas, unless angered, they are cautious on bare ground. He halted, and then walking slowly to one side; and then slowly forward toward his house.

The lions followed him with their eyes, and when he had passed they rose and slouched after him. They were not pleasant followers, but to hurry would have been fatal; and he walked slowly on along the road, while for a mile he kept catching glimpses of the tawny bodies of the beasts as they trod stealthily forward through the sunburned grass, alongside or a little behind him. Then the grass grew short, and the lions halted and continued to gaze after him until he disappeared over a rise.

Everywhere throughout the country we were crossing were signs that the lion was lord and that his reign was cruel. There were many lions, for the game on which they feed was extraordinarily abundant. They occasionally took the ostriches or stock of the settlers, or ravaged the herds and flocks of the natives, but not often; for their favorite food was yielded by the swarming herds of kongoni and zebras, on which they could prey at will. Later we found that in this region they rarely molested the buffalo, even where they lived in the same reedbeds; and this though elsewhere they habitually prey on the buffalo. But where zebras and hartebeests could be obtained without effort, it was evidently not worth their will to challenge such formidable quarry. Every "kill" I saw was a kongoni or a zebra; probably I came across fifty of each. One zebra kill, which was not more than eighteen hours old (after the lapse of that time the vultures and marabouts, not to speak of the hyenas and jackals, leave only the bare bones), showed just what had occurred. The bones were all in place, and the skin still on the lower legs and head. The animal was lying on its belly, the legs spread out, the neck vertebra crushed; evidently the lion had sprung clean on it, bearing it down by his weight while he bit through the back of the neck, and the zebra's legs had spread out as the body yielded under the lion. One fresh kongoni kill showed no marks on the haunches, but a broken neck and claw marks on the face and withers; in this case the lion's hind legs had remained on the ground, while with his fore paws he grasped the kongoni's head and shoulders, holding it until the teeth splintered the neck bone.

One or two of our efforts to get lions failed, of course; the ravines we beat did not contain them, or we failed to make them leave some particularly difficult hill or swamp- for lions lie close. But Sir Alfred knew just the right place to go to, and was bound to get us lions- and he did.

One day we started from the ranch house in good season for an all-day lion hunt. Besides Kermit and myself, there was a fellow-guest, Medlicott, and not only our host, but our hostess and her daughter; and we were joined by Percival at lunch, which we took under a great fig-tree at the foot of a high, rocky hill. Percival had with him a little mongrel bull-dog, and a Masai "boy," a fine, bold-looking savage, with a handsome head-dress and the usual formidable spear; master, man, and dog evidently all looked upon any form of encounter with lions simply in the light of a spree.

After lunch we began to beat down a long donga, or dry watercourse- a creek, as we should call it in the Western plains country. The watercourse, with low, steep banks, wound in curves, and here and there were patches of brush, which might contain anything in the shape of lion, cheetah, hyena, or wild dog. Soon we came upon lion spoor in the sandy bed; first the footprints of a big male, then those of a lioness. We walked cautiously along each side of the donga, the horses following close behind so that if the lion were missed we could gallop after him and round him up on the plain. The dogs- for besides the little bull, we had a large brindled mongrel named Ben, whose courage belied his looks- began to show signs of scenting the lion; and we beat out each patch of brush, the natives shouting and throwing in stones, while we stood with the rifles where we could best command any probable exit. After a couple of false alarms the dogs drew toward one patch, their hair bristling, and showing such eager excitement that it was evident something big was inside; and in a moment one of the boys called, "simba" (lion), and pointed with his finger. It was just across the little ravine, there about four yards wide and as many feet deep; and I shifted my position, peering eagerly into the bushes for some moments before I caught a glimpse of tawny hide; as it moved, there was a call to me to "shoot," for at that distance, if the lion charged, there would be scant time to stop it; and I fired into what I saw. There was a commotion in the bushes, and Kermit fired; and immediately afterward there broke out on the other side, not the hoped-for big lion, but two cubs the size of mastiffs. Each was badly wounded and we finished them off; even if unwounded, they were too big to take alive.

This was a great disappointment, and as it was well on in the afternoon, and we had beaten the country most apt to harbor our game, it seemed unlikely that we would have another chance. Percival was on foot and a long way from his house, so he started for it; and the rest of us also began to jog homeward. But Sir Alfred, although he said nothing, intended to have another try. After going a mile or two he started off to the left at a brisk canter; and we, the other riders, followed, leaving behind our gun-bearers, saises, and porters. A couple of miles away was another donga, another shallow watercourse with occasional big brush patches along the winding bed; and toward this we cantered. Almost as soon as we reached it our leader found the spoor of two big lions; and with ever sense acock, we dismounted and approached the first patch of tall bushes. We shouted and threw in stones, but nothing came out; and another small patch showed the same result. Then we mounted our horses again, and rode toward another patch a quarter of a mile off. I was mounted on Tranquility; the stout and quiet sorrel.

This patch of tall, thick brush stood on the hither bank- that is, on our side of the watercourse. We rode up to it and shouted loudly. The response was immediate, in the shape of loud gruntings, and crashings through the thick brush. We were off our horses in an instant, I throwing the reins over the head of mine; and without delay the good old fellow began placidly grazing, quite unmoved by the ominous sounds immediately in front.

I sprang to one side; and for a second or two we waited, uncertain whether we should see the lions charging out ten yards distant or running away. Fortunately, they adopted the latter course. Right in front of me, thirty yards off, there appeared, from behind the bushes which had first screened him from my eyes, the tawny, galloping form of a big maneless lion. Crack! the Winchester spoke; and as the soft-nosed bullet ploughed forward through his flank the lion swerved so that I missed him with the second shot; but my third bullet went through the spine and forward into his chest. Down he came, sixty yards off, his hind quarters dragging, his head up, his ears back, his jaws open and lips drawn up in a prodigious snarl, as he endeavored to turn to face us. His back was broken; but of this we could not at the moment be sure, and if it had merely been grazed, he might have recovered, and then, even though dying, his charge might have done mischief. So Kermit, Sir Alfred, and I fired, almost together, into his chest. His head sank, and he died.

This lion had come out on the left of the bushes; the other, to the right of them, had not been hit, and we saw him galloping off across the plain, six or eight hundred yards away. A couple more shots missed, and we mounted our horses to try to ride him down. The plain sloped gently upward for three-quarters of a mile to a low crest or divide, and long before we got near him he disappeared over this. Sir Alfred and Kermit were tearing along in front and to the right, with Miss Pease close behind; while Tranquility carried me, as fast as he could, on the left, with Medlicott near me. On topping the divide Sir Alfred and Kermit missed the lion, which had swung to the left, and they raced ahead too far to the right. Medlicott and I, however, saw the lion, loping along close behind some kongoni; and this enabled me to get up to him as quickly as the lighter men on the faster horses. The going was now slightly downhill, and the sorrel took me along very well, while Medlicott, whose horse was slow, bore to the right and joined the other two men. We gained rapidly, and finding out this, the lion suddenly halted and came to bay in a slight hollow, where the grass was rather long. The plain seemed flat, and we could see the lion well from horseback; but, especially when he lay down, it was most difficult to make him out on foot, and impossible to do so when kneeling.

We were about a hundred and fifty yards from the lion, Sir Alfred, Kermit, Medlicott, and Miss Pease off to one side, and slightly above him on the slope, while I was on the level, about equidistant from him and them. Kermit and I tried shooting from the horses; but at such a distance this was not effective. Then Kermit got off, but his horse would not let him shoot; and when I got off I could not make out the animal through the grass with sufficient distinctness to enable me to take aim. Old Ben the dog had arrived, and barking loudly, was strolling about near the lion, which paid him not the slightest attention. At this moment my black sais, Simba, came running up to me and took hold of the bridle; he had seen the chase from the line of march and had cut across to join me. There was no other sais or gun-bearer anywhere near, and his action was plucky, for he was the only man afoot, with the lion at bay. Lady Pease had also ridden up and was an interested spectator only some fifty yards behind me.

Now, an elderly man with a varied past which includes rheumatism does not vault lightly into the saddle; as his sons, for instance, can; and I had already made up my mind that in the event of the lion's charging it would be wise for me to trust to straight powder rather than to try to scramble into the saddle and get under way in time. The arrival of my two companions settled matters. I was not sure of the speed of Lady Pease's horse; and Simba was on foot and it was of course out of the question for me to leave him. So I said, "Good, Simba, now we'll see this thing through," and gentle-mannered Simba smiled a shy appreciation of my tone, though he could not understand the words. I was still unable to see the lion when I knelt, but he was now standing up, looking first at one group of horses and then at the other, his tail lashing to and fro, his head held low, his lips dropped over his mouth in peculiar fashion, while his harsh and savage growling rolled thunderously over the plain. Seeing Simba and me on foot, he turned toward us, his tail lashing quicker and quicker. Resting my elbow on Simba's bent shoulder, I took steady aim and pressed the trigger; the bullet went in between the neck and shoulder, and the lion fell over on his side, one foreleg in the air. He recovered in a moment and stood up, evidently very sick, and once more faced me, growling hoarsely. I think he was on the eve of charging. I fired again at once, and this bullet broke his back just behind the shoulders; and with the next I killed him outright, after we had gathered round him.

These were two good-sized maneless lions; and very proud of them I was. I think Sir Alfred was at least as proud, especially because we had performed the feat alone, without any professional hunters being present. "We were all amateurs, only gentleman riders up," said Sir Alfred. It was late before we got the lions skinned. Then we set off toward the ranch, two porters carrying each lion skin, strapped to a pole; and two others carrying the cub skins. Night fell long before we were near the ranch; but the brilliant tropic moon lighted the trail. The stalwart savages who carried the bloody lion skins swung along at a faster walk as the sun went down and the moon rose higher; and they began to chant in unison, one uttering a single word or sentence, and the others joining in a deep-toned, musical chorus. The men on a safari, and indeed African natives generally, are always excited over the death of a lion, and the hunting tribes then chant their rough hunting songs, or victory songs, until the monotonous, rhythmical repetitions make them grow almost frenzied. The ride home through the moonlight, the vast barren landscape shining like silver on either hand, was one to be remembered; and above all, the sight of our trophies and of their wild bearers.

Three days later we had another successful lion hunt. Our camp was pitched at a waterhole in a little stream called Potha, by a hill of the same name. Pease, Medlicott, and both the Hills were with us, and Heller came too; for he liked, when possible, to be with the hunters so that he could at once care for any beast that was shot. As the safari was stationary, we took fifty or sixty porters as beaters. It was thirteen hours before we got into camp that evening. The Hills had with them as beaters and water-carriers half a dozen of the Wakamba who were working on their farm. It was interesting to watch these naked savages, with their teeth, their heads shaved in curious patterns, and carrying for arms little bows and arrows.

Before lunch we beat a long, low hill. Harold Hill was with me; Medlicott and Kermit were together. We placed ourselves, one couple on each side of a narrow neck, two-thirds of the way along the crest of the hill; and soon after we were in position we heard the distant shouts of the beaters as they came toward us, covering the crest and the tops of the slopes on both sides. It was rather disconcerting to find how much better Hill's eyes were than mine. He saw everything first, and it usually took some time before he could make me see it. In this first drive nothing came my way except some mountain reedbuck does, at which I did not shoot. But a fine male cheetah came to Kermit, and he bowled it over in good style as it ran.

Then the beaters halted, and waited before resuming their march until the guns had gone clear round and established themselves at the base of the farther end of the hill. This time Kermit, who was a couple of hundred yards from me, killed a reedbuck and a steinbuck. Suddenly Hill said, "Lion," and endeavored to point it out to me, as it crept cautiously among the rocks on the steep hill-side, a hundred and fifty yards away. At first I could not see it; finally I though I did and fired, but, as it proved, at a place just above him. However, it made him start up, and I immediately put the next bullet behind his shoulders; it was a fatal shot;

but, growling, he struggled down the hill, and I fired again and killed him. It was not much of a trophy, however, turning out to be a half-grown male.

We lunched under a tree, and then arranged for another beat. There was a long, wide valley, or rather a slight depression in the ground- for it was only three or four feet below the general level- in which the grass grew tall, as the soil was quite wet. It was the scene of Percival's adventure with the lion that chased him. Hill and I stationed ourselves on one side of this valley or depression, toward the upper end; Pease took Kermit to the opposite side; and we waited, our horses some distance behind us. The beaters were put in at the lower end, formed a line across the valley, and beat slowly toward us, making a great noise.

They were still some distance away when Hill saw three lions, which had slunk stealthily off ahead of them through the grass. I have called the grass tall, but this was only by comparison with the short grass of the dry plains. In the depression or valley it was some three feet high. In such grass a lion, which is marvellously adept at hiding, can easily conceal itself, not merely when lying down, but when advancing at a crouching gait. It if stands erect, however, it can be seen.

There were two lions near us, one directly in our front, a hundred and ten yards off. Some seconds passed before Hill could make me realize that the dim yellow smear in the yellow-brown grass was a lion; and then I found such difficulty in getting a bead on him that I overshot. However, the bullet must have passed very close- indeed I think it just grazed him- for he jumped up and faced us, growling savagely. Then, his head lowered, he threw his tail straight into the air and began to charge. The first few steps he took at a trot, and before he could start into a gallop I put the soft-nosed Winchester bullet in between the neck and shoulder. Down he went with a roar; the wound was fatal, but I was taking no chances, and I put two more bullets in him. Then we walked toward where Hill had already seen another lion- the lioness, as it proved. Again he had some difficulty in making me see her; but he succeeded and I walked toward her through the long grass, repressing the zeal of my two gun-bearers, who were stanch, but who showed a tendency to walk a little ahead of me on each side, instead of a little behind. I walked toward her because I could not kneel to shoot in grass so tall; and when shooting off-hand I like to be fairly close, so as to be sure that my bullets go in the right place. At sixty yards I could make her out clearly, snarling at me as she faced me; and I shot her full in the chest. She at once performed a series of extraordinary antics, tumbling about on her head, just as if she were throwing somersaults, first to one side and then to the other. I fired again, but managed to shoot between the somersaults, so to speak, and missed her. The shot seemed to bring her to herself, and away she tore; but instead of charging us she charged the line of beaters. She was dying fast, however, and in her weakness failed to catch any one; and she sank down into the long grass. Hill and I advanced to look her up, our rifles at full cock, and the gun-bearers close behind. It is ticklish work to follow a wounded lion in tall grass, and we walked carefully, every sense on the alert. We passed Heller, who had been with the beaters. He spoke to us with an amused smile. His only weapon was a pair of field-glasses, but he always took things as they came, with entire coolness, and to be close to a wounded lioness when she charged merely interested him. A beater came running up and pointed toward where he had seen her, and we walked toward the place. At thirty yards distance Hill pointed, and, eagerly peering, I made out the form of the lioness showing indistinctly through the grass. She was half crouching, half sitting, her head bent down; but she still had strength to do mischief. She saw us, but before she could turn I sent a bullet through her shoulders; down she went, and was dead when we walked up. A cub had been seen, and another full-grown lion, but they had slunk off and we got neither.

This was a full-grown, but young, lioness of average size; her cubs must have been several months old. We took her entire to camp to weigh; she weighed two hundred and eighty-three pounds. The first lion, which we had difficulty in finding, as there were no identifying marks in the plain of tall grass, was a good-sized male, weighing about four hundred pounds, but not yet full-grown; although he was probably the father of the cubs.

We were a long way from camp, and, after beating in vain for the other lion, we started back; it was after nightfall before we saw the camp-fires. It was two hours later before the porters appeared, bearing on poles the skin of the dead lion, and the lioness entire. The moon was nearly full, and it was interesting to see them come swinging down the trail in the bright silver light, chanting in deep tones, over and over again, a line or phrase that sounded like:

"**Zou-zou-boule ma ja guntai; zou-zou-boule ma ja gunatai.**"

Occasionally they would interrupt it by repetition in unison, at short intervals, of a guttural ejaculation, sounding like "huzlem." They marched into camp, then up and down the lines, before the rows of small fires; then, accompanied by all the rest of the porters, they paraded up to the big fire where I was standing. Here they stopped and ended the ceremony by a minute or two's vigorous dancing amid singing and wild shouting. The firelight gleamed and flickered across the grim dead beasts, and the shining eyes and black features of the excited savages, while all around the moon flooded the landscape with her white light.

# A Trek Through the Thirst

*African Game Trails*

On June 5th we started south from Kijabe to trek through the thirst, through the waterless country which lies across the way to the Sotik.

The preceding Sunday, at Nairobi, I had visited the excellent French Catholic Mission, had been most courteously received by the fathers, had gone over their plantations and the school in which they taught the children of the settlers (much to my surprise, among them were three Parsee children, who were evidently put on a totally different plane from the other Indians, even the Goanese), and had been keenly interested in their account of their work and of the obstacles with which they met.

At Kijabe I spent several exceedingly interesting hours at the American Industrial Mission. Its head, Mr. Hurlburt, had called on me in Washington at the White House, in the preceding October, and I had then made up my mind that if the chance occurred I must certainly visit his mission. It is an interdenominational mission, and is carried on in a spirit which combines to a marked degree broad sanity and common-sense with disinterested fervor. Of course, such work, under the conditions which necessarily obtain in East Africa, can only show gradual progress; but I am sure that missionary work of the Kijabe kind will be an indispensable factor in the slow uplifting of the natives. There is full recognition of the fact that industrial training is a foundation stone in the effort to raise ethical and moral standards. Industrial teaching must go hand in hand with moral teaching- and in both the mere force of example and the influence of firm, kindly sympathy and understanding, count immeasurably. There is further recognition of the fact that in such a country the missionary should either already know how to, or else at once learn how to, take the lead himself in all kinds of industrial and mechanical work. Finally the effort is made consistently to teach the native how to live a more comfortable, useful, and physically and morally clean life, not under white conditions, but under the conditions which he will actually have to face when he goes back to his people, to live among them, and, if things go well, to be in his turn a conscious or unconscious missionary for good.

At lunch, in addition to the missionaries and their wives and children, there were half a dozen of the neighboring settlers, with their families. It is always a good thing to see the missionary and the settler working shoulder to shoulder. Many parts of East Africa can, and I believe will, be made into a white man's country; and the process will be helped, not hindered, by treating the black man well. At Kijabe, nearly under the equator, the beautiful scenery was almost northern in type; at night we needed blazing camp-fires and the days were as cool as September on Long Island or by the southern shores of the Great Lakes. It is a very healthy region; the children of the missionaries and settlers, of all ages, were bright and strong; those of Mr. and Mrs. Hurlburt had not been out of the country for eight years, and showed no ill effects whatever; on the contrary,I quite believed Mrs. Hurlburt when she said that she regarded the fertile wooded hills of Kijabe, with their forests and clear brooks, as forming a true health resort.

The northern look of the place was enhanced by the fact that the forests contained junipers; but they also contained monkeys, a small green monkey, and the big guerza, with its long silky hair and bold black-and-white coloring. Kermit, Heller, and Loring shot several. There were rhinoceros and buffalo in the neighborhood. A few days previously some buffalo had charged, unprovoked, a couple of the native boys of the emission, who had escaped only by their agility in tree-climbing. On one of his trips to an outlying mission station, Mr. Hurlburt had himself narrowly escaped a serious accident. Quite wantonly, a cow rhino, with a calf, charged the safari almost before they knew of its presence. It attacked Hurlburt's mule, which fortunately he was not riding, and tossed and killed it; it passed through the line, and then turned and again charged it, this time attacking one of the porters. The porter dodged behind a tree, and the rhino hit the tree, knocked off a huge flake of bark and wood, and galloped away.

The trek across "the thirst," as any waterless country is apt to be called by an Africander, is about sixty miles, by the road. On our horses we could have ridden it in a night; but on a serious trip of any kind loads must be carried, and laden porters cannot go fast, and must rest at intervals. We had rather more than our porters could carry, and needed additional transportation for the water for the safari; and we had hired four ox wagons. They were under the lead of a fine young colonial Englishman named Ulyate, whose great-grandfather had come to South Africa in 1820, as part of the most important English emigration that ever went thither. His father and sisters had lunched with us at the mission-aries' the day before; his wife's baby was too young for her to come. It was the best kind of pioneer family; all the members, with some of their fellow-colo-nials, had spent much of the preceding three years in adventurous explo-ration of the country in their ox wagons, the wives and daughters as valiant as the men; one of the two daughters I met had driven one of the ox wagons on the hardest and most dangerous trip they made, while her younger sister led the oxen. It was on this trip that they had pioneered the way across the water-less route I was to take. For those who, like ourselves, followed the path they had thus blazed, there was no danger to the men, and merely discomfort to the oxen; but the first trip was a real feat, for no one could tell what lay ahead, or what exact route would be practicable. The family had now settled on a big farm, but also carried on the business of "transport riding," as freighting with wag-ons is called in Africa; and they did it admirably.

With Ulyate were three other with wagon-drivers, all colonials; two of them English, the third Dutch, or Boer. There was also a Cape boy, a Kaffir wagon-driver; utterly different from any of the East African natives, and dressed in ordinary clothes. In addition there were various natives- primitive savages in dress and habit, but coming from the cattle-owning tribes. Each ox-team was guided by one of these savages, who led the first yoke by a leathern thong, while the wagon-driver, with his long whip, stalked to and fro beside the line of oxen, or rode in the wagon. The huge wagons, with their white tops or "sails," were larger than those our own settlers and freighters used. Except one small one, to which there were but eight oxen, each was drawn by a span of seven or eight yoke; they were all native humped cattle.

We had one hundred and ninety-six porters, in addition to the askaris, tent boys, gun-bearers, and saises. The management of such a safari is a work of difficulty; but no better man for the purpose than Cuninghame could be found anywhere, and he had chosen his headmen well. In the thirst, the march goes on by day and night. The longest halt is made in the day, for men and animals both travel better at night than under the blazing noon. We were fortunate in that it was just after the full of the moon, so that our night treks were made in good light. Of course, on such a march the porters must be spared as much as possible; camp is not pitched, and each white man uses for the trip only what he wears, or carries on his horse- and the horse also must be loaded as lightly as possible. I took nothing but my army overcoat, rifle and cartridges, and three canteens of water. Kermit did the same.

The wagons broke camp about ten, to trek to the water, a mile and a half off, where the oxen would be outspanned to take the last drink for three days; stock will not drink early in the morning nearly as freely as if the march is begun later. We, riding our horses, followed by the long line of burdened porters, left at half-past twelve, and in a couple of hours overtook the wagons. The porters were in high spirits. In the morning, before the start, they twice held regular dances, the chief musician being one of their own number who carried an extraordinary kind of native harp; and after their loads were allotted they marched out of camp singing and blowing their horns and whistles. Three askaris brought up the rear to look after laggards, and see that no weak or sick man fell out without our knowing or being able to give him help.

The trail led first through open brush, or low, dry forest, and then out on the vast plains, where the withered grass was dotted here and there with low, scantily leaved thorn-trees, from three to eight feet high. Hour after hour we drew slowly ahead under the shimmering sunlight. The horsemen walked first, with the gun-bearers, saises, and usually a few very energetic and powerful porters; then came the safari in single file; and then the lumbering white-topped wagons, the patient oxen walking easily, each team led by a half-naked savage with frizzed hair and a spear or throwing-stick in his hand, while at intervals the long whips of the drivers cracked like rifles. The dust rose in clouds from the dry earth, and soon covered all of us; in the distance herds of zebra and hartebeest gazed at us as we passed, and we saw the old spoor of rhino, beasts we hoped to avoid, as they often charge such a caravan.

Slowly the shadows lengthened; the light wanted, the glare of the white, dusty plain was softened, and the bold outlines of the distant mountains grew dim. Just before nightfall we halted on the further side of a dry watercourse. The safari came up singing and whistling, and the men put down their loads, lit fires, and with chatter and laughter prepared their food. The crossing was not good, the sides of the watercourse being steep; and each wagon was brought through by a double span, the whips cracking lustily as an accompaniment to the shouts of the drivers, as the thirty oxen threw their weight into the yokes by which they were attached to the long trek tow. The horses were fed. We had tea, with bread and cold meat- and a most delicious meal it was- and then lay dozing or talking beside the bush-fires. At half-past eight, the moon having risen, we were off again. The safari was still in high spirits, and started with the usual chanting and drumming.

We pushed steadily onward across the plain, the dust rising in clouds under the spectral moonlight. Sometimes we rode, sometimes we walked to ease our horses. The Southern Cross was directly ahead, not far above the horizon. Higher and higher rose the moon, and brighter grew the flood of her light. At intervals the barking call of zebras was heard on either hand. It was after midnight when we again halted. The porters were tied, and did not sing as they came up; the air was cool, almost nipping, and they at once huddled down in their blankets, some of them building fires. We, the white men, after seeing our horses staked out, each lay down in his overcoat or jacket and slicker, with his head on his saddle, and his rifle beside him, and had a little over two hours' sleep. At three we were off again, the shivering porters making no sound as they started; but once under way the more irrepressible spirits speedily began a kind of intermittent chant, and most of the rest by degrees joined in the occasional grunt or hum that served as chorus.

For four hours we travelled steadily, first through the moonlight, and then through the reddening dawn. Jackals shrieked, and the plains plover wailed and scolded as they circled round us. When the sun was well up, we halted; the desolate flats stretched far and wide on every side and rose into lofty hills ahead of us. The porters received their water and food, and lay down to sleep, some directly in the open, others rigging little sun shelters under the scattering thorn-bushes. The horses were fed, were given half a pail of water apiece, and were turned loose to graze with the oxen; this was the last time the oxen would feed freely, unless there was rain; and this was to be our longest halt. We had an excellent breakfast, like our supper the night before, and then slept as well as we could.

Noon came, and son afterward we again started. The country grew hilly, and brushy. It was too dry for much game, but we saw a small herd of giraffe, which are independent of water. Now riding our horses, now leading them, we travelled until nearly sunset, when we halted at the foot of a steep divide, beyond which our course lay across slopes that gradually fell to the stream for which we were heading. Here the porters had all the food and water they wished, and so did the horses; and, each with a double span of oxen, the wagons were driven up the slope, the weary cattle straining hard in the yokes.

Black clouds had risen and thickened in the west, boding rain. Three-fourths of our journey was over; and it was safe to start the safari and then leave it to come on by itself, while the ox wagons followed later. At nine, before the moon struggled above the hill-crests to our left, we were off. Soon we passed the wagons, drawn up abreast, a lantern high on a pole, while the tired oxen lay in their yokes, attached to the trek tow. An hour afterward we left the safari behind, and rode ahead, with only our saises and gun-bearers. Gusts of rain blew in our faces, and gradually settled into a steady, gentle downpour. Our horses began to slip in the greasy soil; we knew the rain would refresh the cattle, but would make the going harder.

At one we halted, in the rain, for a couple hours' rest. Just before this we heard two lions roaring, or rather grunting, not far in front of us; they were after prey. Lions are bold on rainy nights, and we did not wish to lose any of our horses; so a watch was organized, and we kept ready for immediate action, but the lions did not come. The native boys built fires, and lay close to them, relieving one another, and us, as sentinels. Kermit and I had our army overcoats, which are warm and practically water-proof; the others had coats almost as good. We lay down in the rain, on the drenched grass, with our saddle-cloths over our feet, and our heads on our saddles, and slept comfortably for two hours.

At three we mounted and were off again, the rain still falling. There were steep ravines to cross, slippery from the wet; but we made good time, and soon after six off-saddled on the farther side of a steep drift or ford in the little Suavi River. It is a rapid stream flowing between high, well-wooded banks; it was an attractive camp site, and, as we afterwards found, the nights were so cool as to make great camp-fires welcome. At half-past ten the safari appeared, in excellent spirits, the flag waving, to an accompaniment of chanting and horn-blowing; and, to their loudly expressed satisfaction, the porters were told that they should have an extra day's rations, as well as a day's rest. Camp was soon pitched; and all, of every rank, slept soundly that night, though the lions moaned near by. The wagons did not get in until ten the following morning. By that time the oxen had been nearly three days without water, so, by dawn, they were unyoked and driven down to drink before the drift was attempted, the wagons being left a mile or two back. The approaches to the drift were steep and difficult, and, with two spans to each, the wagons swayed and plunged, over the twisted bowlder-choked trails down into the river-bed, crossed it, and, without lurching and straining, men shouting and whip cracking, drew slowly up on the opposite bank.

After a day's rest, we pushed on, in two days' easy travelling, to the Guaso Nyero of the south. Our camps were pleasant, by running streams of swift water; one was really beautiful, in a grassy bend of a rapid little river, by huge African yew-trees, with wooded cliffs in front. It was cool, rainy weather, with overcast skies and misty mornings, so that it seemed strangely unlike the tropics. The country was alive with herds of Masai cattle, sheep, and donkeys. The Masai, herdsmen by profession and warrior by preference, with their great spears and ox-hide shields, were stalwart savages, and showed the mixture of types common to this part of Africa, which is the edge of an ethnic whirlpool. Some of them were of seemingly pure negro type; others except in their black skin had little negro about them, their features being as clear-cut as those of ebony Nilotic Arabs. They were dignified, but friendly and civil, shaking hands as soon as they came up to us.

On the Guaso Nyero was a settler from South Africa, with his family; and we met another settler travelling with a big flock of sheep which he had bough for trading purposes. The latter, while journeying over our route with cattle, a month before, had been attacked by lions one night. They seized his cook as he lay by the fire, but fortunately grabbed his red blanket, which they carried off, and the terrified man escaped; and they killed a cow and a calf. Ulyate's brother-in-law, Smith, had been rendered a hopeless cripple for life, six months previously, by a lioness he had wounded. Another settler while at one of our camping-places lost two of his horses, which were killed although within a boma. One night lions came within threatening neighborhood of our ox wagons; and we often heard them moaning in the early part of the night, roaring when full fed toward morning; but we were not molested.

The safari was in high feather, for the days were cool, the work easy, and we shot enough game to give them meat. When we broke camp after breakfast, the porters would all stand ranged by their loads; then Tarlton would whistle, and a chorus of whistles, horns, and tomtoms would answer, as each porter lifted and adjusted his burden, fell into his place, and then joined in some shrill or guttural chorus as the long line swung off at its marching pace. After nightfall the camp-fires blazed in the cool air, and as we stood or sat around them each man had tales to tell: Cuninghame and Tarlton of elephant hunting in the Congo, and of perilous adventures hunting lion and buffalo; Mearns of long hikes and fierce fighting in the steaming Philippine forests; Loring and Heller of hunting and collecting in Alaska, in the Rockies, and among the deserts of the Mexican border; and always our talk came back to strange experiences with birds and beast, both great and small, and to the ways of the great game. The three naturalists revelled in the teeming bird life, with its wealth of beauty and color- nor was the beauty only of color and shape, for at dawn the bird songs made real music. The naturalists trapped many small mammals: big eared mice looking like our white-footed mice, mice with spiny fur, mice that lived in trees, rats striped like our chipmunks, rats that jumped like jerboas, big cane-rats, dormice, and tiny shrews. Meercats, things akin to a small mongoose, lived out in the open plains, burrowing in companies like prairie dogs, very spry and active, and looking like picket pins when they stood up on end to survey us. I killed a nine-foot python which had swallowed a rabbit. Game was not plentiful, but we killed enough for the table. I shot a wildebeest bull one day, having edged up to it on foot, after missing it standing; I broke it down with a bullet through the hips as it galloped across my front at three hundred yards. Kermit killed our first topi, a bull; a beautiful animal, the size of a hartebeest, its glossy coat with a satin sheen, varying from brown to silver and purple.

By the Guaso Nyero we halted for several days; and we arranged to leave Mearns and Loring in a permanent camp, so that they might seriously study and collect the birds and small mammals while the rest of us pushed wherever we wished after the big game. The tents were pitched, and the ox wagons drawn up on the southern side of the muddy river, by the edge of a wide plain, on which we could see the game grazing as we walked around camp. The alluvial flats bordering the river, and some of the higher plains, were covered with an open forest growth, the most common tree looking exactly like a giant sage-brush, thirty feet high; and there were tall aloes and cactus and flat-topped mimosa. We found a wee hedgehog, with much white about it. He would cuddle up in my hand snuffing busily with his funny little nose. We did not have the heart to turn the tame, friendly little fellow over to the naturalists, so we let him go. Birds abounded. One kind of cuckoo called like a whippoorwill in the early morning and late evening, and after nightfall. Among our friendly visitors were the pretty, rather strikingly colored little chats- Livingstone's wheatear- which showed real curiosity in coming into camp. They were nesting in burrows on the open plains round about. Mearns got a white egg and a nest at the end of a little burrow two feet long; wounded, the birds ran into holes or burrows. They sang attractively on the wing, often at night. The plover-like coursers, very pretty birds, continually circled round us with querulous clamor. Gorgeously colored, diminutive sunbirds, of many different kinds, were abundant; they had an especial fondness for the gaudy flowers of the tall mint which grew close to the river. We got a small cobra, less than eighteen inches long; it had swallowed another snake almost as big as itself; unfortunately the head of the swallowed snake was digested, but the body looked like that of a young puff adder.

The day after reaching this camp I rode off for a hunt, accompanied by my two gun-bearers, Mahomet, though a good man in the field, had proved in other respects so unsatisfactory that he had been replaced by another, a Wakamba heathen named Gouvimali- I could never remember his name until, as a mnemonic aid, Kermit suggested that I think of Governor

Morris, the old Federalist statesman, whose life I had once studied. He was a capital man for the work.

Half a mile from camp I saw a buck tommy with a good head, and as we needed his delicious venison for our own table, I dismounted and after a little care killed him as he faced me at two hundred and ten yards. Sending him back by one of the porters, I rode on toward two topi was saw far in front. But there were zebra, hartebeest, and wildebeest in between, all of which ran; and the topi proved wary. I was still walking after them when we made out two eland bulls ahead and to our left. The ground was too open to admit of the possibility of a stalk; but leaving my horse and the porters to follow slowly, the gunbearers and I walked quartering toward them. They hesitated about going, and when I had come as close as I dared, I motioned to the two gun-bearers to continue walking, and dropped to one knee. I had the little Springfield, and was anxious to test the new sharp-pointed military bullet on some large animal. The biggest bull was half facing me, just two hundred and eighty yards off; I fired a little bit high and a trifle to the left; but the tiny ball broke his back and the splendid beast, heavy as a prize steer, came plunging and struggling to the ground. The other bull started to run off, but after I had walked a hundred yards forward, he actually trotted back toward his companion; then halted, turned, and galloped across my front at a distance of a hundred and eighty years; and him too I brought down with a single shot. The little full-jacketed, sharp-pointed bullet made a terrific rending compared with the heavier, ordinary-shaped bullet of the same composition.

I was much pleased with my two prizes, for the National Museum particularly desired a good group of eland. They were splendid animals, like beautiful heavy cattle; and I could not sufficiently admire their sleek, handsome, striped coats, their shapely heads, fine horns, and massive bodies. The big bull, an old one, looked blue at a distance; he was very heavy and his dewlap hung down just as with cattle. His companion, although much less heavy, was a full-grown bull in his prime, with longer horns; for the big one's horns had begun to wear down at the tips. In their stomachs were grass blades and, rather to my surprise, aloe leaves.

We had two canvas cloths with us, which Heller had instructed me to put over anything I shot, in order to protect it from the sun; so, covering both bulls, I left a porter with them, and sent in another to notify Heller- who came out with an ox wagon to bring in the skins and mea. I had killed these two eland bulls, as well as the buck gazelle (bringing down each with a single bullet) within three- quarters of an hour after leaving camp.

I wanted a topi, and continued to hunt. The country swarmed with the herds and flocks of the Masai, who own a wealth of live stock. Each herd of cattle and donkeys or flock of sheep was guarded by its herdsmen; bands of stalwart, picturesque warriors, with their huge spears and ox-hide shields, occasionally strolled by us; and we passed many bomas, the kraals where the stock is gathered at night, with the mud huts of the owners ringing them. Yet there was much game in the country also, chiefly zebra and hartebeest; the latter, according to their custom, continually jumping up on ant-hills to get a clearer view of me, and sometimes standing on them motionless for a considerable time, as sentries to scan the country around.

At last we spied a herd of topi, distinguishable from the hartebeest at a very long distance by their dark coloring, the purples and browns giving the coat a heavy shading which when far off, in certain lights, looks almost black. Topi, hartebeest, and wildebeest belong to the same group, and are specialized, and their peculiar physical and mental traits developed, in the order named. The wildebeest is the least normal and most grotesque and odd-looking of the three, and his idiosyncrasies of temper are also the most marked. The hartebeest comes next, with his very high withers, long face, and queerly shaped horns; while the topi, although with a general hartebeest look, has the features of shape and horn less pronounced, and bears a greater resemblance to his more ordinary kinsfolk. In the same way, though it will now and then buck and plunge when it begins to run after being startled, its demeanor is less pronounced in this respect. The topi's power of leaping is great; I have seen one when frightened bound clear over a companion, and immediately afterward over a high ant-hill.

The herd of topi we saw was more shy than the neighboring zebra and hartebeest. There was no cover and I spent an hour trying to walk up to them by manoeuvring in one way and another. They did not run clear away, but kept standing and letting me approach to distances varying from four hundred and fifty to six hundred yards; tempting me to shoot, while nevertheless I could not estimate the range accurately, and was not certain whether I was over or under shooting. So I fired more times than I care to mention before I finally got my topi- at just five hundred and twenty yards. It was a handsome cow, weighing two hundred and sixty pounds; for topi are somewhat smaller than kongoni. The beauty of its coat, in texture and coloring, struck me afresh as I looked at the sleek creature stretched out on the grass. Like the eland, it was free from ticks; for the hideous pests do not frequent this part of the country in any great numbers.

I reached camp early in the afternoon, and sat down at the mouth of my tent to enjoy myself. It was on such occasions that the Pigskin Library proved itself indeed a blessing. In addition to the original books we had picked up one or two old favorites on the way: Alice's Adventures, for instance, and Fitzgerald- I say Fitzgerald, because reading other versions of Omar Khayyam always leaves me with the feeling that Fitzgerald is the major partner in the book we really like. Then there was a book I had not read, Dumas's "Louves de Machecoul." This was presented to me at Port Said by M. Jusserand, the brother of an old and valued friend, the French ambassador at Washington- the vice-president of the "Tennis Cabinet." We had been speaking of Balzac, and I mentioned regretfully that I did not at heart care for his longer novels excepting the "Chouans"; and, as John Hay once told me, in the eye of all true Balzacians to like the "Chouans" merely aggravates the offence of not liking the novels which they deem really great. M. Jusserand thereupon asked me if I knew Dumas's Vandean novel; being a fairly good Dumas man, I was rather ashamed to admit that I did not; whereupon he sent it to me, and I enjoyed it to the full.

The next day was Kermit's red-letter day. We were each out until after dark; I merely got some of the ordinary game, taking the skins for the naturalists, the flesh for our following; he killed two cheetahs, and a fine maned lion, finer than any previously killed. There were three cheetahs together. Kermit, who was with Tarlton, galloped the big male, and, although it had a mile's start, ran into it in three miles, and shot it as it lay under a bush. He afterward shot another, a female, who was lying on a stone koppie. Neither made any attempt to charge; the male had been eating a tommy. The lion was with a lioness, which wheeled to one side as the horsemen galloped after her maned mate. He turned to bay after a run of less than a mile, and started to charge from a distance of two hundred yards; but Kermit's first bullets mortally wounded him and crippled him so that he could not come at any pace and was easily stopped before covering half the distance. Although nearly a foot longer than the biggest of the lions I had already killed, he was so gaunt- whereas they were very fat- that he weighed but little more, only four hundred and twelve pounds.

The following day I was out by myself, after impalla and Roberts' gazelle; and the day after I went out with Tarlton to try for lion. We were away from camp for over fifteen hours. Each was followed by his sais and gun-bearers, and we took a dozen porters also. The day may be worth describing, as a sample of the days when we did not start before dawn for a morning's hunt.

We left camp at seven, steering for a high, rocky hill, four miles off. We passed zebra and hartebeest, and on the hill came upon Chanler's reedbuck; but we wanted none of these. Continually, Tarlton stopped to examine some distant object with his glasses, and from the hills we scanned the country far and wide; but we saw nothing we desired and continued on our course. The day was windy and cool, and the sky often overcast. Slowly we walked across the stretches of brown grassland, sometimes treeless, sometimes scantily covered with an open growth of thorn-trees, each branch armed with long spikes, needle-sharp; and among the thorns here and there stood the huge cactus-like euphorbias, shaped like candelabra, groups of tall aloes, and gnarled wild olives of great age, with hoary trunks and twisted branches. Now and then there would be a dry watercourse, with flat-topped acacias bordering it, and perhaps someone pool of thick green-ish water. There was game always in view, and about noon we sighted three rhi-nos, a bull, a cow, and a big calf, nearly a mile ahead of us. We were travelling down wind, and they scented us, but did not charge, making off in a semicircle and halt-ing when abreast of us. We examined them carefully through the glasses. The cow was bigger than the bull, and had fair horns, but nothing extraordinary; and as we were twelve miles from camp, so that Heller would have had to come out for the night if we shot her, we decided to leave her alone. Then our attention was attracted by seeing the game all gazing in one direction, and we made out a hyena; I got a shot at it, at three hundred yards, but missed. Soon afterward we saw another rhino, but on approaching it proved to be about two-thirds grown, with a stubby horn. We did not wish to shoot it, and therefore desired to avoid a charge; and so we passed three or four hundred yards to leeward, trusting to its bad eyesight. Just opposite it, when it was on our right, we saw another hyena on our left, about as far off as the rhino. I decided to take a shot, and run the chance of disturbing the rhino. So I knelt down and aimed with the little Springfield, keeping the Holland by me to be ready for events. I never left camp, on foot or on horseback, for any distance, no matter how short, without carrying one of the repeating rifles; and when on a hunt my two gun-bearers car-ried, on the other magazine rifle, and one the double-barrelled Holland.

Tarlton, whose eye for distance was good, told me the hyena was over three hundred yards off; it was walking slowly to the left. I put up the three-hundred yard sight, and drew a rather coarse bead; and down went the hyena with its throat cut; the little sharp-pointed, full-jacketed bullet makes a slash-ing wound. The distance was just three hundred and fifty long paces. As soon as I had pulled trigger I wheeled to watch the rhino. It started round at the shot and gazed toward us with its ears cocked forward, but made no movement to advance. While a couple of porters were dressing the hyena, I could not help laughing at finding that we were the centre of a thoroughly African circle of deeply interested spectators. We were in the middle of a vast plain, covered with sun-scorched grass and here and there a stunted thorn; in the background were isolated barren hills, and the mirage wavered in the distance. Vultures wheeled overhead. The rhino, less than half a mile away, stared steadily at us. Wildebeest-their heavy forequarters and the carriage of their heads making them look like bison- and hartebeest were somewhat nearer, in a ring all round us, intent upon our proceedings. Four topi became so much interested that they approached within two hundred and fifty yards and stood motionless. A buck tommy came even closer, and a zebra trotted by at about the same distance, uttering its queer bark or neigh. It continued its course past the rhino, and started a new train of ideas in the latter's muddled reptilian brain; round it wheeled, gazed after the zebra, and then evidently concluded that everything was normal, for it lay down to sleep.

On we went, past a wildebeest herd lying down; at a distance they looked exactly like bison as they used to lie out on the prairie in the old days. We halted for an hour and a half to rest the men and horses, and took our lunch under a thick-trunked olive-tree that must have been a couple of centuries old. Again we went on, ever scanning through the glasses every distant object which we though might possibly be a lion, and ever being disappointed. A serval cat jumped up ahead of us in the tall grass, but I missed it. Then, trotting on foot, I got ahead of two warthog boars, and killed the biggest; making a bad initial miss and then emptying my magazine at it as it ran. We sent it in to camp, and went on, following a donga, or small watercourse, fringed with big acacias. The afternoon was wearing away, and it was time for the lions to be abroad.

The sun was near the horizon when Tarlton though he saw something tawny in the watercourse ahead of us, behind a grassy ant-hill, toward which we walked after dismounting. Some buck were grazing peacefully beyond it, and for a moment we supposed that this was what he had seen. But as we stood, one of the porters behind called out "Simba"; and we caught a glimpse of a big lioness galloping down beside the trees, just beyond the donga; she was out of sight in an instant. Mounting our horses, we crossed the donga; she was not to be seen, and we loped at a smart pace parallel with the line of trees, hoping to see her in the open. But, as it turned out, as soon as she saw us pass, she crouched in the bed of the donga; we had gone by her a quarter of a mile when a shout from one of our followers announced that he had seen her, and back we galloped, threw ourselves from our horses, and walked toward where the man was pointing. Tarlton took his big double-barrel and advised me to take mine, as the sun had just set and it was likely to be close work; but I shook my head, for the Winchester. 405 is, at least for me personally, the "medicine gun" for lions. In another moment up she jumped, and galloped slowly down the other side of the donga, switching her tail and growling; I scrambled across the donga, and just before she went round a clump of trees, eighty yards off, I fired. The bullet hit her fair, and going forward injured her spine. Over she rolled, growling savagely, and dragged herself into the watercourse; and running forward I finished her with two bullets behind the shoulder. She was a big, fat lioness, very old, with two cubs inside her; her lower canines were much worn and injured. She was very heavy, and probably weighed considerably over three hundred pounds.

The light was growing dim, and camp was eight or ten miles away. The porters- they are always much excited over the death of a lion- wished to carry the body whole to camp, and I let them try. While they were lashing it to a pole another lion began to moan hungrily half a mile away. Then we started; there was no moon, but the night was clear and we could guide ourselves by the stars. The porters staggered under their heavy load, and we made slow progress; most of the time Tarlton and I walked, with our double-barrels in our hands, for it was a dangerous neighborhood. Again and again we heard lions, and twice one accompanied us for some distance, grunting occasionally, while we kept the men closed. Once the porters were thrown into a panic by a succession of steam-engine-like snorts on our left, which announced the immediate proximity of a rhino. They halted in a huddle while Tarlton and I ran forward and crouched to try to catch the great beast's loom against the sky-line; but it moved off. Four miles from camp was a Masai kraal, and we went toward this when we caught the gleam of the fires; for the porters were getting exhausted.

The kraal was in shape a big oval, with a thick wall of thorn-bushes, eight feet high, the low huts standing just within this wall, while the cattle and sheep were crowded into small bomas in the centre. The fires gleamed here and there within, and as we approached we heard the talking and laughing of men and women, and the lowing and bleating of the pent-up herds and flocks. We hailed loudly, explaining our needs. At first they were very suspicious. They told us, we could not bring the lion within, because it would frighten the cattle, but after some parley consented to our building a fire outside, and skinning the animal. They passed two brands over the thorn fence, and our men speedily kindled a blaze, and drew the lioness beside it. By this time the Masai were reassured, and a score of their warriors, followed soon by half a dozen women, came out through a small opening in the fence, and crowded close around the fire, with boisterous, noisy good-humor. They showed a tendency to chaff our porters. One, the humorist of the crowd, excited much merriment by describing, with pantomimic accompaniment of gestures, how when the white man shot a lion it might bite a Swahili, who thereupon would call for his mother. But they were entirely friendly, and offered me calabashes of milk. The men were tall, finely shaped savages, their hair plastered with red mud, and drawn out into longish ringlets; they were naked except for a blanket worn, not round the loins, but over the shoulders; their ears were slit, and from them hung bone and wooden ornaments; they wore metal bracelets and anklets, and chains which passed around their necks, or else over one side of the neck and under the opposite arm. The women had pleasant faces, and were laden with metal ornaments- chiefly wire anklets, bracelets, and necklaces- of many pounds of weight. The features of the men we bold and clear-cut, and their bearing warlike and self-reliant; as the flame of the fire glanced over them, and brought their faces and bronze figures into lurid relief against the darkness, the likeness was striking, not to the West Coast negroes, but to the engravings on the tombs, temples, and palaces of ancient Egypt; they might have been soldiers in the armies of Thothmes or Rameses. They stood resting on their long staffs, and looked at me as I leaned on my rifle; and they laughed and jested with their women, who felt the lion's teeth and claws and laughed back at the men; our gun-bearers worked at the skinning, and answered the jests of their warlike friends with the freedom of men who themselves followed a dangerous trade; the two horses stood quiet just outside the circle; and over all the firelight played and leaped.

It was after ten when we reached camp, and I enjoyed a hot bath and a shave before sitting down to a supper of eland venison and broiled spurfowl; and surely no supper ever tasted more delicious.

Next day we broke camp. My bag for the five days illustrates ordinary African shooting in this part of the continent. Of course I could have killed many other things; but I shot nothing that was not absolutely needed, both for scientific purposes and for food; the skin of every animal I shot was preserved for the National Museum. The bag included fourteen animals, of ten different species: one lioness, one hyena, one wart-hog board, two zebra, two eland, one wildebeest, two topi, two impalla, one Roberts' gazelle, one Thomson's gazelle. Except the lioness and one impalla (both of which I shot running), all were shot at rather long ranges; seven were shot standing, two walking, five running. The average distance at which they were shot was a little over two hundred and twenty yards. I used sixty-five cartridges, an amount which will seem excessive chiefly to those who are not accustomed actually to count the cartridges they expend, to measure the distances at which they fire, and to estimate for themselves the range, on animals in the field when they are standing or running a good way off. Only one wounded animal got away; and eight of the animals I shot had to be finished with one bullet- two in the case of the lioness- as they lay on the ground. Many of the cartridges expended really represented range-finding.

When it was all over the Roosevelts had bagged eleven elephants, twenty rhinos, both black and white, seventeen lions, seven hippos, and a variety of other animals to the number of about 1,100. The four naturalists on the trip had brought back smaller animals for the most part: rodents of all kinds, four species of hyrax, nine species of shrew, bats, monkeys. There were large numbers of gazelles, dikdiks, koodoos, antelopes, oribis, and so on and so on. Was it wasteful? By modern lights, yes, it probably was. But the life histories of many of these animals were not known before Roosevelt's safari went into the field. A lot of natural history got done on this trip. The Smithsonian, and science, benefited. But there was one thing the trip did not accomplish. It did not teach Theodore Roosevelt to be an ex-President.

Almost as soon as he got back to the United States, in fact, he started sticking his toe into the political waters again. Taft had fired Roosevelt's friend and personal choice, Gifford Pinchot, from the job of head of the Forest Service, which Roosevelt had created. Taft was not actively pursuing the anti-trust measures that were so important to Roosevelt. Taft was not active, period. He was a reactive President, not a doer. A judgeship would have suited him perfectly. When Warren Harding named him to the Supreme Court in 1921, he finally got what he had always wanted. Roosevelt in contrast was all action, all push and energy. He loved power and sought it out. He was uncomfortable not being President. The office suited him perfectly. He decided in 1912 that he wanted it back.

He might have gotten it back, too, if he hadn't split the Republican Party. But it was not to be. Instead he and his Progressive Party (or Bull Moose Party, as it was dubbed when Roosevelt declared himself as fit as a bull moose) pulled enough votes away from Taft to make sure that Woodrow Wilson became President of the United States in 1912. Roosevelt was once again at loose ends. He had been shot during the campaign, interestingly enough, by a saloonkeeper who had gone over the edge mentally, but he *gave the speech he was scheduled to give that evening anyway, and only then went to the hospital. The bullet had broken a rib. He was indeed as fit as a bull moose.*

*Fit enough for another expedition, certainly. This one was, in its way, even more ambitious than the African safari, but it was not planned that way. It started out as a simple hunting trip into the Brazilian wilderness to shoot the most elusive large American feline of all, the jaguar. At the time, in 1913, his son Kermit, who had gone with him to Africa, was working in Brazil as a supervisor for an English company engaged in building bridges and other large construction projects. Roosevelt thought it would be easy to combine a visit to Kermit with two weeks hunting in the interior. But the trip grew rapidly. Roosevelt was acquainted with an explorer, who also happened to be a priest, named John Augustine Zahm, and Zahm had been urging him for years to visit South America with him. At the same time, Roosevelt was receiving invitations to speak in South America for substantial fees. Roosevelt, to be sure, was always being asked to speak, but he was minded to go. He could arrange a series of talks in Brazil and Argentina, which had also invited him south, and then in Chile, which joined the tour. After the speaking tour he and Kermit could hunt.*

*Then Frank Chapman at the American Museum of Natural History in New York decided Roosevelt's trip would be a nice opportunity to send a couple of naturalists south and collect specimens. Roosevelt was himself a naturalist, after all, and the publicity could only do the museum good. By the time he finally arrived in Brazil the whole thing had ballooned into a rather elaborate journey. More air was pumped into it there. The Brazilian government asked Roosevelt on arrival if he would mind if they sent a Brazilian army officer with him. His name was Col. Candido Mariano de Salva Rondon. He was one of Brazil's best-known explorers. He wanted Roosevelt to take him along, and he wanted to explore in a totally unknown portion of western Matto Grosso (which means "great wilderness" in Portuguese). Rondon had discovered a river there, and no one knew where it ran. Its name: Rio da Duvida. River of Doubt. Would Roosevelt lead such an expedition? Roosevelt would.*

*It proved to be the most dangerous and difficult expedition Roosevelt was ever on. The book he wrote about his experiences is called* Through the Brazilian Wilderness, *and we have chosen the heart of it for this anthology, the two chapters which describe the running of the Rio da Duvida, Chapters VIII and IX, "The River of Doubt" and "Down an Unknown River." One man drowned on the expedition, as the reader will see, and another man was murdered. What Roosevelt does not mention is how badly he fared during the trip. His left leg, injured years before in an accident, was infected during the trip by the bites of sandflies, causing a disease known as cutaneous leishmaniasis, which manifests itself in fever, anemia, and weight loss. Roosevelt lost 55 pounds on the trip. An abscess on the leg had to be drained. The fever was so bad that*

Roosevelt spent a night in delirium, reciting the opening line of Samuel Taylor Coleridge's poem "Kubla Khan" again and again and again. He was lucky to escape alive. But the expedition was a success. The Rio da Duvida is a major tributary to the Amazon. It is as long as the Rhine. The Brazilian government, in his honor and over his objections, renamed it the Rio Teodoro. This time the naturalists brought back some 1500 specimens, most of them birds. Many of them were new to science.

# The River of Doubt

*Through the Brazilian Wilderness*

On February 27, 1914, shortly after midday, we started down the River of Doubt into the unknown. We were quite uncertain whether after a week we should find ourselves in the Gy-Paraná, or after six weeks in the Madeira, or after three months we knew not where. That was why the river was rightly christened the Dúvida.

We had been camped close to the river, where the trail that follows the telegraph-line crosses it by a rough bridge. As our laden dugouts swung into the stream, Amilcar and Miller and all the others of the Gy-Paraná party were on the banks and the bridge to wave farewell and wish us good-by and good luck. It was the height of the rainy season, and the swollen torrent was swift and brown. Our camp was at about 12° 1′ latitude south and 60° 15′ longitude west of Greenwich. Our general course was to be northward toward the equator, by waterway through the vast forest.

We had seven canoes, all of them dugouts. One was small, one was cranky, and two were old, waterlogged, and leaky. The other three were good. The two old canoes were lashed together, and the cranky one was lashed to one of the others. Kermit with two paddlers went in the smallest of the good canoes; Colonel Rondon and Lyra with three other paddlers in the next largest; and the doctor, Cherrie, and I in the largest with three paddlers. The remaining eight camaradas—there were sixteen in all—were equally divided between our two pairs of lashed canoes. Although our personal baggage was cut down to the limit necessary for health and efficiency, yet on such a trip as ours, where scientific work has to be done and where food for twenty-two men for an unknown period of time has to be carried, it is impossible not to take a good deal of stuff; and the seven dugouts were too heavily laden.

The paddlers were a strapping set. They were expert river-men and men of the forest, skilled veterans in wilderness work. They were lithe as panthers and brawny as bears. They swam like water-dogs. They were equally at home with pole and paddle, with axe and machete; and one was a good cook and others were good men around camp. They looked like pirates in the pictures of Howard Pyle or Maxfield Parrish; one or two of them were pirates, and one worse than a pirate; but most of them were hard-working, willing, and cheerful. They were white,— or, rather, the olive of southern Europe,—black, copper-colored, and of all inter- mediate shades. In my canoe Luiz the steersman, the headman, was a Matto Grosso negro; Julio the bowsman was from Bahia and of pure Portuguese blood; and the third man, Antonio, was a Parecís Indian.

The actual surveying of the river was done by Colonel Rondon and Lyra, with Kermit as their assistant. Kermit went first in his little canoe with the sighting- rod, on which two disks, one red and one white, were placed a metre apart. He selected a place which commanded as long vistas as possible up-stream and down, and which therefore might be at the angle of a bend; landed; cut away the branches which obstructed the view; and set up the sighting-pole—incidentally encountering maribundi wasps and swarms of biting and singing ants. Lyra, from his station up-stream, with his telemetre established the distance, while Colonel Rondon with the compass took the direction, and made the records. Then they moved on to the point Kermit had left, and Kermit established a new point within their sight. The first half-day's work was slow. The general course of the stream was a trifle east of north, but at short intervals it bent and curved liter- ally toward every point of the compass. Kermit landed nearly a hundred times, and we made but nine and a third kilometres.

My canoe ran ahead of the surveying canoes. The height of the water made the going easy, for most of the snags and fallen trees were well beneath the surface. Now and then, however, the swift water hurried us toward ripples that marked ugly spikes of sunken timber, or toward uprooted trees that stretched almost across the stream. Then the muscles stood out on the backs and arms of the paddlers as stroke on stroke they urged us away from and past the obstacle. If the leaning or fallen trees were the thorny, slender-stemmed boritana palms, which love the wet, they were often, although plunged beneath the river, in full and vigorous growth, their stems curving upward, and their frond-crowned tops shaken by the rushing water. It was interesting work, for no civilized man, no white man, had ever gone down or up this river or seen the country through which we were passing. The lofty and matted forest rose like a green wall on either hand. The trees were stately and beautiful. The looped and twisted vines hung from them like great ropes. Masses of epiphytes grew both on the dead trees and the living; some had huge leaves like elephants' ears. Now and then fragrant scents were blown to us from flowers on the banks. There were not many birds, and for the most part the forest was silent; rarely we heard strange calls from the depths of the woods, or saw a cormorant or ibis.

My canoe ran only a couple of hours. Then we halted to wait for the others. After a couple of hours more, as the surveyors had not turned up, we landed and made camp at a spot where the bank rose sharply for a hundred yards to a level stretch of ground. Our canoes were moored to trees. The axemen cleared a space for the tents; they were pitched, the baggage was brought up, and fires were kindled. The woods were almost soundless. Through them ran old tapir trails, but there was no fresh sign. Before nightfall the surveyors arrived. There were a few piums and gnats, and a few mosquitoes after dark, but not enough to make us uncomfortable. The small stingless bees, of slightly aromatic odor, swarmed while daylight lasted and crawled over our faces and hands; they were such tame, harmless little things that when they tickled too much I always tried to brush them away without hurting them. But they became a great nuisance after a while. It had been raining at intervals, and the weather was overcast; but after the sun went down the sky cleared. The stars were brilliant overhead, and the new moon hung in the west. It was a pleasant night, the air almost cool, and we slept soundly.

Next morning the two surveying canoes left immediately after breakfast. An hour later the two pairs of lashed canoes pushed off. I kept our canoe to let Cherrie collect, for in the early hours we could hear a number of birds in the woods near by. The most interesting birds he shot were a cotinga, brilliant turquoise-blue with a magenta-purple throat, and a big woodpecker, black above and cinnamon below with an entirely red head and neck. It was almost noon before we started. We saw a few more birds; there were fresh tapir and paca tracks at one point where we landed; once we heard howler monkeys from the depth of the forest, and once we saw a big otter in midstream. As we drifted and paddled down the swirling brown current, through the vivid rain-drenched green of the tropic forest, the trees leaned over the river from both banks. When those that had fallen in the river at some narrow point were very tall, or where it happened that two fell opposite each other, they formed barriers which the men in the leading canoes cleared with their axes. There were many palms, both the burity with its stiff fronds like enormous fans, and a handsome species of bacaba, with very long, gracefully curving fronds. In places the palms stood close together, towering and slender, their stems a stately colonnade, their fronds an arched fretwork against the sky. Butterflies of many hues fluttered over the river. The day was overcast, with showers of rain. When the sun broke through rifts in the clouds, his shafts turned the forest to gold.

In mid-afternoon we came to the mouth of a big and swift affluent entering from the right. It was undoubtedly the Bandeira, which we had crossed well toward its head, some ten days before, on our road to Bonofacio. The Nhambiquaras had then told Colonel Rondon that it flowed into the Dúvida. After its junction, with the added volume of water, the river widened without losing its depth. It was so high that it had overflowed and stood among the trees on the lower levels. Only the higher stretches were dry. On the sheer banks where we landed we had to push the canoes for yards or rods through the branches of the submerged trees, hacking and hewing. There were occasional bays and ox-bows from which the current had shifted. In these the coarse marsh grass grew tall.

This evening we made camp on a flat of dry ground, densely wooded, of course, directly on the edge of the river and five feet above it. It was fine to see the speed and sinewy ease with which the choppers cleared an open space for the tents. Next morning, when we bathed before sunrise, we dived into deep water right from the shore, and from the moored canoes. This second day we made sixteen and a half kilometres along the course of the river, and nine kilometres in a straight line almost due north.

The following day, March 1, there was much rain—sometimes showers, sometimes vertical sheets of water. Our course was somewhat west of north and we made twenty and a half kilometres. We passed signs of Indian habitation. There were abandoned palm-leaf shelters on both banks. On the left bank we came to two or three old Indian fields, grown up with coarse fern and studded with the burned skeletons of trees. At the mouth of a brook which entered from the right some sticks stood in the water, marking the site of an old fish-trap. At one point we found the tough vine hand-rail of an Indian bridge running right across the river, a couple of feet above it. Evidently the bridge had been built at low water. Three stout poles had been driven into the stream-bed in a line at right angles to the current. The bridge had consisted of poles fastened to these supports, leading between them and from the support at each end to the banks. The rope of tough vines had been stretched as a hand-rail, necessary with such precarious footing. The rise of the river had swept away the bridge, but the props and the rope hand-rail remained. In the afternoon, from the boat, Cherrie shot a large dark-gray monkey with a prehensile tail. It was very good eating.

We camped on a dry level space, but a few feet above, and close beside, the river—so that our swimming-bath was handy. The trees were cleared and camp was made with orderly hurry. One of the men almost stepped on a poisonous coral-snake, which would have been a serious thing, as his feet were bare. But I had on stout shoes, and the fangs of these serpents—unlike those of the pit-vipers—are too short to penetrate good leather. I promptly put my foot on him, and he bit my shoe with harmless venom. It has been said that the brilliant hues of the coral-snake when in its native haunts really confer on it a concealing coloration. In the dark and tangled woods, and to an only less extent in the ordinary varied landscape, anything motionless, especially if partially hidden, easily eludes the eye. But against the dark-brown mould of the forest floor on which we found this coral-snake its bright and varied coloration was distinctly revealing; infinitely more so than the duller mottling of the jararaca and other dangerous snakes of the genus lachecis. In the same place, however, we found a striking example of genuine protective or mimetic coloration and shape. A rather large insect larva—at least we judged it to be a larval form, but we were none of us entomologists—bore a resemblance to a partially curled dry leaf which was fairly startling. The tail exactly resembled the stem or continuation of the midrib of the dead leaf. The flattened body was curled up at the sides, and veined and colored precisely like the leaf. The head, colored like the leaf, projected in front.

We were still in the Brazilian highlands. The forest did not teem with life. It was generally rather silent; we did not hear such a chorus of birds and mammals as we had occasionally heard even on our overland journey, when more than once we had been awakened at dawn by the howling, screaming, yelping, and chattering of monkeys, toucans, macaws, parrots, and parakeets. There were, however, from time to time, queer sounds from the forest, and after nightfall different kinds of frogs and insects uttered strange cries and calls. In volume and frequency these seemed to increase until midnight. Then they died away and before dawn everything was silent.

At this camp the carregadores ants completely devoured the doctor's undershirt, and ate holes in his mosquito-net; and they also ate the strap of Lyra's gun-case. The little stingless bees, of many kinds, swarmed in such multitudes, and were so persevering, that we had to wear our head-nets when we wrote or skinned specimens.

The following day was almost without rain. It was delightful to drift and paddle slowly down the beautiful tropical river. Until mid-afternoon the current was not very fast, and the broad, deep, placid stream bent and curved in every direction, although the general course was northwest. The country was flat, and more of the land was under than above water. Continually we found ourselves travelling between stretches of marshy forest where for miles the water stood or ran among the trees. Once we passed a hillock. We saw brilliantly colored parakeets and trogons. At last the slow current quickened. Faster it went, and faster, until it began to run like a mill-race, and we heard the roar of rapids ahead. We pulled to the right bank, moored the canoes, and while most of the men pitched camp two or three of them accompanied us to examine the rapids. We had made twenty kilometres.

We soon found that the rapids were a serious obstacle. There were many curls, and one or two regular falls, perhaps six feet high. It would have been impossible to run them, and they stretched for nearly a mile. The carry, however, which led through woods and over rocks in a nearly straight line, was somewhat shorter. It was not an easy portage over which to carry heavy loads and drag heavy dugout canoes. At the point where the descent was steepest there were great naked flat of friable sandstone and conglomerate. Over parts of these, where there was a surface of fine sand, there was a growth of coarse grass. Other parts were bare and had been worn by the weather into fantastic shapes—one projection looked like an old-fashioned beaver hat upside down. In this place, where the naked flats of rock showed the projection of the ledge through which the river had cut its course, the torrent rushed down a deep, sheer-sided, and extremely narrow channel. At one point it was less than two yards across, and for quite a distance not more than five or six yards. Yet only a mile or two above the rapids the deep, placid river was at least a hundred yards wide. It seemed extraordinary, almost impossible, that so broad a river could in so short a space of time contract its dimensions to the width of the strangled channel through which it now poured its entire volume.

This has for long been a station where the Nhambiquaras at intervals built their ephemeral villages and tilled the soil with the rude and destructive cultivation of savages. There were several abandoned old fields, where the dense growth of rank fern hid the tangle of burnt and fallen logs. Nor had the Nhambiquaras been long absent. In one trail we found what gypsies would have called a "pateran," a couple of branches arranged crosswise, eight leaves to a branch; it had some special significance, belonging to that class of signals, each with some peculiar and often complicated meaning, which are commonly used by many wild peoples. The Indians had thrown a simple bridge, consisting of four long poles, without a hand-rail, across one of the narrowest parts of the rock gorge through which the river foamed in its rapid descent. This sub-tribe of Indians was called the Navaïté; we named the rapids after them, Navaïté Rapids. By observation Lyra found them to be (in close approximation to) latitude 11° 44´ south and longitude 60° 18´ west from Greenwich.

We spent March 3 and 4 and the morning of the 5th in portaging around the rapids. The first night we camped in the forest beside the spot where we had halted. Next morning we moved the baggage to the foot of the rapids, where we intended to launch the canoes, and pitched our tents on the open sandstone flat. It rained heavily. The little bees were in such swarms as to be a nuisance. Many small stinging bees were with them, which stung badly. We were bitten by huge horse-flies, the size of bumblebees. More serious annoyance was caused by the pium and boroshuda flies during the hours of daylight, and by the polvora, the sand-flies, after dark. There were a few mosquitoes. The boroshudas were the worst pests; they brought the blood at once, and left marks that lasted for weeks. I did my writing in head-net and gauntlets. Fortunately we had with us several bottles of "fly dope" —so named on the label—put up, with the rest of our medicine, by Doctor Alexander Lambert; he had tested it in the north woods and found it excellent. I had never before been forced to use such an ointment, and had been reluctant to take it with me; but now I was glad enough to have it, and we all of us found it exceedingly useful. I would never again go into mosquito or sand-fly country without it. The effect of an application wears off after half an hour or so, and under many conditions, as when one is perspiring freely, it is of no use; but there are times when minute mosquitoes and gnats get through head-nets and under mosquito-bars, and when the ointment occasionally renewed may permit one to get sleep or rest which would otherwise be impossible of attainment. The termites got into our tent on the sand-flat, ate holes in Cherrie's mosquito-net and poncho, and were starting to work at our duffel-bags, when we discovered them.

Packing the loads across was simple. Dragging the heavy dugouts was labor. The biggest of the two water-logged ones was the heaviest. Lyra and Kermit did the job. All the men were employed at it except the cook, and one man who was down with fever. A road was chopped through the forest and a couple of hundred stout six-foot poles, or small logs, were cut as rollers and placed about two yards apart. With block and tackle the seven dugouts were hoisted out of the river up the steep banks, and up the rise of ground until the level was reached. Then the men harnessed themselves two by two on the drag-rope, while one of their number pried behind with a lever, and the canoe, bumping and sliding, was twitched through the woods. Over the sandstone flats there were some ugly ledges, but on the whole the course was down-hill and relatively easy. Looking at the way the work was done, at the good-will, the endurance, and the bull-like strength of the camaradas, and at the intelligence and the unwearied efforts of their commanders, one could but wonder at the ignorance of those who do not realize the energy and the power that are so often possessed by, and that may be so readily developed in, the men of the tropics. Another subject of perpetual wonder is the attitude of certain men who stay at home, and still more the attitude of certain men who travel under easy conditions, and who belittle the achievements of the real explorers of, the real adventures in, the great wilderness. The impostors and romancers among explorers or would-be explorers and wilderness wanderers have been unusually prominent in connection with South America (although the conspicuous ones are not South Americans, by the way); and these are fit subjects for condemnation and derision. But the work of the genuine explorer and wilderness wanderer is fraught with fatigue, hardship, and danger. Many of the men of little knowledge talk glibly of portaging as if it were simple and easy. A portage over rough and unknown ground is always a work of difficulty and of some risk to the canoe; and in the untrodden, or even in the unfrequented, wilderness risk to the canoe is a serious matter. This particular portage at Navaïté Rapids was far from being unusually difficult; yet it not only cost two and a half days of severe and incessant labor, but it cost something in damage to the canoes. One in particular, the one in which I had been journeying, was split in a manner which caused us serious uneasiness as to how long, even after being patched, it would last. Where the canoes were launched, the bank was sheer, and one of the water-logged canoes filled and went to the bottom; and there was more work in raising it.

We were still wholly unable to tell where we were going or what lay ahead of us. Round the camp-fire, after supper, we held endless discussions and hazarded all kinds of guesses on both subjects. The river might bend sharply to the west and enter the Gy-Paraná high up or low down, or go north to the Madeira, or bend eastward and enter the Tapajos, or fall into the Canumá and finally through one of its mouths enter the Amazon direct. Lyra inclined to the first, and Colonel Rondon to the second, of these propositions. We did not know whether we had one hundred or eight hundred kilometres to go, whether the stream would be fairly smooth or whether we would encounter waterfalls, or rapids, or even some big marsh or lake. We could not tell whether or not we would meet hostile Indians, although no one of us ever went ten yards from camp without his rifle.

We had no idea how much time the trip would take. We had entered a land of unknown possibilities.

We started down-stream again early in the afternoon of March 5. Our hands and faces were swollen from the bites and stings of the insect pests at the sand-flat camp, and it was a pleasure once more to be in the middle of the river, where they did not come, in any numbers, while we were in motion. The current was swift, but the river was so deep that there were no serious obstructions. Twice we went down over slight riffles, which in the dry season were doubtless rapids; and once we struck a spot where many whirlpools marked the presence underneath of bowlders which would have been above water had not the river been so swollen by the rains. The distance we covered in a day going down-stream would have taken us a week if we had been going up. The course wound hither and thither, sometimes in sigmoid curves; but the general direction was east of north. As usual, it was very beautiful; and we never could tell what might appear around any curve. In the forest that rose on either hand were tall rubber-trees. The surveying canoes, as usual, went first, while I shepherded the two pairs of lashed cargo canoes. I kept them always between me and the surveying canoes—ahead of me until I passed the surveying canoes, then behind me until, after an hour or so, I had chosen a place to camp. There was so much overflowed ground that it took us some little time this afternoon before we found a flat place high enough to be dry. Just before reaching camp Cherrie shot a jacu, a handsome bird somewhat akin to, but much smaller than, a turkey; after Cherrie had taken its skin, its body made an excellent canja. We saw parties of monkeys; and the false bell-birds uttered their ringing whistles in the dense timber around our tents. The giant ants, an inch and a quarter long, were rather too plentiful around this camp; one stung Kermit; it was almost like the sting of a small scorpion, and pained severely for a couple of hours. This half-day we made twelve kilometres.

On the following day we made nineteen kilometres, the river twisting in every direction, but in its general course running a little west of north. Once we stopped at a bee-tree, to get honey. The tree was a towering giant, of the kind called milk-tree, because a thick milky juice runs freely from any cut. Our camaradas eagerly drank the white fluid that flowed from the wounds made by their axes. I tried it. The taste was not unpleasant, but it left a sticky feeling in the mouth. The helmsman of my boat, Luiz, a powerful negro, chopped into the tree, balancing himself with springy ease on a slight scaffolding. The honey was in a hollow, and had been made by medium-sized stingless bees. At the mouth of the hollow they had built a curious entrance of their own, in the shape of a spout of wax about a foot long. At the opening the walls of the spout showed the wax formation, but elsewhere it had become in color and texture indistinguishable from the bark of the tree. The honey was delicious, sweet and yet with a tart flavor. The comb differed much from that of our honey-bees. The honey-cells were very large, and the brood-cells, which were small, were in a single instead of a double row. By this tree I came across an example of genuine concealing coloration. A huge tree-toad, the size of a bullfrog, was seated upright—not squatted flat—on a big rotten limb. It was absolutely motionless; the yellow brown of its back, and its dark sides, exactly harmonized in color with the light and dark patches on the log; the color was as concealing, here in its natural surroundings, as is the color of our common wood-frog among the dead leaves of our woods. When I stirred it up it jumped to a small twig, catching hold with the disks of its finger-tips, and balancing itself with unexpected ease for so big a creature, and then hopped to the ground and again stood motionless. Evidently it trusted for safety to escaping observation. We saw some monkeys and fresh tapir sign, and Kermit shot a jacu for the pot.

At about three o'clock I was in the lead, when the current began to run more quickly. We passed over one or two decided ripples, and then heard the roar of rapids ahead, while the stream began to race. We drove the canoe into the bank, and then went down a tapir trail, which led alongside the river, to reconnoitre. A quarter of a mile's walk showed us that there were big rapids, down which the canoes could not go; and we returned to the landing. All the canoes had gathered there, and Rondon, Lyra, and Kermit started down-stream to explore. They returned in an hour, with the information that the rapids continued for a long distance, with falls and steep pitches of broken water, and that the portage would take several days. We made camp just above the rapids. Ants swarmed, and some of them bit savagely. Our men, in clearing away the forest for our tents, left several very tall and slender accashy palms; the bole of this palm is as straight as an arrow and is crowned with delicate, gracefully curved fronds. We had come along the course of the river almost exactly a hundred kilometres; it had twisted so that we were only about fifty-five kilometres north of our starting-point. The rock was porphyritic.

The 7th, 8th, and 9th we spent in carrying the loads and dragging and floating the dugouts past the series of rapids at whose head we had stopped.

The first day we shifted camp a kilometre and a half to the foot of this series of rapids. This was a charming and picturesque camp. It was at the edge of the river, where there was a little, shallow bay with a beach of firm sand. In the water, at the middle point of the beach, stood a group of three burity palms, their great trunks rising like columns. Round the clearing in which our tents stood were several very big trees; two of them were rubber-trees. Kermit went downstream five or six kilometres, and returned, having shot a jacu and found that at the point which he had reached there was another rapids, almost a fall, which would necessitate our again dragging the canoes over a portage. Antonio, the Parecís, shot a big monkey; of this I was glad because portaging is hard work, and the men appreciated the meat. So far Cherrie had collected sixty birds on the Dúvida, all of them new to the collection, and some probably new to science. We saw the fresh sign of paca, agouti, and the small peccary, and Kermit with the dogs roused a tapir, which crossed the river right through the rapids; but no one got a shot at it.

Except at one or perhaps two points a very big dugout, lightly loaded, could probably run all these rapids. But even in such a canoe it would be silly to make the attempt on an exploring expedition, where the loss of a canoe or of its contents means disaster; and moreover such a canoe could not be taken, for it would be impossible to drag it over the portages on the occasions when the portages became inevitable. Our canoes would not have lived half a minute in the wild water.

On the second day the canoes and loads were brought down to the foot of the first rapids. Lyra cleared the path and laid the logs for rollers, while Kermit dragged the dugouts up the bank from the water with block and tackle, with strain of rope and muscle. Then they joined forces, as over the uneven ground it needed the united strength of all their men to get the heavy dugouts along. Meanwhile the colonel with one attendant measured the distance, and then went on a long hunt, but saw no game. I strolled down beside the river for a couple of miles, but also saw nothing. In the dense tropical forest of the Amazonian basin hunting is very difficult, especially for men who are trying to pass through the country as rapidly as possible. On such a trip as ours getting game is largely a matter of chance.

On the following day Lyra and Kermit brought down the canoes and loads, with hard labor, to the little beach by the three palms where our tents were pitched. Many pacovas grew round about. The men used their immense leaves, some of which were twelve feet long and two and a half feet broad, to roof the flimsy shelters under which they hung their hammocks. I went into the woods, but in the tangle of vegetation it would have been a mere hazard had I seen any big animal. Generally the woods were silent and empty. Now and then little troops of birds of many kinds passed—wood-hewers, ant-thrushes, tanagers, flycatchers; as in the spring and fall similar troops of warblers, chickadees, and nuthatches pass through our northern woods. On the rocks and on the great trees by the river grew beautiful white and lilac orchids—the sobralia, of sweet and delicate fragrance. For the moment my own books seemed a trifle heavy, and perhaps I would have found the day tedious if Kermit had not lent me the Oxford Book of French Verse. Eustache Deschamp, Joachim du Bellay, Ronsard, the delightful La Fontaine, the delightful but appalling Villon, Victor Hugo's "Guitare," Madame Desbordes-Valmore's lines on the little girl and her pillow, as dear little verses about a child as ever were written—these and many others comforted me much, as I read them in head-net and gauntlets, sitting on a log by an unknown river in the Amazonian forest.

On the 10th we again embarked and made a kilometre and a half, spending most of the time in getting past two more rapids. Near the first of these we saw a small cayman, a jacaré-tinga. At each set of rapids the canoes were unloaded and the loads borne past on the shoulders of the camaradas; three of the canoes were paddled down by a couple of naked paddlers apiece; and the two sets of double canoes were let down by ropes, one of one couple being swamped but rescued and brought safely to shore on each occasion. One of the men was upset while working in the swift water, and his face was cut against the stones. Lyra and Kermit did the actual work with the camaradas. Kermit, dressed substantially like the camaradas themselves, worked in the water, and, as the overhanging branches were thronged with crowds of biting and stinging ants, he was marked and blistered over his whole body. Indeed, we all suffered more or less from these ants; while the swarms of biting flies grew constantly more numerous. The termites ate holes in my helmet and also in the cover of my cot. Every one else had a hammock. At this camp we had come down the river about 102 kilometres, according to the surveying records, and in height had descended nearly 100 metres, as shown by the aneroid—although the figure in this case is only an approximation, as an aneroid cannot be depended on for absolute accuracy of results.

Next morning we found that during the night we had met with a serious misfortune. We had halted at the foot of the rapids. The canoes were moored to trees on the bank, at the tail of the broken water. The two old canoes, although one of them was our biggest cargo-carrier, were water-logged and heavy, and one of them was leaking. In the night the river rose. The leaky canoe, which at best was too low in the water, must have gradually filled from the wash of the waves. It sank, dragging down the other; they began to roll, bursting their moorings; and in the morning they had disappeared. A canoe was launched to look for them; but, rolling over the bowlders on the rocky bottom, they had at once been riven asunder, and the big fragments that were soon found, floating in eddies, or along the shore, showed that it was useless to look farther. We called these rapids Broken Canoe Rapids.

It was not pleasant to have to stop for some days; thanks to the rapids, we had made slow progress, and with our necessarily limited supply of food, and no knowledge whatever of what was ahead of us, it was important to make good time. But there was no alternative. We had to build either one big canoe or two small ones. It was raining heavily as the men started to explore in different directions for good canoe trees. Three—which ultimately proved not very good for the purpose—were found close to camp; splendid-looking trees, one of them five feet in diameter three feet from the ground. The axemen immediately attacked this one under the superintendence of Colonel Rondon. Lyra and Kermit started in opposite directions to hunt. Lyra killed a jacu for us, and Kermit killed two monkeys for the men. Toward nightfall it cleared. The moon was nearly full, and the foaming river gleamed like silver.

Our men were "regional volunteers," that is, they had enlisted in the service of the Telegraphic Commission especially to do this wilderness work, and were highly paid, as was fitting, in view of the toil, hardship, and hazard to life and health. Two of them had been with Colonel Rondon during his eight months' exploration in 1909, at which time his men were regulars, from his own battalion of engineers. His four aides during the closing months of this trip were Lieutenants Lyra, Amarante, Alencarliense, and Pyrineus. The naturalist Miranda Ribeiro also accompanied him. This was the year when, marching on foot through an absolutely unknown wilderness, the colonel and his party finally reached the Gy-Paraná, which on the maps was then (and on most maps is now) placed in an utterly wrong course, and over a degree out of its real position. When they reached the affluents of the Gy-Paraná a third of the members of the party were so weak with fever that they could hardly crawl. They had no baggage. Their clothes were in tatters, and some of the men were almost naked. For months they had had no food except what little game they shot, and especially the wild fruits and nuts; if it had not been for the great abundance of the Brazil-nuts they would all have died. At the first big stream they encountered they built a canoe, and Alencarliense took command of it and descended to map the course of the river. With him went Ribeiro, the doctor Tanageira, who could no longer walk on account of the ulceration of one foot, three men whom the fever had rendered unable longer to walk, and six men who were as yet well enough to handle the canoe. By the time the remainder of the party came to the next navigable river eleven more fever-stricken men had nearly reached the end of their tether. Here they ran across a poor devil who had for four months been lost in the forest and was dying of slow starvation. He had eaten nothing but Brazil-nuts and the grubs of insects. He could no longer walk, but could sit erect and totter feebly for a few feet. Another canoe was built, and in it Pyrineus started down-stream with the eleven fever patients and the starving wanderer. Colonel Rondon kept up the morale of his men by still carrying out the forms of military discipline. The ragged bugler had his bugle. Lieutenant Pyrineus had lost every particle of his clothing except a hat and a pair of drawers. The half-naked lieutenant drew up his eleven fever patients in line; the bugle sounded; every one came to attention; and the haggard colonel read out the orders of the day. Then the dugout with its load of sick men started down-stream, and Rondon, Lyra, Amarante, and the twelve remaining men resumed their weary march. When a fortnight later they finally struck a camp of rubber-gatherers three of the men were literally and entirely naked. Meanwhile Amilcar had ascended the Jacyparaná a month or two previously with provisions to meet them; for at that time the maps incorrectly treated this river as larger, instead of smaller, than the Gy-Paraná, which they were in fact descending; and Colonel Rondon had supposed that they were going down the former stream. Amilcar returned after himself suffering much hardship and danger. The different parties finally met at the mouth of the Gy-Paraná, where it enters the Madeira. The lost man whom they had found seemed on the road to recovery, and they left him at a ranch, on the Madeira, where he could be cared for; yet after they had left him they heard that he had died.

On the 12th the men were still hard at work hollowing out the hard wood of the big tree, with axe and adze, while watch and ward were kept over them to see that the idlers did not shirk at the expense of the industrious. Kermit and Lyra again hunted; the former shot a curassow, which was welcome, as we were endeavoring in all ways to economize our food supply. We were using the tops of palms also. I spent the day hunting in the woods, for the most part by the river, but saw nothing. In the season of the rains game is away from the river and fish are scarce and turtles absent. Yet it was pleasant to be in the great silent forest. Here and there grew immense trees, and on some of them mighty buttresses sprang from the base. The lianas and vines were of every size and shape. Some were twisted and some were not. Some came down straight and slender from branches a hundred feet above. Others curved like long serpents around the trunks. Others were like knotted cables. In the shadow there was little noise. The wind rarely moved the hot, humid air. There were few flowers or birds. Insects were altogether too abundant, and even when travelling slowly it was impossible always to avoid them—not to speak of our constant companions the bees, mosquitoes, and especially the boroshudas or bloodsucking flies. Now while bursting through a tangle I disturbed a nest of wasps, whose resentment was active; now I heedlessly stepped among the outliers of a small party of the carnivorous foraging ants; now, grasping a branch as I stumbled, I shook down a shower of fireants; and among all these my attention was particularly arrested by the bite of one of the giant ants, which stung like a hornet, so that I felt it for three hours. The camaradas generally went barefoot or only wore sandals; and their ankles and feet were swollen and inflamed from the bites of the boroshudas and ants, some being actually incapacitated from work. All of us suffered more or less, our faces and hands swelling slightly from the boroshuda bites; and in spite of our clothes we were bitten all over our bodies, chiefly by ants and the small forest ticks. Because of the rain and the heat our clothes were usually wet when we took them off at night, and just as wet when we put them on again in the morning.

All day on the 13th the men worked at the canoe, making good progress. In rolling and shifting the huge , heavy tree-trunk every one had to assist now and then. The work continued until ten in the evening, as the weather was clear. After nightfall some of the men held candles and the others plied axe or adze, standing within or beside the great, half-hollowed logs, while the flicker of the lights showed the tropic forest rising in the darkness round about. The night air was hot and still and heavy with moisture. The men were stripped to the waist. Olive and copper and ebony, their skins glistened as if oiled, and rippled with the ceaseless play of the thews beneath.

On the morning of the 14th the work was resumed in a torrential tropic downpour. The canoe was finished, dragged down to the water, and launched soon after midday, and another hour or so saw us under way. The descent was marked, and the swollen river raced along. Several times we passed great whirlpools, sometimes shifting, sometimes steady. Half a dozen times we ran over rapids, and, although they were not high enough to have been obstacles to loaded Canadian canoes, two of them were serious to us. Our heavily laden, clumsy dugouts were sunk to within three or four inches of the surface of the river, and, although they were buoyed on each side with bundles of burity-palm branch-stems, they shipped a great deal of water in the rapids. The two biggest rapids we only just made, and after each we had hastily to push ashore in order to bail. In one set of big ripples or waves my canoe was nearly swamped. In a wilderness, where what is ahead is absolutely unknown, alike in terms of time, space, and method—for we had no idea where we would come out, how we would get out, or when we would get out—it is of vital consequence not to lose one's outfit, especially the provisions; and yet it is of only less consequence to go as rapidly as possible lest all the provisions be exhausted and the final stages of the expedition be accomplished by men weakened from semi-starvation, and therefore ripe for disaster. On this occasion, of the two hazards, we felt it necessary to risk running the rapids; for our progress had been so very slow that unless we made up the time, it was probable that we would be short of food before we got where we could expect to procure any more except what little the country in the time of the rains and floods, might yield. We ran until after five, so that the work of pitching camp was finished in the dark. We had made nearly sixteen kilometres in a direction slightly east of north. This evening the air was fresh and cool.

The following morning, the 15th of March, we started in good season. For six kilometres we drifted and paddled down the swift river without incident. At times we saw lofty Brazil-nut trees rising above the rest of the forest on the banks; and back from the river these trees grow to enormous proportions, towering like giants. There were great rubber-trees also, their leaves always in sets of threes. Then the ground on either hand rose into bowlder-strewn, forest-clad hills and the roar of broken water announced that once more our course was checked by dangerous rapids. Round a bend we came on them; a wide descent of white water, with an island in the middle, at the upper edge. Here grave misfortune befell us, and graver misfortune was narrowly escaped.

Kermit, as usual, was leading in his canoe. It was the smallest and least seaworthy of all. He had in it little except a week's supply of our boxed provisions and a few tools; fortunately none of the food for the camaradas. His dog Trigueiro was with him. Besides himself, the crew consisted of two men: João, the helmsman, or pilot, as he is called in Brazil, and Simplicio, the bowsman. Both were negroes and exceptionally good men in every way. Kermit halted his canoe on the left bank, above the rapids, and waited for the colonel's canoe. Then the colonel and Lyra walked down the bank to see what was ahead. Kermit took his canoe across to the island to see whether the descent could be better accomplished on the other side. Having made his investigation, he ordered the men to return to the bank he had left, and the dugout was headed up-stream accordingly. Before they had gone a dozen yards, the paddlers digging their paddles with all their strength into the swift current, one of the shifting whirlpools of which I have spoken came down-stream, whirled them around, and swept them so close to the rapids that no human power could avoid going over them. As they were drifting into them broadside on, Kermit yelled to the steersman to turn her head, so as to take them in the only way that offered any chance whatever of safety. The water came aboard, wave after wave, as they raced down. They reached the bottom with the canoe upright, but so full as barely to float, and the paddlers urged her toward the shore. They had nearly reached the bank when another whirlpool or whirling eddy tore them away and hurried them back to midstream, where the dugout filled and turned over. João, seizing the rope, started to swim ashore; the rope was pulled from his hand, but he reached the bank. Poor Simplicio must have been pulled under at once, and his life beaten out on the bowlders beneath the racing torrent. He never rose again, nor did we ever recover his body. Kermit clutched his rifle, his favorite 405 Winchester with which he had done most of his hunting both in Africa and America, and climbed on the bottom of the upset boat. In a minute he was swept into the second series of rapids, and whirled away from the rolling boat, losing his rifle. The water beat his helmet down over his head and face and drove him beneath the surface; and when he rose at last he was almost drowned, his breath and strength almost spent. He was in swift but quiet water, and swam toward an overhanging branch. His jacket hindered him, but he knew he was too nearly gone to be able to get it off, and, thinking with the curious calm one feels when death is but a moment away, he realized that the utmost his failing strength could do was to reach the branch. He reached, and clutched it, and then almost lacked strength to haul himself out on the land. Good Trigueiro had faithfully swum alongside him through the rapids, and now himself scrambled ashore. It was a very narrow escape. Kermit was a great comfort and help to me on the trip; but the fear of some fatal accident befalling him was always a nightmare to me. He was to be married as soon as the trip was over; and it did not seem to me that I could bear to bring bad tidings to his betrothed and to his mother.

Simplicio was unmarried. Later we sent to his mother all the money that would have been his had he lived. The following morning we put on one side of the post erected to mark our camping-spot the following inscription, in Portuguese:

"IN THESE RAPIDS DIED POOR SIMPLICIO."

On an expedition such as ours death is one of the accidents that may at any time occur, and narrow escapes from death are too common to be felt as they would be felt elsewhere. One mourns sincerely, but mourning cannot interfere with labor. We immediately proceeded with the work of the portage. From the head to the tail of this series of rapids the distance was about six hundred yards. A path was cut along the bank, over which the loads were brought. The empty canoes ran the rapids without mishap, each with two skilled paddlers. One of the canoes almost ran into a swimming tapir at the head of the rapids; it went down the rapids, and then climbed out of the river. Kermit accompanied by João, went three or four miles down the river, looking for the body of Simplicio and for the sunk canoe. He found neither. But he found a box of provisions and a paddle, and salvaged both by swimming into midstream after them. He also found that a couple of kilometres below there was another stretch of rapids, and following them on the left-hand bank to the foot he found that they were worse than the ones we had just passed, and impassable for canoes on this left-hand side.

We camped at the foot of the rapids we had just passed. There were many small birds here, but it was extremely difficult to see or shoot them in the lofty tree tops, and to find them in the tangle beneath if they were shot. However, Cherrie got four species new to the collection. One was a tiny hummer, one of the species known as woodstars, with dainty but not brilliant plumage; its kind is never found except in the deep, dark woods, not coming out into the sunshine. Its crop was filled with ants; when shot it was feeding at a cluster of long red flowers. He also got a very handsome trogon and an exquisite little tanager, as brilliant as a cluster of jewels; its throat was lilac, its breast turquoise, its crown and forehead topaz, while above it was glossy purple-black, the lower part of the back ruby-red. This tanager was a female; I can hardly imagine that the male is more brilliantly colored. The fourth bird was a queer hawk of the genus *ibycter,* black, with a white belly, naked red cheeks and throat and red legs and feet. Its crop was filled with the seeds of fruits and a few insect remains; an extraordinary diet for a hawk.

The morning of the 16th was dark and gloomy. Through sheets of blinding rain we left our camp of misfortune for another camp where misfortune also awaited us. Less than half an hour took our dugouts to the head of the rapids below. As Kermit had already explored the left-hand side, Colonel Rondon and Lyra went down the right-hand side and found a channel which led round the worst part, so that they deemed it possible to let down the canoes by ropes from the bank. The distance to the foot of the rapids was about a kilometre. While the loads were being brought down the left bank, Luiz and Antonio Correa, our two best watermen, started to take a canoe down the right side, and Colonel Rondon walked ahead to see anything he could about the river. He was accompanied by one of our three dogs, Lobo. After walking about a kilometre he heard ahead a kind of howling noise, which he thought was made by spider-monkeys. He walked in the direction of the sound and Lobo ran ahead. In a minute he heard Lobo yell with pain, and then, still yelping, come toward him, while the creature that was howling also approached, evidently in pursuit. In a moment a second yell from Lobo, followed by silence, announced that he was dead; and the sound of the howling, when near, convinced Rondon that the dog had been killed by an Indian, doubtless with two arrows. Probably the Indian was howling to lure the spider-monkeys toward him. Rondon fired his rifle in the air, to warn off the Indian or Indians, who in all probability had never seen a civilized man, and certainly could not imagine that one was in the neighborhood. He then returned to the foot of the rapids, where the portage was still going on, and, in company with Lyra, Kermit, and Antonio Parecis, the Indian, walked back to where Lobo's body lay. Sure enough he found him, slain by two arrows. One arrow-head was in him, and near by was a strange stick used in the very primitive method of fishing of all these Indians. Antonio recognized its purpose. The Indians, who were apparently two or three in number, had fled. Some beads and trinkets were left on the spot to show that we were not angry and were friendly.

Meanwhile Cherrie stayed at the head and I at the foot of the portage as guards. Luiz and Antonio Correa brought down one canoe safely. The next was the new canoe, which was very large and heavy, being made of wood that would not float. In the rapids the rope broke, and the canoe was lost, Luiz being nearly drowned.

It was a very bad thing to lose the canoe, but it was even worse to lose the rope and pulleys. This meant that it would be physically impossible to hoist big canoes up even small hills or rocky hillocks, such as had been so frequent beside the many rapids we had encountered. It was not wise to spend the four days necessary to build new canoes where we were, in danger of attack from the Indians. Moreover, new rapids might be very near, in which case the new canoes would hamper us. Yet the four remaining canoes would not carry all the loads and all the men, no matter how we cut the loads down; and we intended to cut everything down at once. We had been gone eighteen days. We had used over a third of our food. We had gone only 125 kilometres, and it was probable that we had at least five times, perhaps six or seven times, this distance still to go. We had taken a fortnight to descend rapids amounting in the aggregate to less than seventy yards of fall; a very few yards of fall makes a dangerous rapid when the river is swollen and swift and there are obstructions. We had only one aneroid to determine our altitude, and therefore could make merely a loose approximation to it, but we probably had between two and three times this descent in the aggregate of rapids ahead of us. So far the country had offered little in the way of food except palm-tops. We had lost four canoes and one man. We were in the country of wild Indians, who shot well with their bows. It behooved us to go warily, but also to make all speed possible, if we were to avoid serious trouble.

The best plan seemed to be to march thirteen men down along the bank, while the remaining canoes, lashed two and two, floated down beside them. If after two or three days we found no bad rapids, and there seemed a reasonable chance of going some distance at decent speed, we could then build the new canoes—preferably two small ones, this time, instead of one big one. We left all the baggage we could. We were already down as far as comfort would permit; but we now struck off much of the comfort. Cherrie, Kermit, and I had been sleeping under a very light fly; and there was another small light tent for one person, kept for possible emergencies. The last was given to me for my cot, and all five of the others swung their hammocks under the big fly. This meant that we left two big and heavy tents behind. A box of surveying instruments was also abandoned. Each of us got his personal belongings down to one box or duffel-bag—although there was only a small diminution thus made; because we had so little that the only way to make a serious diminution was to restrict ourselves to the clothes on our backs.

The biting flies and ants were to us a source of discomfort and at times of what could fairly be called torment. But to the camaradas, most of whom went barefoot or only wore sandals—and they never did or would wear shoes—the effect was more serious. They wrapped their legs and feet in pieces of canvas or hide; and the feet of three of them became so swollen that they were crippled and could not walk any distance. The doctor, whose courage and cheerfulness never flagged, took excellent care of them. Thanks to him, there had been among them hitherto but one or two slight cases of fever. He administered to each man daily a half-gram—nearly eight grains—of quinine, and every third or fourth day a double dose.

The following morning Colonel Rondon, Lyra, Kermit, Cherrie, and nine of the camaradas started in single file down the bank, while the doctor and I went in the two double canoes, with six camaradas, three of them the invalids with swollen feet. We halted continually, as we went about three times as fast as the walkers; and we traced the course of the river. After forty minutes' actual going in the boats we came to some rapids; the unloaded canoes ran them without difficulty, while the loads were portaged. In an hour and a half we were again under way, but in ten minutes came to other rapids, where the river ran among islands, and there were several big curls. The clumsy, heavily laden dugouts, lashed in couples, were unwieldy and hard to handle. The rapids came just round a sharp bend, and we got caught in the upper part of the swift water and had to run the first set of rapids in consequence. We in the leading pair of dugouts were within an ace of coming to grief on some big bowlders against which we were swept by a cross current at the turn. All of us paddling hard—scraping and bumping—we got through by the skin of our teeth, and managed to make the bank and moor our dugouts. It was a narrow escape from grave disaster. The second pair of lashed dugouts profited by our experience, and made the run—with risk, but with less risk—and moored beside us. Then all the loads were taken out, and the empty canoes were run down through the least dangerous channels among the islands.

This was a long portage, and we camped at the foot of the rapids, having made nearly seven kilometres. Here a little river, a rapid stream of volume equal to the Dúvida at the point where we first embarked, joined from the west. Colonel Rondon and Kermit came to it first, and the former named it Rio Kermit. There was in it a waterfall about six or eight feet high, just above the junction. Here we found plenty of fish. Lyra caught two pacu, good-sized, deep-bodied fish. They were delicious eating. Antonio the Parecís said that these fish never came up heavy rapids in which there were falls they had to jump. We could only hope that he was correct, as in that case the rapids we would encounter in the future would rarely be so serious as to necessitate our dragging the heavy dugouts overland. Passing the rapids we had hitherto encountered had meant severe labor and some danger. But the event showed that he was mistaken. The worst rapids were ahead of us.

While our course as a whole had been almost due north, and sometimes east of north, yet where there were rapids the river had generally, although not always, turned westward. This seemed to indicate that to the east of us there was a low northward projection of the central plateau across which we had travelled on mule-back. This is the kind of projection that appears on the maps of this region as a sierra. Probably it sent low spurs to the west, and the farthest points of these spurs now and then caused rapids in our course (for the rapids generally came where there were hills) and for the moment deflected the river westward from its general down-hill trend to the north. There was no longer any question that the Dúvida was a big river, a river of real importance. It was not a minor affluent of some other affluent. But we were still wholly in the dark as to where it came out. It was still possible, although exceedingly improbable, that it entered the Gy-Paraná, as another river of substantially the same size, near its mouth. It was much more likely, but not probable, that it entered the Tapajos. It was probable, although far from certain, that it entered the Madeira low down, near its point of junction with the Amazon. In this event it was likely, although again far from certain, that its mouth would prove to be the Aripuanan. The Aripuanan does not appear on the maps as a river of any size; on a good standard map of South America which I had with me its name does not appear at all, although a dotted indication of a small river or creek at about the right place probably represents it. Nevertheless, from the report of one of his lieutenants who had examined its mouth, and from the stories of the rubber-gatherers, or seringuerros, Colonel Rondon had come to the conclusion that this was the largest affluent of the Madeira, with such a body of water that it must have a big drainage basin. He thought that the Dúvida was probably one of its head streams—although every existing map represented the lay of the land to be such as to render impossible the existence of such a river system and drainage basin. The rubber-gatherers reported that they had gone many days' journey up the river, to a point where there was a series of heavy rapids with above them the junction-point of two large rivers, one entering from the west. Beyond this they had difficulties because of the hostility of the Indians; and where the junction-point was no one could say. On the chance Colonel Rondon had directed one of his subordinate officers, Lieutenant Pyrineus, to try to meet us, with boats and provisions, by ascending the Aripuanan to the point of entry of its first big affluent. This was the course followed when Amilcar had been directed to try to meet the explorers who in 1909 came down the Gy-Paraná. At that time the effort was a failure, and the two parties never met; but we might have better luck, and in any event the chance was worth taking.

On the morning following our camping by the mouth of the Rio Kermit, Colonel Rondon took a good deal of pains in getting a big post set up at the entry of the smaller river into the Dúvida. Then he summoned me, and all the others, to attend the ceremony of its erection. We found the camaradas drawn up in line, and the colonel preparing to read aloud "the orders of the day." To the post was nailed a board with "Rio Kermit" on it; and the colonel read the orders reciting that by the direction of the Brazilian Government, and inasmuch as the unknown river was evidently a great river, he formally christened it the Rio Roosevelt. This was a complete surprise to me. Both Lauro Muller and Colonel Rondon had spoken to me on the subject, and I had urged, and Kermit had urged, as strongly as possible, that the name be kept as Rio da Dúvida. We felt that the "River of Doubt" was an unusually good name; and it is always well to keep a name of this character. But my kind friends insisted otherwise, and it would have been churlish of me to object longer. I was much touched by their action, and by the ceremony itself. At the conclusion of the reading Colonel Rondon led in cheers for the United States and then for me and for Kermit; and the camaradas cheered with a will. I proposed three cheers for Brazil and then for Colonel Rondon, and Lyra, and the doctor, and then for all the camaradas. Then Lyra said that everybody had been cheered except Cherrie; and so we all gave three cheers for Cherrie, and the meeting broke up in high good humor.

Immediately afterward the walkers set off on their march down-stream, looking for good canoe-trees. In a quarter of an hour we followed with the canoes. As often as we overtook them we halted until they had again gone a good distance ahead. They soon found fresh Indian sign, and actually heard the Indians; but the latter fled in panic. They came on a little Indian fishing village, just abandoned. The three low, oblong huts, of palm-leaves, had each an entrance for a man on all fours, but no other opening. They were dark inside, doubtless as a protection against the swarms of biting flies. On a pole in this village an axe, a knife, and some strings of red beads were left, with the hope that the Indians would return, find the gifts, and realize that we were friendly. We saw further Indian sign on both sides of the river.

After about two hours and a half we came on a little river entering from the east. It was broad but shallow, and at the point of entrance rushed down, green and white, over a sharply inclined sheet of rock. It was a lovely sight and we halted to admire it. Then on we went, until, when we had covered about eight kilometres, we came on a stretch of rapids. The canoes ran them with about a third of the loads, the other loads being carried on the men's shoulders. At the foot of the rapids we camped, as there were several good canoe-trees near, and we had decided to build two rather small canoes. After dark the stars came out; but in the deep forest the glory of the stars in the night of the sky, the serene radiance of the moon, the splender of sunrise and sunset, are never seen as they are seen on the vast open plains.

The following day, the 19th, the men began work on the canoes. The ill-fated big canoe had been made of wood so hard that it was difficult to work, and so heavy that the chips sank like lead in the water. But these trees were araputangas, with wood which was easier to work and which floated. Great buttresses, or flanges, jutted out from their trunks at the base, and they bore big hard nuts or fruits which stood erect at the ends of the branches. The first tree felled proved rotten, and moreover it was chopped so that it smashed a number of lesser trees into the kitchen, overthrowing everything, but not inflicting serious damage. Hard-working, willing, and tough though the camaradas were, they naturally did not have the skill of northern lumberjacks.

We hoped to finish the two canoes in three days. A space was cleared in the forest for our tents. Among the taller trees grew huge-leafed pacovas, or wild bananas. We bathed and swam in the river, although in it we caught piranhas. Carregadores ants swarmed all around our camp. As many of the nearest of their holes as we could we stopped with fire; but at night some of them got into our tents and ate things we could ill spare. In the early morning a column of foraging ants appeared, and we drove them back, also with fire. When the sky was not overcast the sun was very hot, and we spread out everything to dry. There were many wonderful butterflies round about, but only a few birds. Yet in the early morning and late afternoon there was some attractive bird music in the woods. The two best performers were our old friend the false bell-bird, with its series of ringing whistles, and a shy, attractive ant-thrush. The latter walked much on the ground, with dainty movements, courtesying and raising its tail; and in accent and sequence, although not in tone or time, its song resembled that of our white-throated sparrow.

It was three weeks since we had started down the River of Doubt. We had come along its winding course about 140 kilometres, with a descent of somewhere in the neighborhood of 124 metres. It had been slow progress. We could not tell what physical obstacles were ahead of us, nor whether the Indians would be actively hostile. But a river normally describes in its course a parabola, the steep descent being in the upper part; and we hoped that in the future we should not have to encounter so many and such difficult rapids as we had already encountered, and that therefore we would make better time—a hope destined to failure.

# Down an Unknown River

*Through the Brazilian Wilderness*

THE MIGHTIEST RIVER IN THE WORLD IS THE AMAZON. IT RUNS FROM west to east, from the sunset to the sunrise, from the Andes to the Atlantic. The main stream flows almost along the equator, while the basin which contains its affluents extends many degrees north and south of the equator. The gigantic equatorial river basin is filled with an immense forest, the largest in the world, with which no other forests can be compared save those of western Africa and Malaysia. We were within the southern boundary of this great equatorial forest, on a river which was not merely unknown but unguessed at, no geographer having ever suspected its existence. This river flowed northward toward the equator, but whither it would go, whether it would turn one way or another, the length of its course, where it would come out, the character of the stream itself, and the character of the dwellers along its banks—all these things were yet to be discovered.

One morning while the canoes were being built Kermit and I walked a few kilometres down the river and surveyed the next rapids below. The vast still forest was almost empty of life. We found old Indian signs. There were very few birds, and these in the tops of the tall trees. We saw a recent tapir-track; and under a cajazeira-tree by the bank there were the tracks of capybaras which had been eating the fallen fruit. This fruit is delicious and would make a valuable addition to our orchards. The tree although tropical is hardy, thrives when domesticated, and propagates rapidly from shoots. The Department of Agriculture should try whether it would not grow in southern California and Florida. This was the tree from which the doctor's family name was taken.

His parental grandfather, although of Portuguese blood, was an intensely patriotic Brazilian. He was a very young man when the independence of Brazil was declared, and did not wish to keep the Portuguese family name; so he changed it to that of the fine Brazilian tree in question. Such change of family names is common in Brazil. Doctor Vital Brazil, the student of poisonous serpents, was given his name by his father, whose own family name was entirely different; and his brother's name was again different.

There were tremendous downpours of rain, lasting for a couple of hours and accompanied by thunder and lightning. But on the whole it seemed as if the rains were less heavy and continuous than they had been. We all of us had to help in building the canoes now and then. Kermit, accompanied by Antonio the Parecis and João, crossed the river and walked back to the little river that had entered from the east, so as to bring back a report of it to Colonel Rondon. Lyra took observations, by the sun and by the stars. We were in about latitude 11° 21' acute; south, and due north of where we had started. The river had wound so that we had gone two miles for every one we made northward. Our progress had been very slow; and until we got out of the region of incessant rapids, with their attendant labor and hazard, it was not likely that we should go much faster.

On the morning of March 22 we started in our six canoes. We made ten kilometres. Twenty minutes after starting we came to the first rapids. Here every one walked except the three best paddlers, who took the canoes down in succession—an hour's job. Soon after this we struck a bees' nest in the top of a tree overhanging the river; our steersman climbed out and robbed it, but, alas! lost the honey on the way back. We came to a small steep fall which we did not dare run in our overladen, clumsy, and cranky dugouts. Fortunately, we were able to follow a deep canal which led off for a kilometre, returning just below the falls, fifty yards from where it had started. Then, having been in the boats and in motion only one hour and a half, we came to a long stretch of rapids which it took us six hours to descend, and we camped at the foot. Everything was taken out of the canoes, and they were run down in succession. At one difficult and perilous place they were let down by ropes; and even thus we almost lost one.

We went down the right bank. On the opposite bank was an Indian village, evidently inhabited only during the dry season. The marks on the stumps of trees showed that these Indians had axes and knives; and there were old fields in which maize, beans, and cotton had been grown. The forest dripped and steamed. Rubber-trees were plentiful. At one point the tops of a group of tall trees were covered with yellow-white blossoms. Others bore red blossoms. Many of the big trees, of different kinds, were buttressed at the base with great thin walls of wood. Others, including both palms and ordinary trees, showed an even stranger peculiarity. The trunk, near the base, but sometimes six or eight feet from the ground, was split into a dozen or twenty branches or small trunks which sloped outward in tent-like shape, each becoming a root. The larger trees of this type looked as if their trunks were seated on the tops of the pole frames of Indian tepees. At one point in the stream, to our great surprise, we saw a flying-fish. It skimmed the water like a swallow for over twenty yards.

Although we made only ten kilometres we worked hard all day. The last canoes were brought down and moored to the bank at nightfall. Our tents were pitched in the darkness.

Next day we made thirteen kilometres. We ran, all told, a little over an hour and three-quarters. Seven hours were spent in getting past a series of rapids at which the portage, over rocky and difficult ground, was a kilometre long. The canoes were run down empty—a hazardous run, in which one of them upset.

Yet while we were actually on the river, paddling and floating down-stream along the reaches of swift, smooth water, it was very lovely. When we started in the morning the day was overcast and the air was heavy with vapor. Ahead of us the shrouded river stretched between dim walls of forest, half-seen in the mist. Then the sun burned up the fog, and loomed through it in a red splendor that changed first to gold and then to molten white. In the dazzling light, under the brilliant blue of the sky, every detail of the magnificent forest was vivid to the eye: the great trees, the network of bush ropes, the caverns of greenery, where thick-leaved vines covered all things else. Wherever there was a hidden bowlder the surface of the current was broken by waves. In one place, in midstream, a pyramidal rock thrust itself six feet above the surface of the river. On the banks we found fresh Indian sign.

At home in Vermont Cherrie is a farmer, with a farm of six hundred acres, most of it woodland. As we sat at the foot of the rapids, watching for the last dugouts with their naked paddlers to swing into sight round the bend through the white water, we talked of the northern spring that was just beginning. He sells cream, eggs, poultry, potatoes, honey, occasionally pork and veal; but at this season it was the time for the maple-sugar crop. He has a sugar orchard, where he taps twelve hundred trees and hopes soon to tap as many more in addition. Said Cherrie: "It's a busy time now for Fred Rice" —Fred Rice is the hired man, and in sugar time the Cherrie boys help him with enthusiasm, and, moreover, are paid with exact justice for the work they do. There is much wild life about the farm, although it is near Brattleboro. One night in early spring a bear left his tracks near the sugar-house; and now and then in summer

Cherrie has had to sleep in the garden to keep the deer away from the beans, cabbages, and beets.

There was not much bird life in the forest, but Cherrie kept getting species new to the collection. At this camp he shot an interesting little ant-thrush. It was the size of a warbler, jet-black, with white under-surfaces of the wings and tail, white on the tail-feathers, and a large spot of white on the back, normally almost concealed, the feathers on the back being long and fluffy. When he shot the bird, a male, it was showing off before a dull-colored little bird, doubtless the female; and the chief feature of the display was this white spot on the back. The white feathers were raised and displayed so that the spot flashed like the "chrysanthemum" on a prongbuck whose curiosity has been aroused. In the gloom of the forest the bird was hard to see, but the flashing of this patch of white feathers revealed it at once, attracting immediate attention. It was an excellent example of a coloration mark which served a purely advertising purpose; apparently it was part of a courtship display. The bird was about thirty feet up in the branches.

In the morning, just before leaving this camp, a tapir swam across stream a little way above us; but unfortunately we could not get a shot at it. An ample supply of tapir beef would have meant much to us. We had started with fifty days' rations; but this by no means meant full rations, in the sense of giving every man all he wanted to eat. We had two meals a day, and were on rather short commons—both our mess and the camaradas'—except when we got plenty of palm-tops. For our mess we had the boxes chosen by Fiala, each containing a day's rations for six men, our number. But we made each box last a day and a half, or at times two days, and in addition we gave some of the food to the camaradas. It was only on the rare occasions when we had killed some monkeys or curassows, or caught some fish, that everybody had enough. We would have welcomed that tapir. So far the game, fish, and fruit had been too scarce to be an element of weight in our food supply. In an exploring trip like ours, through a difficult and utterly unknown country, especially if densely forested, there is little time to halt, and game cannot be counted on. It is only in lands like our own West thirty years ago, like South Africa in the middle of the last century, like East Africa to-day that game can be made the chief food supply. On this trip our only substantial food supply from the country hitherto had been that furnished by the palm-tops. Two men were detailed every day to cut down palms for food.

A kilometre and a half after leaving this camp we came on a stretch of big rapids. The river here twists in loops, and we had heard the roaring of these rapids the previous afternoon. Then we passed out of earshot of them; but

Antonio Correa, our best waterman, insisted all along that the roaring meant rapids worse than any we had encountered for some days. "I was brought up in the water, and I know it like a fish, and all its sounds," said he. He was right. We had to carry the loads nearly a kilometre that afternoon, and the canoes were pulled out on the bank so that they might be in readiness to be dragged overland next day. Rondon, Lyra, Kermit, and Antonio Correa explored both sides of the river. On the opposite or left bank they found the mouth of a considerable river, bigger than the Rio Kermit, flowing in from the west and making its entrance in the middle of the rapids. This river we christened the Taunay, in honor of a distinguished Brazilian, an explorer, a soldier, a senator, who was also a writer of note. Kermit had with him two of his novels, and I had read one of his books dealing with a disastrous retreat during the Paraguayan war.

Next morning, the 25th, the canoes were brought down. A path was chopped for them and rollers laid; and half-way down the rapids Lyra and Kermit, who were overseeing the work as well as doing their share of the pushing and hauling, got them into a canal of smooth water, which saved much severe labor. As our food supply lowered we were constantly more desirous of economizing the strength of the men. One day more would complete a month since we had embarked on the Dúvida—as we had started in February, the lunar and calendar months coincided. We had used up over half our provisions. We had come only a trifle over 160 kilometres, thanks to the character and number of the rapids. We believed we had three or four times the distance yet to go before coming to a part of the river where we might hope to meet assistance, either from rubber-gatherers, or from Pyrineus, if he were really coming up the river which we were going down. If the rapids continued to be as they had been it could not be much more than three weeks before we were in straits for food, aside from the ever-present danger of accident in the rapids; and if our progress were no faster than it had been—and we were straining to do our best—we would in such event still have several hundreds of kilometres of unknown river before us. We could not even hazard a guess at what was in front. The river was now a really big river, and it seemed impossible that it could flow either into the Gy-Paraná or the Tapajos. It was possible that it went into the Canumá, a big affluent of the Madeira low down, and next to the Tapajos. It was more probable that it was the headwaters of the Aripuanan, a river which, as I have said, was not even named on the excellent English map of Brazil I carried. Nothing but the mouth had been known to any geographer; but the lower course had long been known to rubber-gatherers, and recently a commission from the government of Amazonas had part-way ascended one branch of it—not as far as the rubber-gatherers had gone, and, as it turned out, not the branch we came down.

Two of our men were down with fever. Another man, Julio, a fellow of powerful frame, was utterly worthless, being an inborn, lazy shirk with the heart of a ferocious cur in the body of a bullock. The others were good men, some of them very good indeed. They were under the immediate supervision of Pedrinho Craveiro, who was first-class in every way.

This camp was very lovely. It was on the edge of a bay, into which the river broadened immediately below the rapids. There was a beach of white sand, where we bathed and washed our clothes. All around us, and across the bay, and on both sides of the long water-street made by the river, rose the splendid forest. There were flocks of parakeets colored green, blue, and red. Big toucans called overhead, lustrous green-black in color, with white throats, red gorgets, red-and-yellow tail coverts, and huge black-and-yellow bills. Here the soil was fertile; it will be a fine site for a coffee-plantation when this region is open to settlement. Surely such a rich and fertile land cannot be permitted to remain idle, to lie as a tenantless wilderness, while there are such teeming swarms of human beings in the overcrowded, overpeopled countries of the Old World. The very rapids and waterfalls which now make the navigation of the river so difficult and dangerous would drive electric trolleys up and down its whole length and far out on either side, and run mills and factories, and lighten the labor on farms. With the incoming of settlement and with the steady growth of knowledge how to fight and control tropical diseases, fear of danger to health would vanish. A land like this is a hard land for the first explorers, and perhaps for their immediate followers, but not for the people who come after them.

In mid-afternoon we were once more in the canoes; but we had paddled with the current only a few minutes, we had gone only a kilometre, when the roar of rapids in front again forced us to haul up to the bank. As usual, Rondon, Lyra, and Kermit, with Antonio Correa, explored both sides while camp was being pitched. The rapids were longer and of steeper descent than the last, but on the opposite or western side there was a passage down which we thought we could get the empty dugouts at the cost of dragging them only a few yards at one spot. The loads were to be carried down the hither bank, for a kilometre, to the smooth water. The river foamed between great rounded masses of rock, and at one point there was a sheer fall of six or eight feet. We found and ate wild pineapples. Wild beans were in flower. At dinner we had a toucan and a couple of parrots, which were very good.

All next day was spent by Lyra in superintending our three best watermen as they took the canoes down the west side of the rapids, to the foot, at the spot to which the camp had meantime been shifted. In the forest some of the huge sipas, or rope vines, which were as big as cables, bore clusters of fragrant flowers. The men found several honey-trees, and fruits of various kinds, and small cocoanuts; they chopped down an ample number of palms, for the palm-cabbage; and, most important of all, they gathered a quantity of big Brazil-nuts, which when roasted tasted like the best of chestnuts and are nutritious; and they caught a number of big piranhas, which were good eating. So we all had a feast, and everybody had enough to eat and was happy.

By these rapids, at the fall, Cherrie found some strange carvings on a bare mass of rock. They were evidently made by men a long time ago. As far as is known, the Indians thereabouts make no such figures now. They were in two groups, one on the surface of the rock facing the land, the other on that facing the water. The latter were nearly obliterated. The former were in good preservation, the figures sharply cut into the rock. They consisted, upon the upper flat part of the rock, of four multiple circles with a dot in the middle (O), very accurately made and about a foot and a half in diameter; and below them, on the side of the rock, four multiple m's or inverted w's (M). What these curious symbols represented, or who made them, we could not, of course, form the slightest idea. It may be that in a very remote past some Indian tribes of comparatively advanced culture had penetrated to this lovely river, just as we had now come to it. Before white men came to South America there had already existed therein various semicivilizations, some rude, others fairly advanced, which rose, flourished, and persisted through immemorial ages, and then vanished. The vicissitudes in the history of humanity during its stay on this southern continent have been as strange, varied, and inexplicable as paleontology shows to have been the case, on the same continent, in the history of the higher forms of animal life during the age of mammals. Colonel Rondon stated that such figures as these are not found anywhere else in Matto Grosso where he has been, and therefore it was all the more strange to find them in this one place on the unknown river, never before visited by white men, which we were descending.

Next morning we went about three kilometers before coming to some steep hills, beautiful to look upon, clad as they were in dense, tall, tropical forest, but ominous of new rapids. Sure enough, at their foot we had to haul up and prepare for a long portage. The canoes we ran down empty. Even so, we were within an ace of losing two, the lashed couple in which I ordinarily journeyed. In a sharp bend of the rapids, between two big curls, they were swept among the bowlders and under the matted branches which stretched out from the bank. They filled, and the racing current pinned them where they were, one partly on the other. All of us had to help get them clear. Their fastenings were chopped asunder with axes. Kermit and half a dozen of the men, stripped to the skin, made their way to a small rock island in the little falls just above the canoes, and let down a rope which we tied to the outermost canoe. The rest of us, up to our armpits and barely able to keep our footing as we slipped and stumbled among the bowlders in the swift current, lifted and shoved while Kermit and his men pulled the rope and fastened the slack to a half-submerged tree. Each canoe in succession was hauled up the little rock island, baled, and then taken down in safety by two paddlers. It was nearly four o'clock before we were again ready to start, having been delayed by a rain-storm so heavy that we could not see across the river. Ten minutes' run took us to the head of another series of rapids; the exploring party returned with the news that we had an all day's job ahead of us; and we made camp in the rain, which did not matter much, as we were already drenched through. It was impossible, with the wet wood, to make a fire sufficiently hot to dry all our soggy things, for the rain was still falling. A tapir was seen from our boat, but, as at the moment we were being whisked round in a complete circle by a whirlpool, I did not myself see it in time to shoot.

Next morning we went down a kilometre, and then landed on the other side of the river. The canoes were run down, and the loads carried to the other side of a little river coming in from the west, which Colonel Rondon christened Cherrie River. Across this we went on a bridge consisting of a huge tree felled by Macario, one of our best men. Here we camped, while Rondon, Lyra, Kermit, and Antonio Correa explored what was ahead. They were absent until mid-afternoon. Then they returned with the news that we were among ranges of low mountains, utterly different in formation from the high plateau region to which the first rapids, those we had come to on the 2d of March, belonged. Through the first range of these mountains the river ran in a gorge, some three kilometres long, immediately ahead of us. The ground was so rough and steep that it would be impossible to drag the canoes over it and difficult enough to carry the loads; and the rapids were so bad, containing several falls, one of at least ten metres in height, that it was doubtful how many of the canoes we could get down them. Kermit, who was the only man with much experience of rope work, was the only man who believed we could get the canoes down at all; and it was, of course, possible that we should have to build new ones at the foot to supply the place of any that were lost or left behind. In view of the length and character of the portage, and of all the unpleasant possibilities that were ahead, and of the need of keeping every pound of food, it was necessary to reduce weight in every possible way and to throw away everything except the barest necessities.

We thought we had reduced our baggage before; but now we cut to the bone. We kept the fly for all six of us to sleep under. Kermit's shoes had gone, thanks to the amount of work in the water which he had been doing; and he took the pair I had been wearing, while I put on my spare pair. In addition to the clothes I wore, I kept one set of pajamas, a spare pair of drawers, a spare pair of socks, half a dozen handkerchiefs, my wash-kit, my pocket medicine-case, and a little bag containing my spare spectacles, gun-grease, some adhesive plaster, some needles and thread, the "fly-dope," and my purse and letter of credit, to be used at Manaos. All of these went into the bag containing my cot, blanket, and mosquito-net. I also carried a cartridge-bag containing my cartridges, head-net, and gauntlets. Kermit cut down even closer; and the others about as close.

The last three days of March we spent in getting to the foot of the rapids in this gorge. Lyra and Kermit, with four of the best watermen, handled the empty canoes. The work was not only difficult and laborious in the extreme, but hazardous; for the walls of the gorge were so sheer that at the worst places they had to cling to narrow shelves on the face of the rock, while letting the canoes down with ropes. Meanwhile Rondon surveyed and cut a trail for the burden-bearers, and superintended the portage of the loads. The rocky sides of the gorge were too steep for laden men to attempt to traverse them. Accordingly the trail had to go over the top of the mountain, both the ascent and the descent of the rock-strewn, forest-clad slopes being very steep. It was hard work to carry loads over such a trail. From the top of the mountain, through an opening in the trees on the edge of a cliff, there was a beautiful view of the country ahead. All around and in front of us there were ranges of low mountains about the height of the lower ridges of the Alleghanies. Their sides were steep and they were covered with the matted growth of the tropical forest. Our next camping-place, at the foot of the gorge, was almost beneath us, and from thence the river ran in a straight line, flecked with white water, for about a kilometre. Then it disappeared behind and between mountain ridges, which we supposed meant further rapids. It was a view well worth seeing; but, beautiful although the country ahead of us was, its character was such as to promise further hardships, difficulty, and exhausting labor, and especially further delay; and delay was a serious matter to men whose food supply was beginning to run short, whose equipment was reduced to the minimum, who for a month, with the utmost toil, had made very slow progress, and who had no idea of either the distance or the difficulties of the route in front of them.

There was not much life in the woods, big or little. Small birds were rare, although Cherrie's unwearied efforts were rewarded from time to time by a species new to the collection. There were tracks of tapir, deer, and agouti; and if we had taken two or three days to devote to nothing else than hunting them we might perchance have killed something; but the chance was much too uncertain, the work we were doing was too hard and wearing, and the need of pressing forward altogether too great to permit us to spend any time in such manner. The hunting had to come in incidentally. This type of well-nigh impenetrable forest is the one in which it is most difficult to get even what little game exists therein. A couple of curassows and a big monkey were killed by the colonel and Kermit. On the day the monkey was brought in Lyra, Kermit, and their four associates had spent from sunrise to sunset in severe and at moments dangerous toil among the rocks and in the swift water, and the fresh meat was appreciated. The head, feet, tail, skin, and entrails were boiled for the gaunt and ravenous dogs. The flesh gave each of us a few mouthfuls; and how good those mouthfuls tasted!

Cherrie, in addition to being out after birds in every spare moment, helped in all emergencies. He was a veteran in the work of the tropic wilderness. We talked together often, and of many things, for our views of life, and of a man's duty to his wife and children, to other men, and to women, and to the state in peace and war, were in all essentials the same. His father had served all through the Civil War, entering an Iowa cavalry regiment as a private and coming out as a captain; his breast-bone was shattered by a blow from a musket-butt, in hand-to-hand fighting at Shiloh.

During this portage the weather favored us. We were coming toward the close of the rainy season. On the last day of the month, when we moved camp to the foot of the gorge, there was a thunder-storm; but on the whole we were not bothered by rain until the last night, when it rained heavily, driving under the fly so as to wet my cot and bedding. However, I slept comfortably enough, rolled in the damp blanket. Without the blanket I should have been uncomfortable; a blanket is a necessity for health. On the third day Lyra and Kermit, with their daring and hard-working watermen, after wearing labor, succeeded in getting five canoes through the worst of the rapids to the chief fall. The sixth, which was frail and weak, had its bottom beaten out on the jagged rocks of the broken water. On this night, although I thought I had put my clothes out of reach, both the termites and the carregadores ants got at them, ate holes in one boot, ate one leg of my drawers, and riddled my handkerchief; and I now had nothing to replace anything that was destroyed.

Next day Lyra, Kermit, and their camaradas brought the five canoes that were left down to camp. They had in four days accomplished a work of incredible labor and of the utmost importance; for at the first glance it had seemed an absolute impossibility to avoid abandoning the canoes when we found that the river sank into a cataract-broken torrent at the bottom of a canyon-like gorge between steep mountains. On April 2 we once more started, wondering how soon we should strike other rapids in the mountains ahead, and whether in any reasonable time we should, as the aneroid indicated, be so low down that we should necessarily be in a plain where we could make a journey of at least a few days without rapids. We had been exactly a month going through an uninterrupted succession of rapids. During that month we had come only about 110 kilometres, and had descended nearly 150 metres—the figures are approximate but fairly accurate. We had lost four of the canoes with which we started, and one other, which we had built, and the life of one man; and the life of a dog which by its death had in all probability saved the life of Colonel Rondon. In a straight line northward, toward our supposed destination, we had not made more than a mile and a quarter a day; at the cost of bitter toil for most of the party, of much risk for some of the party, and of some risk and some hardship for all the party. Most of the camaradas were downhearted, naturally enough, and occasionally asked one of us if we really believed that we should ever get out alive; and we had to cheer them up as best we could.

There was no change in our work for the time being. We made but three kilometres that day. Most of the party walked all the time; but the dugouts carried the luggage until we struck the head of the series of rapids which were to take up the next two or three days. The river rushed through a wild gorge, a chasm or canyon, between two mountains. Its sides were very steep, mere rock walls, although in most places so covered with the luxuriant growth of the trees and bushes that clung in the crevices, and with green moss, that the naked rock was hardly seen. Rondon, Lyra, and Kermit, who were in front, found a small level spot, with a beach of sand, and sent back word to camp there, while they spent several hours in exploring the country ahead. The canoes were run down empty, and the loads carried painfully along the face of the cliffs; so bad was the trail that I found it rather hard to follow, although carrying nothing but my rifle and cartridge-bag. The explorers returned with the information

that the mountains stretched ahead of us, and that there were rapids as far as
they had gone. We could only hope that the aneroid was not hopelessly out of
kilter, and that we should, therefore, fairly soon find ourselves in comparatively
level country. The severe toil, on a rather limited food supply, was telling on
the strength as well as on the spirits of the men; Lyra and Kermit, in addition
to their other work, performed as much actual physical labor as any of them.

Next day, the 3d of April, we began the descent of these sinister rapids of
the chasm. Colonel Rondon had gone to the summit of the mountain in order
to find a better trail for the burden-bearers, but it was hopeless, and they had
to go along the face of the cliffs. Such an exploring expedition as that in
which we were engaged of necessity involves hard and dangerous labor, and
perils of many kinds. To follow down-stream an unknown river, broken by innumerable cataracts and rapids, rushing through mountains of which the existence has never been even guessed, bears no resemblance whatever to following
even a fairly dangerous river which has been thoroughly explored and has
become in some sort a highway, so that experienced pilots can be secured as
guides, while the portages have been pioneered and trails chopped out, and
every dangerous feature of the rapids is known beforehand. In this case no one
could foretell that the river would cleave its way through steep mountain
chains, cutting narrow clefts in which the cliff walls rose almost sheer on either
hand. When a rushing river thus "canyons," as we used to say out West, and the
mountains are very steep, it becomes almost impossible to bring the canoes
down the river itself and utterly impossible to portage them along the cliff sides,
while even to bring the loads over the mountain is a task of extraordinary labor
and difficulty. Moreover, no one can tell how many times the task will have
to be repeated, or when it will end, or whether the food will hold out; every
hour of work in the rapids is fraught with the possibility of the gravest disaster, and yet it is imperatively necessary to attempt it; and all this is done in an
uninhabited wilderness, or else a wilderness tenanted only by unfriendly savages, where failure to get through means death by disease and starvation.
Wholesale disasters to South American exploring parties have been frequent.
The first recent effort to descend one of the unknown rivers to the Amazon from
the Brazilian highlands resulted in such a disaster. It was undertaken in 1889
by a party about as large as ours under a Brazilian engineer officer, Colonel Telles
Peres. In descending some rapids they lost everything—canoes, food, medicine,
implements—everything. Fever smote them, and then starvation. All of them
died except one officer and two men, who were rescued months later. Recently,
in Guiana, a wilderness veteran, André, lost two-thirds of his party by

starvation. Genuine wilderness exploration is as dangerous as warfare. The conquest of wild nature demands the utmost vigor, hardihood, and daring, and takes from the conquerors a heavy toll of life and health.

Lyra, Kermit, and Cherrie, with four of the men, worked the canoes half-way down the canyon. Again and again it was touch and go whether they could get by a given point. At one spot the channel of the furious torrent was only fifteen yards across. One canoe was lost, so that of the seven with which we had started only two were left. Cherrie labored with the other men at times, and also stood as guard over them, for, while actually working, of course no one could carry a rifle. Kermit's experience in bridge building was invaluable in enabling him to do the rope work by which alone it was possible to get the canoes down the canyon. He and Lyra had now been in the water for days. Their clothes were never dry. Their shoes were rotten. The bruises on their feet and legs had become sores. On their bodies some of the insect bites had become festering wounds, as indeed was the case with all of us. Poisonous ants, biting flies, ticks, wasps, bees were a perpetual torment. However, no one had yet been bitten by a venomous serpent, a scorpion, or a centiped, although we had killed all of the three within camp limits.

Under such conditions whatever is evil in men's natures comes to the front. On this day a strange and terrible tragedy occurred. One of the camaradas, a man of pure European blood, was the man named Julio, of whom I have already spoken. He was a very powerful fellow and had been importunately eager to come on the expedition; and he had the reputation of being a good worker. But, like so many men of higher standing, he had had no idea of what such an expedition really meant, and under the strain of toil, hardship, and danger his nature showed its true depths of selfishness, cowardice, and ferocity. He shirked all work. He shammed sickness. Nothing could make him do his share; and yet unlike his self-respecting fellows he was always shamelessly begging for favors. Kermit was the only one of our party who smoked; and he was continually giving a little tobacco to some of the camaradas, who worked especially well under him. The good men did not ask for it; but Julio, who shirked every labor, was always, and always in vain, demanding it. Colonel Rondon, Lyra, and Kermit each tried to get work out of him, and in order to do anything with him had to threaten to leave him in the wilderness. He threw all his tasks on his comrades; and, moreover, he stole their food as well as ours. On such an expedition the theft of food comes next to murder as a crime, and should by rights be punished as such. We could not trust him to cut down palms or gather nuts, because he would stay out and eat what ought to have gone into the common store. Finally, the men on several occasions themselves detected him stealing their food. Alone of the whole party, and thanks to the stolen food, he had kept in full flesh and bodily vigor.

One of our best men was a huge negro named Paixão—Paishon—a corporal and acting sergeant in the engineer corps. He had, by the way, literally torn his trousers to pieces, so that he wore only the tatters of a pair of old drawers until I gave him my spare trousers when we lightened loads. He was a stern disciplinarian. One evening he detected Julio stealing food and smashed him in the mouth. Julio came crying to us, his face working with fear and malignant hatred; but after investigation he was told that he had gotten off uncommonly lightly. The men had three or four carbines, which were sometimes carried by those who were not their owners.

On this morning, at the outset of the portage, Pedrinho discovered Julio stealing some of the men's dried meat. Shortly afterward Paishon rebuked him for, as usual, lagging behind. By this time we had reached the place where the canoes were tied to the bank and then taken down one at a time. We were sitting down, waiting for the last loads to be brought along the trail. Pedrinho was still in the camp we had left. Paishon had just brought in a load, left it on the ground with his carbine beside it, and returned on the trail for another load. Julio came in, put down his load, picked up the carbine, and walked back on the trail, muttering to himself but showing no excitement. We thought nothing of it, for he was always muttering; and occasionally one of the men saw a monkey or big bird and tried to shoot it, so it was never surprising to see a man with a carbine.

In a minute we heard a shot; and in a short time three or four of the men came up the trail to tell us that Paishon was dead, having been shot by Julio, who had fled into the woods. Colonel Rondon and Lyra were ahead; I sent a messenger for them, directed Cherrie and Kermit to stay where they were and guard the canoes and provisions, and started down the trail with the doctor— an absolutely cool and plucky man, with a revolver but no rifle—and a couple of the camaradas. We soon passed the dead body of poor Paishon. He lay in a huddle, in a pool of his own blood, where he had fallen, shot through the heart. I feared that Julio had run amuck, and intended merely to take more lives before he died, and that he would begin with Pedrinho, who was alone and unarmed in the camp we had left. Accordingly I pushed on, followed by my companions, looking sharply right and left; but when we came to the camp the doctor quietly walked by me, remarking, "My eyes are better than yours, colonel; if he is in sight I'll point him out to you, as you have the rifle." However, he was not there, and the others soon joined us with the welcome news that they had found the carbine.

The murderer had stood to one side of the path and killed his victim, when a dozen paces off, with deliberate and malignant purpose. Then evidently his murderous hatred had at once given way to his innate cowardice; and, perhaps hearing some one coming along the path, he fled in panic terror into the wilderness. A tree had knocked the carbine from his hand. His footsteps showed that after going some rods he had started to return, doubtless for the carbine, but had fled again, probably because the body had then been discovered. It was questionable whether or not he would live to reach the Indian villages, which were probably his goal. He was not a man to feel remorse—never a common feeling; but surely that murderer was in a living hell, as, with fever and famine leering at him from the shadows, he made his way through the empty desolation of the wilderness. Franca, the cook, quoted out of the melancholy proverbial philosophy of the people the proverb: "No man knows the heart of any one" ; and then expressed with deep conviction a weird ghostly belief I had never encountered before: "Paishon is following Julio now, and will follow him until he dies; Paishon fell forward on his hands and knees, and when a murdered man falls like that his ghost will follow the slayer as long as the slayer lives."

We did not attempt to pursue the murderer. We could not legally put him to death, although he was a soldier who in cold blood had just deliberately killed a fellow soldier. If we had been near civilization we would have done our best to bring him in and turn him over to justice. But we were in the wilderness, and how many weeks' journey were ahead of us we could not tell. Our food was running low, sickness was beginning to appear among the men, and both their courage and their strength were gradually ebbing. Our first duty was to save the lives and the health of the men of the expedition who had honestly been performing, and had still to perform, so much perilous labor. If we brought the murderer in he would have to be guarded night and day on an expedition where there were always loaded firearms about, and where there would continually be opportunity and temptation for him to make an effort to seize food and a weapon and escape, perhaps murdering some other good man. He could not be shackled while climbing along the cliff slopes; he could not be shackled in the canoes, where there was always chance of upset and drowning; and standing guard would be an additional and severe penalty on the weary, honest men already exhausted by overwork. The expedition was in peril, and it was wise to take every chance possible that would help secure success. Whether the murderer lived or died in the wilderness was of no moment compared with the duty of doing everything to secure the safety of the rest of the party. For the two days following we were always on the watch against his return, for he could have readily killed some one else by rolling rocks down on any of the men working on the cliff sides or in the bottom of the gorge. But we did not see him until the morning of the third day. We had passed the last of the rapids of the chasm, and the four boats were going downstream when he appeared behind some trees on the bank and called out that he wished to surrender and be taken aboard; for the murderer was an arrant craven at heart, a strange mixture of ferocity and cowardice. Colonel Rondon's boat was far in advance; he did not stop nor answer. I kept on in similar fashion with the rear boats, for I had no intention of taking the murderer aboard, to the jeopardy of the other members of the party, unless Colonel Rondon told me that it would have to be done in pursuance of his duty as an officer of the army and a servant of the Government of Brazil. At the first halt Colonel Rondon came up to me and told me that this was his view of his duty, but that he had not stopped because he wished first to consult me as the chief of the expedition. I answered that for the reasons enumerated above I did not believe that in justice to the good men of the expedition we should jeopardize their safety by taking the murderer along, and that if the responsibility were mine I should refuse to take him; but that he, Colonel Rondon, was the superior officer of both the murderer and of all the other enlisted men and army officers on the expedition, and in return was responsible for his actions to his own governmental superiors and to the laws of Brazil; and that in view of this responsibility he must act as his sense of duty bade him. Accordingly, at the next camp he sent back two men, expert woodsmen, to find the murderer and bring him in. They failed to find him.

I have anticipated my narrative because I do not wish to recur to the horror more than is necessary. I now return to my story. After we found that Julio had fled, we returned to the scene of the tragedy. The murdered man lay with a handkerchief thrown over his face. We buried him beside the place where he fell. With axes and knives the camaradas dug a shallow grave while we stood by with bared heads. Then reverently and carefully we lifted the poor body which but half an hour before had been so full of vigorous life. Colonel Rondon and I bore the head and shoulders. We laid him in the grave, and heaped a mound over him, and put a rude cross at his head. We fired a volley for a brave and loyal soldier who had died doing his duty. Then we left him forever, under the great trees beside the lonely river.

That day we got only half-way down the rapids. There was no good place to camp. But at the foot of one steep cliff there was a narrow, bowlder-covered slope where it was possible to sling hammocks and cook; and a slanting spot was found for my cot, which had sagged until by this time it looked like a broken-backed centiped. It rained a little during the night, but not enough to wet us much. Next day Lyra, Kermit, and Cherrie finished their job, and brought the four remaining canoes to camp, one leaking badly from the battering on the rocks. We then went down-stream a few hundred yards, and camped on the opposite side; it was not a good camping-place, but it was better than the one we left.

The men were growing constantly weaker under the endless strain of exhausting labor. Kermit was having an attack of fever, and Lyra and Cherrie had touches of dysentery, but all three continued to work. While in the water trying to help with an upset canoe I had by my own clumsiness bruised my leg against a bowlder; and the resulting inflammation was somewhat bothersome. I now had a sharp attack of fever, but thanks to the excellent care of the doctor, was over it in about forty-eight hours; but Kermit's fever grew worse and he too was unable to work for a day or two. We could walk over the portages, however. A good doctor is an absolute necessity on an exploring expedition in such a country as that we were in, under penalty of a frightful mortality among the members; and the necessary risks and hazards are so great, the chances of disaster so large, that there is no warrant for increasing them by the failure to take all feasible precautions.

The next day we made another long portage round some rapids, and camped at night still in the hot, wet, sunless atmosphere of the gorge. The following day, April 6, we portaged past another set of rapids, which proved to be the last of the rapids of the chasm. For some kilometres we kept passing hills, and feared lest at any moment we might again find ourselves fronting another mountain gorge; with, in such case, further days of grinding and perilous labor ahead of us, while our men were disheartened, weak, and sick. Most of them had already begun to have fever. Their condition was inevitable after over a month's uninterrupted work of the hardest kind in getting through the long series of rapids we had just passed; and a long further delay, accompanied by wearing labor, would have almost certainly meant that the weakest among our party would have begun to die. There were already two of the camaradas who were too weak to help the others, their condition being such as to cause us serious concern.

However, the hills gradually sank into a level plain, and the river carried us through it at a rate that enabled us during the remainder of the day to reel off thirty-six kilometres, a record that for the first time held out promise. Twice tapirs swam the river while we passed, but not near my canoe. However, the previous evening Cherrie had killed two monkeys and Kermit one, and we all had a few mouthfuls of fresh meat; we had already had a good soup made out of a turtle Kermit had caught. We had to portage by one short set of rapids, the unloaded canoes being brought down without difficulty. At last, at four in the afternoon, we came to the mouth of a big river running in from the right. We thought it was probably the Ananás, but, of course, could not be certain. It was less in volume than the one we had descended, but nearly as broad; its breadth at this point being ninety-five yards as against one hundred and twenty for the larger river. There were rapids ahead, immediately after the junction, which took place in latitude 10° 58' south. We had come 216 kilometres all told, and were nearly north of where we had started. We camped on the point of land between the two rivers. It was extraordinary to realize that here about the eleventh degree we were on such a big river, utterly unknown to the cartographers and not indicated by even a hint on any map. We named this big tributary Rio Cardozo, after a gallant officer of the commission who had died of beriberi just as our expedition began. We spent a day at this spot, determining our exact position by the sun, and afterward by the stars, and sending on two men to explore the rapids in advance. They returned with the news that there were big cataracts in them, and that they would form an obtacle to our progress. They had also caught a huge siluroid fish, which furnished an excellent meal for everybody in camp. This evening at sunset the view across he broad river, from our camp where the two rivers joined, was very lovely; and for the first time we had an open space in front of and above us, so that after nightfall the stars, and the great waxing moon, were glorious overhead, and against the rocks in midstream the broken water gleamed like tossing silver.

The huge catfish which the men had caught was over three feet and a half long, with the usual enormous head, out of all proportion to the body, and the enormous mouth, out of all proportion to the head. Such fish, although their teeth are small, swallow very large prey. This one contained the nearly digested remains of a monkey. Probably the monkey had been seized while drinking from the end of a branch; and once engulfed in that yawning cavern there was no escape. We Americans were astounded at the idea of a catfish making prey of a monkey; but our Brazilian friends told us that in the lower Madeira and the part of the Amazon near its mouth there is a still more gigantic catfish which in similar fashion occasionally makes prey of man. This is a grayish-white fish over nine feet long, with the usual disproportionately large head and gaping mouth, with a circle of small teeth; for the engulfing mouth itself is the danger, not the teeth. It is called the piraiba—pronounced in four syllables. While stationed at the small city of Itacoatiara, on the Amazon, at the mouth of the

Madeira, the doctor had seen one of these monsters which had been killed by the two men it had attacked. They were fishing in a canoe when it rose from the bottom—for it is a ground fish—and raising itself half out of the water lunged over the edge of the canoe at them, with open mouth. They killed it with their *falcóns,* as machetes are called in Brazil. It was taken round the city in triumph in an oxcart; the doctor saw it, and said it was three metres long. He said that swimmers feared it even more than the big cayman, because they could see the latter, whereas the former lay hid at the bottom of the water. Colonel Rondon said that in many villages where he had been on the lower Madeira the people had built stockaded enclosures in the water in which they bathed, not venturing to swim in the open water for fear of the piraiba and the big cayman.

Next day, April 8, we made five kilometres only, as there was a succession of rapids. We had to carry the loads past two of them, but ran the canoes without difficulty, for on the west side were long canals of swift water through the forest. The river had been higher, but was still very high, and the current raced round the many islands that at this point divided the channel. At four we made camp at the head of another stretch of rapids, over which the Canadian canoes would have danced without shipping a teaspoonful of water, but which our dugouts could only run empty. Cherrie killed three monkeys and Lyra caught two big piranhas, so that we were again all of us well provided with dinner and breakfast. When a number of men, doing hard work, are most of the time on half-rations, they grow to take a lively interest in any reasonably full meal that does arrive.

On the 10th we repeated the proceedings: a short quick run; a few hundred metres' portage, occupying, however, at least a couple of hours; again a few minutes' run; again other rapids. We again made less than five kilometres; in the two days we had been descending nearly a metre for every kilometre we made in advance; and it hardly seemed as if this state of things could last, for the aneroid showed that we were getting very low down. How I longed for a big Maine birch-bark, such as that in which I once went down the Mattawamkeag at high water! It would have slipped down these rapids as a girl trips through a country dance. But our loaded dugouts would have shoved their noses under every curl. The country was lovely. The wide river, now in one channel, now in several channels, wound among hills; the shower-freshened forest glistened in the sunlight; the many kinds of beautiful palm-fronds and the huge pacova-leaves stamped the peculiar look of the tropics on the whole landscape—it was like passing by water through a gigantic botanical garden. In the afternoon we got an elderly toucan, a piranha, and a reasonably edible sidenecked river-turtle; so we had fresh meat again. We slept as usual in earshot of rapids. We had been out six weeks, and almost all the time we had been engaged in wearily working our own way down and past rapid after rapid. Rapids are by far the most dangerous enemies of explorers and travellers who journey along these rivers.

Next day was a repetition of the same work. All the morning was spent in getting the loads to the foot of the rapids at the head of which we were encamped, down which the canoes were run empty. Then for thirty or forty minutes we ran down the swift, twisting river, the two lashed canoes almost coming to grief at one spot where a swirl of the current threw them against some trees on a small submerged island. Then we came to another set of rapids, carried the baggage down past them, and made camp long after dark in the rain—a good exercise in patience for those of us who were still suffering somewhat from fever. No one was in really buoyant health. For some weeks we had been sharing part of the contents of our boxes with the camaradas; but our food was not very satisfying to them. They needed quantity and the mainstay of each of their meals was a mass of palmitas; but on this day they had no time to cut down palms. We finally decided to run these rapids with the empty canoes, and they came down in safety. On such a trip it is highly undesirable to take any save necessary risks, for the consequences of disaster are too serious; and yet if no risks are taken the progress is so slow that disaster comes anyhow; and it is necessary perpetually to vary the terms of the perpetual working compromise between rashness and overcaution. This night we had a very good fish to eat, a big silvery fellow called a pescada, of a kind we had not caught before.

One day Trigueiro failed to embark with the rest of us, and we had to camp where we were next day to find him. Easter Sunday we spent in the fashion with which we were altogether too familiar. We only ran in a clear course for ten minutes all told, and spent eight hours in portaging the loads past rapids down which the canoes were run; the balsa was almost swamped. This day we caught twenty-eight big fish, mostly piranhas, and everybody had all he could eat for dinner, and for breakfast the following morning.

The forenoon of the following day was a repetition of this wearisome work; but late in the afternoon the river began to run in long quiet reaches. We made fifteen kilometres, and for the first time in several weeks camped where we did not hear the rapids. The silence was soothing and restful. The following day, April 14, we made a good run of some thirty-two kilometres. We passed a little river which entered on our left. We ran two or three light rapids, and portaged the loads by another. The river ran in long and usually tranquil stretches. In the morning when we started the view was lovely. There was a mist, and for a couple of miles the great river, broad and quiet, ran between the high walls of tropical forest, the tops of the giant trees showing dim through the haze. Different members of the party caught many fish, and shot a monkey and a couple of jacú-tinga—birds kin to a turkey, but the size of a fowl—so we again had a camp of plenty. The dry season was approaching, but there were still heavy, drenching rains. On this day the men found some new nuts of which they liked the taste; but the nuts proved unwholesome and half of the men were very sick and unable to work the following day. In the balsa only two were left fit to do anything, and Kermit plied a paddle all day long.

Accordingly, it was a rather sorry crew that embarked the following morning, April 15. But it turned out a red-letter day. The day before, we had come across cuttings, a year old, which were probably but not certainly made by pioneer rubber-men. But on this day—during which we made twenty-five kilometres—after running two hours and a half we found on the left bank a board on a post, with the initials J. A., to show the farthest-up point which a rubber-man had reached and claimed as his own. An hour farther down we came on a newly built house in a little planted clearing; and we cheered heartily. No one was at home, but the house, of palm thatch, was clean and cool. A couple of dogs were on watch, and the belongings showed that a man, a woman, and a child lived there, and had only just left. Another hour brought us to a similar house where dwelt an old black man, who showed the innate courtesy of the Brazilian peasant. We came on these rubber-men and their houses in about latitude 10° 24′.

In mid-afternoon we stopped at another clean, cool, picturesque house of palm thatch. The inhabitants all fled at our approach, fearing an Indian raid; for they were absolutely unprepared to have any one come from the unknown regions up-stream. They returned and were most hospitable and communicative; and we spent the night there. Said Antonio Correa to Kermit: "It seems like a dream to be in a house again, and hear the voices of men and women, instead of being among those mountains and rapids." The river was known to them as the Castanho, and was the main affluent, or rather the left or western branch, of the Aripuanan; the Castanho is a name used by the rubber-gatherers only; it is unknown to the geographers. We were, according to our informants, about fifteen days' journey from the confluence of the two rivers; but there were many rubber-men along the banks, some of whom had become permanent settlers. We had come over three hundred kilometres, in forty-eight days, over absolutely unknown ground; we had seen no human being, although we had twice heard Indians. Six weeks had been spent in steadily slogging our way down through the interminable series of rapids. It was astonishing before,

when we were on a river of about the size of the upper Rhine or Elbe, to realize that no geographer had any idea of its existence. But, after all, no civilized
man of any grade had ever been on it. Here, however, was a river with people
dwelling along the banks, some of whom had lived in the neighborhood for
eight or ten years; and yet on no standard map was there a hint of the river's
existence. We were putting on the map a river, running through between five
and six degrees of latitude—of between seven and eight if, as should properly
be done, the lower Aripuanan is included as part of it—of which no geographer,
in any map published in Europe, or the United States, or Brazil had even
admitted the possibility of the existence; for the place actually occupied by it
was filled, on the maps, by other—imaginary—streams, or by mountain ranges.
Before we started, the Amazonas Boundary Commission had come up the lower
Aripuanan and then the eastern branch, or upper Aripuanan, to 8° 48´, following
the course which for a couple of decades had been followed by the rubber-men,
but not going as high. An employee, either of this commission or of one of the
big rubber-men, had been up the Castanho, which is easy of ascent in its
lower course, to about the same latitude, not going nearly as high as the rubber-men had gone; this we found out while we ourselves were descending the
lower Castanho. The lower main stream, and the lower portion of its main affluent, the Castanho, had been commercial highways for rubber-men and settlers
for nearly two decades, and, as we speedily found, were as easy to traverse as
the upper stream, which we had just come down, was difficult to traverse; but
the governmental and scientific authorities, native and foreign, remained in
complete ignorance; and the rubber-men themselves had not the slightest idea
of the headwaters, which were in country never hitherto traversed by civilized
men. Evidently the Castanho was, in length at least, substantially equal, and
probably superior, to the upper Aripuanan; it now seemed even more likely that
the Ananás was the headwaters of the main stream than of the Cardozo. For
the first time this great river, the greatest affluent of the Madiera, was to be put
on the map; and the understanding of its real position and real relationship,
and the clearing up of the complex problem of the sources of all these lower
right-hand affluents of the Madiera, was rendered possible by the seven weeks
of hard and dangerous labor we had spent in going down an absolutely
unknown river, through an absolutely unknown wilderness. At this stage of
the growth of world geography I esteemed it a great piece of good fortune to
be able to take part in such a feat—a feat which represented the capping of the
pyramid which during the previous seven years had been built by the labor
of the Brazilian Telegraphic Commission.

We had passed the period when there was a chance of peril, of disaster, to the whole expedition. There might be risk ahead to individuals, and some difficulties and annoyances for all of us; but there was no longer the least likelihood of any disaster to the expedition as a whole. We now no longer had to face continual anxiety, the need of constant economy with food, the duty of labor with no end in sight, and bitter uncertainty as to the future.

It was time to get out. The wearing work, under very unhealthy conditions, was beginning to tell on every one. Half of the camaradas had been down with fever and were much weakened; only a few of them retained their original physical and moral strength. Cherrie and Kermit had recovered; but both Kermit and Lyra still had bad sores on their legs, from the bruises received in the water work. I was in worse shape. The after effects of the fever still hung on; and the leg which had been hurt while working in the rapids with the sunken canoe had taken a turn for the bad and developed an abscess. The good doctor, to whose unwearied care and kindness I owe much, had cut it open and inserted a drainage tube; an added charm being given the operation, and the subsequent dressings, by the enthusiasm with which the piums and boroshudas took part therein. I could hardly hobble, and was pretty well laid up. But "there aren't no 'stop, conductor,' while a battery's changing ground." No man has any business to go on such a trip as ours unless he will refuse to jeopardize the welfare of his associates by any delay caused by a weakness or ailment of his. It is his duty to go forward, if necessary on all fours, until he drops. Fortunately, I was put to no such test. I remained in good shape until we had passed the last of the rapids of the chasms. When my serious trouble came we had only canoe-riding ahead of us. It is not ideal for a sick man to spend the hottest hours of the day stretched on the boxes in the bottom of a small open dugout, under the well-nigh intolerable heat of the torrid sun of the mid-tropics, varied by blinding, drenching downpours of rain; but I could not be sufficiently grateful for the chance. Kermit and Cherrie took care of me as if they had been trained nurses; and Colonel Rondon and Lyra were no less thoughtful.

The north was calling strongly to the three men of the north—Rocky Dell Farm to Cherrie, Sagamore Hill to me; and to Kermit the call was stronger still. After nightfall we could now see the Dipper well above the horizon—upside down, with the two pointers pointing to a north star below the world's rim; but the Dipper, with all its stars. In our home country spring had now come, the wonderful northern spring of long glorious days, of brooding twilights, of cool delightful nights. Robin and bluebird, meadow-lark and song-sparrow, were singing in the mornings at home; the maple-buds were red;

windflowers and bloodroot were blooming while the last patches of snow still lingered; the rapture of the hermit-thrush in Vermont, the serene golden melody of the wood-thrush on Long Island, would be heard before we were there to listen. Each man to his home, and to his true love! Each was longing for the homely things that were so dear to him, for the home people who were dearer still, and for the one who was dearest of all.

*Theodore Roosevelt died in 1919. He had predicted that he would live sixty years, and that's how long he lived. The expedition had permanently crippled his health and he never again went on one, but he continued to hunt. Our last selection describes a hunt in Quebec in 1915. It is the last chapter in his last book about the outdoors. The selection has all the characteristic grace of Roosevelt's writing and it comes to an end, fittingly, in the fall of the year, when the leaves were turning and the birds were heading south. It has an elegiac note to it, which makes it especially appropriate to end this book.*

# A Curious Experience

*Book–Lover's Holidays in the Open*

IN 1915 I SPENT A LITTLE OVER A FORTNIGHT ON A PRIVATE GAME RESERVE in the province of Quebec. I had expected to enjoy the great northern woods, and the sight of beaver, moose, and caribou; but I had not expected any hunting experience worth mentioning. Nevertheless, toward the end of my trip, there befell me one of the most curious and interesting adventures with big game that have ever befallen me during the forty years since I first began to know the life of the wilderness.

In both Canada and the United States the theory and indeed the practise of preserving wild life on protected areas of land have made astonishing headway since the closing years of the nineteenth century. These protected areas, some of very large size, come in two classes. First, there are those which are public property, where the protection is given by the State. Secondly, there are those where the ownership and the protection are private.

By far the most important, of course, are the public preserves. These by their very existence afford a certain measure of the extent to which democratic government can justify itself. If in a given community unchecked popular rule means unlimited waste and destruction of the natural resources—soil, fertility, water-power, forests, game, wild-life generally—which by right belong as much to subsequent generations as to the present generation, then it is sure proof that the present generation is not yet really fit for self-control, that it is not yet really fit to exercise the high and responsible privilege of a rule which shall be both by the people and for the people. The term "for the people" must always include the people unborn as well as the people now alive, or the democratic ideal is not realized. The only way to secure the chance for hunting, for the enjoyment of vigorous field-sports, to the average man of small means, is to secure such enforced game laws as will prevent anybody and everybody from killing game to a point which means its diminution and therefore ultimate extinction. Only in this way will the average man be able to secure for himself and his children the opportunity of occasionally spending his yearly holiday in that school of hardihood and self-reliance—the chase. New Brunswick, Maine, and Vermont during the last generation have waked up to this fact. Moose and deer in New Brunswick and Maine, deer in Vermont, are so much more plentiful than they were a generation ago that young men of sufficient address and skill can at small cost spend a holiday in the woods, or on the edge of the rough backwoods farm land, and be reasonably sure of a moose or a deer. To all three commonwealths the game is now a real asset because each moose or deer alive in the woods brings in, from the outside, men who spend among the inhabitants much more than the money value of the dead animal; and to the lover of nature the presence of these embodiments of the wild vigor of life adds immensely to the vast majesty of the forests.

In Canada there are many great national reserves; and much—by no means all—of the wilderness wherein shooting is allowed, is intelligently and faithfully protected, so that the game does not diminish. In the summer of 1915 we caught a glimpse of one of these great reserves, that including the wonderful mountains on the line of the Canadian Pacific, from Banff to Lake Louise, and for many leagues around them. The naked or snow-clad peaks, the lakes, the glaciers, the evergreen forest shrouding the mountainsides and valleys, the clear brooks, the wealth of wild flowers, make up a landscape as lovely as it is varied. Here the game—bighorn and white goat-antelope, moose, wapiti, and black-tail deer and white-tail deer—flourish unmolested. The flora and fauna are boreal, but boreal in the sense that the Rocky Mountains are boreal as far south as Arizona; the crimson paint-brush that colors the hillsides, the waterousel in the rapid torrents—these and most of the trees and flowers and birds suggest those of the mountains which are riven asunder by the profound gorges of the Colorado rather than those which dwell among the lower and more rounded Eastern hill-masses from which the springs find their way into the rivers that flow down to the North Atlantic. Around these and similar great nurseries of game, the hunting is still good in places; although there has been a mistaken lenity shown in permitting the Indians to butcher mountain-sheep and deer to the point of local extermination, and although, as is probably inevitable in all new communities, the game laws are enforced chiefly at the expense of visiting sportsmen, rather than at the expense of the real enemies of the game, the professional meat and hide hunters who slaughter for the profit.

In Eastern Canada, as in the Eastern United States, there has been far less chance than in the West to create huge governmental game reserves. But there has been a positive increase of the big game during the last two or three decades. This is partly due to the creation and enforcement of wise game laws—although here also it must be admitted that in some of the Provinces, as in some of the States, the alien sportsman is judged with Rhadamanthine severity, while the home offenders, and even the home Indians, are but little interfered with. It would be well if in this matter other communities copied the excellent example of Maine and New Brunswick. In addition to the game laws, a large part is played in Canadian game preservation by the hunting and fishing clubs. These clubs have policed, and now police many thousands of square miles of wooded wilderness, worthless for agriculture; and in consequence of this policing the wild creatures of the wilderness have thriven, and in some cases have multiplied to an extraordinary degree, on these club lands.

In September, 1915, I visited the Tourilli Club, as the guest of an old friend, Doctor Alexander Lambert, a companion of previous hunting trips in the Louisiana cane-brakes, in the Rockies, on the plains bordering the Red River of the south, and among the Bad Lands through which the Little Missouri flows. The Tourilli Club is an association of Canadian and American sportsmen and lovers of the wilderness. The land, leased from the government by the club, lies northwest of the attractive Old World city of Quebec—the most distinctive city north of the Mexican border, now that the creole element in New Orleans has been almost swamped. The club holds about two hundred and fifty square miles along the main branches and the small tributaries of the Saint Anne River, just north of the line that separates the last bleak farming land from the forest. It is a hilly, almost mountainous region, studded with numerous lakes, threaded by rapid, brawling brooks, and covered with an unbroken forest growth of spruce, balsam, birch and maple.

On the evening of the day I left Quebec I camped in a neat log cabin by the edge of a little lake. I had come in on foot over a rough forest trail with my two guides or porters. They were strapping, good-humored French Canadians, self-respecting and courteous, whose attitude toward their employer was so much like that of Old World guides as to be rather interesting to a man accustomed to the absolute and unconscious democracy of the Western cow camps and hunting trails. One vital fact impressed me in connection with them as in connection with my Spanish-speaking and Portuguese-speaking friends in South America. They were always fathers of big families as well as sons of parents with big families; the big family was normal to their kind, just as it was normal among the men and women I met in Brazil, Argentina, Chile, Uruguay, and Paraguay, to a degree far surpassing what is true of native Americans, Australians, and English-speaking Canadians. If the tendencies thus made evident continue to work unchanged, the end of the twentieth century will witness a reversal in the present positions of relative dominance, in the new and newest worlds, held respectively by the people who speak English, and the people who speak the three Latin tongues. Darwin, in the account of his famous voyage, in speaking of the backwardness of the countries bordering the Plate River, dwells on the way they lag behind, in population and material development, compared to the English settlers in Australia and North America. Were he alive now, the development of the countries around Buenos Ayres and Montevideo would make him revise his judgment. And, whatever may be the case in the future, so far this material development has not, as in the English-speaking world and in old France, been accompanied by a moral change which threatens complete loss of race supremacy because of sheer dwindling in the birth-rate. The men and women of Quebec, Brazil, and Argentina are still primarily fathers and mothers; and unless this is true of a race it neither can nor ought to permanently prosper. The atrophy of the healthy sexual instinct is in its effects equally destructive whether it be due to licentiousness, asceticism, coldness, or timidity; whether it be due to calculated self-indulgence, love of ease and comfort, or absorption in worldly success on the part of the man, or, on the part of the woman, to that kind of shrieking "feminism," the antithesis of all worth calling womanly, which gives fine names to shirking of duty, and to the fear of danger and discomfort, and actually exalts as praiseworthy the abandonment or subordination by women of the most sacred and vitally important of the functions of womanhood. It is not enough that a race shall be composed of good fighters, good workers, and good breeders; but, unless the qualities thus indicated are present in the race foundation, then the superstructure, however seemingly imposing, will topple. As I watched my French guides prepare supper I felt that they offered fine stuff out of which to make a nation.

Beside the lake an eagle-owl was hooting from the depths of the spruce forest; hoohoo—h-o-o-o—hoohoo. From the lake itself a loon, floating high on the water, greeted me with eerie laughter. A sweetheart-sparrow sang a few plaintive bars among the alders. I felt as if again among old friends.

Next day we tramped to the comfortable camp of the president of the club, Mr. Glen Ford McKinney. Half-way there Lambert met me; and for most of the distance he, or one of the guides, carried a canoe, as the route consisted of lakes connected by portages, sometimes a couple of miles long. When we reached the roomy comfortable log houses on Lake McKinney, at nightfall, we were quite ready for our supper of delicious moose venison. Lambert, while fishing in his canoe, a couple of days previously, had killed a young bull as it stood feeding in a lake, and for some days moose meat was our staple food. After that it was replaced by messes of freshly caught trout, and once or twice by a birch-partridge. Mrs. Lambert was at the camp, and Mr. and Mrs. McKinney joined us there. A club reserve such as this, with weather-proof cabins scattered here and there beside the lakes, offers the chance for women of the outdoors type, no less than for men no longer in their first youth, to enjoy the life of the wonderful northern wilderness, and yet to enjoy also such substantial comforts as warmth, dry clothes, and good food at night, after a hard day in the open.

Such a reserve offers a fine field for observation of the life histories of the more shy and rare wild creatures practically unaffected by man. Many persons do not realize how completely on these reserves the wild life is led under natural conditions, wholly unlike those on small artificial reserves. Most wild beasts in the true wilderness lead lives that are artificial in so far as they are primarily conditioned by fear of man. In wilderness reserves like this, on the contrary, there is so much less dread of human persecution that the lives led by such beasts as the moose, caribou, and beaver more closely resemble life in the woods before the appearance of man. As an example, on the Tourilli game reserve wolves, which did not appear until within a decade, have been much more destructive since then than men, and have more profoundly influenced for evil the lives of the other wild creatures.

The beavers are among the most interesting of all woodland beasts. They had been so trapped out that fifteen years ago there were probably not a dozen individuals left on the reserve. Then they were rigidly protected. After ten years they had increased literally a hundredfold. At the end of that time trapping was permitted for a year; hundreds of skins were taken, and then trapping was again prohibited.

The beaver on the reserve at present number between one and two thousand. We saw their houses and dams everywhere. One dam was six feet high; another dam was built to the height of about a foot and a half, near one of our camping places, in a week's time. The architects were a family of beavers; some of the branches bore the big marks of the teeth of the parent beavers, some the marks of the small teeth of the young ones. It was interesting to see the dams grow, stones being heaped on the up-current side to keep the branches in place. Frequently we came across the animals themselves, swimming a stream or lake, and not much bothered by our presence. When left unmolested they are quite as much diurnal as nocturnal. Again and again, as I sat hidden on the lake banks, beaver swam to and fro close beside me, even at high noon. One, which was swimming across a lake at sunset, would not dive until we paddled the canoe straight for it as hard as we could; whereupon it finally disappeared with a slap of its tail. Once at evening Lambert pulled his canoe across the approach to a house, barring the way to the owner—a very big beaver. It did not like to dive under the canoe, and swam close up on the surface, literally gritting its teeth, and now and then it would slap the water with its tail, whereupon the heads of other beaver would pop up above the waters of the lake.

By damming the outlets of some of the lakes and killing the trees and young stuff around the edges, the beaver on this reserve had destroyed some of the favorite haunts of the moose. We saw the old and new houses on the shores of the lakes and beside the streams; some of them were very large, taller than a man, and twice as much across. Some of the old dams, at the pond outlets and across the streams, had become firm causeways, grown-up with trees. The beaver is a fecund animal, its habits are such that few of the beasts of ravin can kill it more than occasionally, and when not too murderously persecuted by man it increases with extraordinary rapidity.

This is primarily due to the character of its food. The forest trees themselves furnish what it eats. This means that its food supply is practically limitless. It has very few food rivals. The trunks of full-grown trees offer what is edible to a most narrowly limited number of vertebrates, and therefore—a fact often lost sight of—until man appears on the scene forests do not support anything like the same number and variety of large beasts as open, grassy plains. There are tree-browsing creatures, but these can only get at the young growth; the great majority of beasts prefer prairies or open scrub to thick forest. The open plains of central North America were thronged with big game to a degree that was never true of the vast American forests, whether subarctic, temperate, or tropical. The great game regions of Africa were the endless dry plains of South and East Africa, and not the steaming West African forests. There are, of course, some big mammals that live exclusively on low plants and bushes that only grow in the forest, and some trees at certain seasons yield fruits and nuts which fall to the ground; but, speaking generally, an ordinary full-grown tree of average size yields food only to beasts of exceptional type, of which the most conspicuous in North America are the tree-porcupine and the beaver. Even these eat only the bark; no vertebrate, so far as I know, eats the actual wood of the trunk.

These bark-eaters, therefore, have almost no food rivals, and the forest furnishes them food in limitless quantities. The beaver has developed habits more interesting and extraordinary than those of any other rodent—indeed as interesting as those of any other beast—and its ways of life are such as to enable it to protect itself from its enemies, and to insure itself against failure of food, to a degree very unusual among animals. It is no wonder that, when protected against man, it literally swarms in its native forests. Its dams, houses, and canals are all wonderful, and on the Tourilli they were easily studied. The height at which many of the tree trunks had been severed showed that the cutting must have been done in winter when the snow was deep and crusted. One tree which had not fallen showed a deep spiral groove going twice round the trunk. Evidently the snow had melted faster than the beavers worked; they were never able to make a complete ring, although they had gnawed twice around the tree, and finally the rising temperature beat the teeth, and the task was perforce abandoned.

I was surprised at the complete absence from the Tourilli of the other northern tree-eater—bark-eater—the porcupine. Inquiry developed the fact that porcupines had been exceedingly numerous until within a score of years or less. Then a mysterious disease smote the slow, clumsy, sluggish creatures, and in the course of two or three years they were absolutely exterminated. In similar fashion from some mysterious disease (or aggregation of diseases, which sometimes all work with virulence when animals become too crowded) almost all the rabbits in the reserve died off some six years ago. In each case it was a universally, or well-nigh universally, fatal epidemic, following a period during which the smitten animals had possessed good health and had flourished and increased greatly in spite of the flesh-eaters that preyed on them. In some vital details the cases differed. Hares, compared to porcupines, are far more prolific, far more active, and with far more numerous foes; and they also seem to be much more liable to these epidemics, although this may be merely because they so much more quickly increase to the point that seems to invite the disease. The porcupines are rather unsocial, and are so lethargic in their movements that the infection took longer to do its full work. But this work was done so thoroughly that evidently the entire race of porcupines over a large tract of country was exterminated. Porcupines have few foes that habitually prey on them, although it is said that there is an exception in the shape of the pekan—the big, savage sable, inappropriately called fisher by the English-speaking woodsmen. But they breed so slowly (for rodents) and move about so little that when exterminated from a district many years elapse before they again begin to spread throughout it. The rabbits, on the contrary, move about so much that infectious diseases spread with extraordinary rapidity and they are the habitual food of every fair-sized bird and beast of prey, but their extraordinary fecundity enables them rapidly to recover lost ground. As regards these northern wood-rabbits, and doubtless other species of hares, it is evident that their beast and bird foes, who prey so freely on their helplessness, nevertheless are incompetent to restrain the overdevelopment of the species. Their real foes, their only real foes, are the minute organisms that produce the diseases which at intervals sweep off their swarming numbers. The devastation of these diseases, whether the agents spreading them are insects or still smaller, microscopic creatures, is clearly proved in the case of these North American rabbits and porcupines; probably it explains the temporary and local extermination of the Labrador meadow-mice after they have risen to the culminating crest of one of those "waves of life" described by Doctor Cabot. It has ravaged among big African ruminants on an even more extensive scale than among these North American rodents. Doubtless such disease-devastation has been responsible for the extinction of many, many species in the past; and where for any cause species and individuals became crowded together, or there was an increase in moisture and change in temperature, so that the insect carriers of disease became more numerous, the extinction might easily befall more than one species.

Of course, such epidemic disease is only one of many causes that may produce such extermination or reduction in numbers. More efficient food rivals may be a factor; just as sheep drive out cattle from the same pasturage, and as, in Australia, rabbits drive out sheep. Or animal foes may be a cause. Fifteen years ago, in the Tourilli, caribou were far more plentiful than moose. Moose have steadily increased in numbers. But some seven years ago wolves, of which none had been seen in these woods for half a century, made their appearance. They did not seriously molest the full-grown moose (nor the black bears), although they occasionally killed moose calves, and very rarely, when in a pack, an adult, but they warred on all the other animals, including the lucivees when they could catch them on the ice in winter. They followed the caribou unceasingly, killing many, and in consequence the caribou are now far less common. Barthelmy Lirette, the most experienced hunter and best observer among the guides—even better than his brother Arthur—told me that the wolves usually made no effort to assail the moose, and that never but once had he heard of their killing a grown moose. But they followed any caribou they came across, big or little. Once on snow-shoes he had tracked such a chase all day long. A single wolf had followed a caribou for twenty-five miles before killing it. Evidently the wolf deliberately set about tiring his victim so that it could not resist. In the snow the caribou sank deep. The wolf ran lightly. His tracks showed that he had galloped whenever the caribou had galloped, and walked behind it when it became too tired to run, and then galloped again when under the terror of his approach the hunted thing once more flailed its fading strength into flight. Its strength was utterly gone when its grim follower at last sprang on it and tore out its life.

An arctic explorer once told me that on a part of the eastern coast of Greenland he found on one visit plenty of caribou and arctic foxes. A few years later he returned. Musk-oxen had just come into the district, and wolves followed them. The musk-ox is helpless in the presence of human hunters, much more helpless than caribou, and can exist only in the appalling solitudes where even arctic man cannot live; but against wolves, its only other foes, its habits of gregarious and truculent self-defense enable it to hold its own as the caribou cannot. The wolves which were hangers-on of the musk-ox herds speedily killed or drove out both the foxes and the caribou on this stretch of Greenland coast, and as a result two once plentiful species were completely replaced by two other species, which change also doubtless resulted in other changes in the smaller wild life.

Here we can explain the reason for the change as regards three of the animals, inasmuch as this change was ultimately conditioned by the movements of the fourth, the musk-ox. But we know nothing of the cause which produced the musk-ox migration, which migration resulted in such unsettling of life conditions for the wolves, caribous, and foxes of this one locality. Neither can we with our present knowledge explain the causes which in Maine and New Brunswick during the last thirty or forty years have brought about a diminution of the caribou, although there has been an increase in the number of moose and deer; wolves cannot have produced this change, for they kill the deer easier than the caribou. Field naturalists have in such questions an ample opportunity for work of the utmost interest. Doubtless they can in the future give us complete or partial explanations of many of these problems which are at present insoluble. In any event these continuous shiftings of faunas at the present day enable us to form some idea of the changes which must have occurred on innumerable occasions during man's history on this planet. Beyond question many of the faunas which seem to us contemporary when their remains are found associated with those of prehistoric man were really successive and may have alternated again and again before one or both finally disappeared. Life is rarely static, rarely in a state of stable equilibrium. Often it is in a condition of unstable equilibrium, with continual oscillations one way and the other. More often still, while there are many shifts to and fro, the general tendency of change is with slow steadiness in one direction.

After a few days the Lamberts and I shifted to Lambert's home camp; an easy two days' journey, tramping along the portage trails and paddling across the many lakes. It was a very comfortable camp, by a beautiful lake. There were four log cabins, each water-tight and with a stove; and the largest was in effect a sitting-room, with comfortable chairs and shelves of books. They stood in a sunny clearing. The wet, dense forest was all around, the deep mossy ground spangled with bright-red partridge-berries. Behind the cabins was a small potato patch. Wild raspberries were always encroaching on this patch, and attracted the birds of the neighborhood, including hermit and olive-back thrushes, both now silent. Chickadees were in the woods, and woodpeck-ers—the arctic, the hairy, and the big log-cock—drummed on the dead trees. One mid-afternoon a great gray owl called repeatedly, uttering a short loud sound like that of some big wild beast. In front of the main cabin were four graceful mountain ashes, brilliant with scarlet berry clusters. On a neighboring lake Coleman Drayton had a camp; the view from it across the lake was very beau-tiful. He killed a moose on the lake next to his and came over to dinner with us the same evening.

On the way to Lambert's camp I went off by myself for twenty-four hours, with my two guides, Arthur Lirette, one of the game wardens of the club, and Odilon Genest. Arthur was an experienced woodsman, intelligent and respon-sible, and with the really charming manners that are so much more common among men of French or Spanish blood than among ourselves. Odilon was a strong young fellow, a good paddler and willing worker. I wished to visit a lake which moose were said to frequent. We carried our canoe thither.

After circling the lake in the canoe without seeing anything, we drew it ashore among some bushes and sat down under a clump of big spruces to watch. Although only partially concealed, we were quiet; and it is movement that attracts the eyes of wild things. A beaver house was near by and the inmates swam about not thirty feet from us; and scaup-ducks and once a grown brood of dusky mallard drifted and swam by only a little farther off. The beaver kept slapping the water with their broad trowel-tails, evidently in play; where they are wary they often dive without slapping the water. No bull appeared, but a cow moose with two calves came down to the lake, directly opposite us, at one in the afternoon and spent two hours in the water. Near where the three of them entered the lake was a bed of tall, coarse reed-grass standing well above the water. Earlier in the season this had been grazed by moose, but these three did not touch it. The cow, having entered the water, did not leave. She fed exclusively with her head under water. Wading out until only the ridge of her back was above the surface, and at times finding that the mud bothered even her long legs, she plunged her huge homely head to the bottom, coming up with between her jaws big tufts of dripping bottom-grass—the moose grass—or the roots and stems of other plants. After a time she decided to change her station, and, striking off into deep water, she swam half a mile farther down the lake. She swam well and powerfully, but sunk rather deep in the water, only her head and the ridge of her withers above it. She continued to feed, usually broadside to me, some three hundred and fifty yards off; her big ears flopped forward and back, and her long snout, with the protuberant nostrils, was thrust out as she turned from time to time to look or smell for her calves. The latter had separated at once from the mother, and spent only a little time in the water, appearing and disappearing among the alders, and among the berry-bushes on a yielding bog of pink and gray moss. Once they played together for a moment, and then one of them cantered off for a few rods.

When moose calves go at speed they usually canter. By the time they are yearlings, however, they have adopted the trot as their usual gait. When grown they walk, trot when at speed, and sometimes pace; but they gallop so rarely that many good observers say that they never gallop or canter. This is too sweeping, however. I have myself, as will be related, seen a heavy old bull gallop for fifty yards when excited, and I have seen the tracks where a full-grown cow or young bull galloped for a longer distance. Lambert came on one close up in a shallow lake, and in its fright it galloped ashore, churning through the mud and water. In very deep snow one will sometimes gallop or bound for a dozen leaps, and under sudden fright from an enemy near by even the biggest moose will sometimes break into a gallop which may last for several rods. More often, even under such circumstances, the animal trots off; and the trot is its habitual, and, save in exceptional circumstances, its only, rapid gait, even when charging.

As the cow and her young ones stood in the water or on the bank it was impossible not to be struck by the conspicuously advertising character of the coloration. The moose is one of the few animals of which the body is inversely countershaded, being black save for the brownish or grayish of the back. The huge black mass at once attracts the eye, and the whitish or grayish legs are also strikingly visible. The bright-red summer coat of the white-tail deer is, if anything, of even more advertising quality; but the huge bulk of a moose, added to its blackness, makes it the most conspicuous of all our beasts.

Moose are naturally just as much diurnal as nocturnal. We found them visiting the lakes at every hour of the day. They are so fond of water as to be almost amphibious. In the winter they feed on the buds and twig tips of young spruce and birch and swamp-maple; and when there is no snow they feed freely on various ground plants in the forest; but for over half the year they prefer to eat the grasses and other plants which grow either above or under the water in the lakes. They easily wade through mud not more than four feet deep, and take delight in swimming. But until this trip I did not know that moose, while swimming, dived to get grass from the bottom. Mr. McKinney told me of having seen this feat himself. The moose was swimming to and fro in a small lake. He plunged his head beneath water, and then at once raised it, looking around, evidently to see if any enemy were taking advantage of his head being concealed to approach him. Then he plunged his head down again, threw his rump above water, and dived completely below the surface, coming up with tufts of bottom-grass in his mouth. He repeated this several times, once staying down and out of sight for nearly half a minute.

After the cow moose left the water she spent an hour close to the bank, near the inlet. We came quite near to her in the canoe before she fled; her calves were farther in the woods. It was late when we started to make our last portage; a heavy rain-storm beat on us, speedily drenching us, and the darkness and the driving downpour made our walk over the rough forest trail one of no small difficulty. Next day we went to Lambert's camp.

Some ten miles northeast of Lambert's camp lies a stretch of wild and mountainous country, containing many lakes, which has been but seldom visited. A good cabin has been built on one of the lakes. A couple of years ago Lambert went thither, but saw nothing, and Coleman Drayton was there the same summer; Arthur, my guide, visited the cabin last spring to see if it was in repair; otherwise the country had been wholly undisturbed. I determined to make a three days' trip to it, with Arthur and Odilon. We were out of meat and I desired to shoot something for the table. My license permitted me to kill one bull moose. It also permitted me to kill two caribou, of either sex; but Lambert felt, and I heartily agreed with him, that no cow ought to be shot.

We left after breakfast one morning. Before we had been gone twenty-five minutes I was able to obtain the wished-for fresh meat. Our course, as usual, lay along a succession of lakes connected by carries, or portages. We were almost at the end of the first portage when we caught a glimpse of a caribou feeding in the thick woods some fifty yards to the right of our trail. It was eating the streamers of gray-green moss which hung from the dead lower branches of the spruces. It was a yearling bull. At first I could merely make out a small patch of its flank between two tree trunks, and I missed it—fortunately, for, if wounded, it would probably have escaped. At the report, instead of running, the foolish young bull shifted his position to look at us; and with the next shot I killed him. While Arthur dressed him Odilon returned to camp and brought out a couple of men. We took a shoulder with us for our provision and sent the rest back to camp. Hour after hour we went forward. We paddled across the lakes. Between them the trails sometimes led up to and down from high divides; at other times they followed the courses of rapid brooks which brawled over smooth stones under the swaying, bending branches of the alders. Off the trail fallen logs and bowlders covered the ground, and the moss covered everything ankle-deep or knee-deep.

Early in the afternoon we reached the cabin. The lake, like most of the lakes thereabouts, was surrounded by low, steep mountains, shrouded in unbroken forest. The light-green domes of the birches rose among the sombre spruce spires; on the mountain crests the pointed spruces made a serrated line against the sky. Arthur and I paddled off across the lake in the light canoe we had been carrying. We had hardly shoved off from shore before we saw a caribou swimming in the middle of the lake. It was a young cow, and doubtless had never before seen a man. The canoe much excited its curiosity. A caribou, thanks probably to its peculiar pelage, is a very buoyant swimmer. Unlike the moose, this caribou had its whole back, and especially its rump, well out of water; the short tail was held erect, and the white under-surface glinted whenever the swimmer turned away from us. At first, however, it did not swim away, being too much absorbed in the spectacle of the canoe. It kept gazing toward us with its ears thrown forward, wheeling to look at us as lightly and readily as a duck. We passed it at a distance of some seventy-five yards, whereupon it took fright and made off, leaving a wake like a paddle-wheel steamer and, when it landed, bouncing up the bank with a great splashing of water and cracking of bushes. A caribou swims even better than a moose, but whereas a moose not only feeds by preference in the water, but half the time has its head under water, the caribou feeds on land, although occasionally cropping water-grass that stands above the surface.

We portaged beside a swampy little stream to the next lake and circled it in the canoe. Silently we went round every point, alert to find what the bay beyond might hold. But we saw nothing; it was night when we returned. As we paddled across the lake the stars were glorious overhead and the mysterious landscape shimmered in the white radiance of the moonlight. Loons called to one another, not only uttering their goblin laughter, but also those long-drawn, wailing cries, which seem to hold all the fierce and mournful loneliness of the northern wastes. Then we reached camp, and feasted on caribou venison, and slept soundly on our beds of fragrant balsam boughs.

Next morning, on September 19, we started eastward, across a short portage, perhaps a quarter of a mile long, beside which ran a stream, a little shallow river. At the farther end of the portage we launched the canoe in a large lake hemmed in by mountains. The lake twisted and turned, and was indented by many bays. A strong breeze was blowing. Arthur was steersman, Odilon bowsman, while I sat in the middle with my Springfield rifle. We skirted the shores, examining each bay.

Half an hour after starting, as we rounded a point, we saw the huge black body and white shovel antlers of a bull moose. He was close to the alders, wading in the shallow water and deep mud and grazing on a patch of fairly tall water-grass. So absorbed was he that he did not notice us until Arthur had skilfully brought the canoe to within eighty yards of him. Then he saw us, tossed his great antlered head aloft, and for a moment stared at us, a picture of burly majesty. He stood broadside on, and a splendid creature he was, of towering stature, the lord of all the deer tribe, as stately a beast of the chase as walks the round world.

The waves were high, and the canoe danced so on the ripple that my first bullet went wild, but with the second I slew the mighty bull.

We had our work cut out to get the bull out of the mud and on the edge of the dry land. The antlers spread fifty-two inches. Some hours were spent in fixing the head, taking off the hide, and cutting up the carcass. Our canoe was loaded to its full capacity with moose meat when we started toward the beginning of the portage leading from the southeastern corner of the lake toward the Lamberts' camp. Here we landed the meat, putting cool moss over it, and left it to be called for on our way back, on the morrow.

It was shortly after three when we again pushed off in the canoe, and headed for the western end of the lake, for the landing from which the portage led to our cabin. It had been a red-letter day, of the ordinary hunting red-letter type. I had no conception that the real adventure still lay in front of us.

When half a mile from the landing we saw another big bull moose on the edge of the shore ahead of us. It looked and was—if anything—even bigger-bodied than the one I had shot in the morning, with antlers almost as large and rather more palmated. We paddled up to within a hundred yards of it, laughing and talking, and remarking how eager we would have been if we had not already got our moose. At first it did not seem to notice us. Then it looked at us but paid us no further heed. We were rather surprised at this but paddled on past it, and it then walked along the shore after us. We still supposed that it did not realize what we were. But another hundred yards put us to windward of it. Instead of turning into the forest when it got our wind, it merely bristled up the hair on its withers, shook its head, and continued to walk after the canoe, along the shore. I had heard of bull moose, during the rut, attacking men unprovoked, if the men were close up, but never of anything as wanton and deliberate as this action, and I could hardly believe the moose meant mischief, but Arthur said it did; and obviously we could not land with the big, evil-looking beast coming for us—and, of course, I was most anxious not to have to shoot it. So we turned the canoe round and paddled on our back track. But the moose promptly turned and followed us along the shore. We yelled at him, and Odilon struck the canoe with his paddle, but with no effect. After going a few hundred yards we again turned and resumed our former course; and as promptly the moose turned and followed us, shaking his head and threatening us. He seemed to be getting more angry, and evidently meant mischief. We now continued our course until we were opposite the portage landing, and about a hundred yards away from it; the water was shallow and we did not wish to venture closer, lest the moose might catch us if he charged. When he came to the portage trail he turned up it, sniffing at our footsteps of the morning, and walked along it into the woods; and we hoped that now he would become uneasy and go off. After waiting a few minutes we paddled slowly toward the landing, but before reaching it we caught his loom in the shadow, as he stood facing us some distance down the trail. As soon as we stopped he rushed down the trail toward us, coming in to the lake; and we backed hastily into deep water. He vented his rage on a small tree, which he wrecked with his antlers. We continued to paddle round the head of the bay, and he followed us; we still hoped we might get him away from the portage, and that he would go into the woods. But when we turned he followed us back, and thus went to and fro with us. Where the water was deep near shore we pushed the canoe close in to him, and he promptly rushed down to the water's edge, shaking his head, and striking the earth with his fore hoofs. We shouted at him, but with no effect. As he paraded along the shore he opened his mouth, lolling out his tongue; and now and then when he faced us he ran out his tongue and licked the end of his muzzle with it. Once, with head down, he bounded or galloped round in a half circle; and from time to time he grunted or uttered a low, menacing roar. Altogether the huge black beast looked like a formidable customer, and was evidently in a most evil rage and bent on man-killing.

For over an hour he thus kept us from the shore, running to meet us wherever we tried to go. The afternoon was waning, a cold wind began to blow, shifting as it blew. He was not a pleasant-looking beast to meet in the woods in the dusk. We were at our wits' ends what to do. At last he turned, shook his head, and with a flourish of his heels galloped—not trotted—for fifty yards up beside the little river which paralleled the portage trail. I called Arthur's attention to this, as he had been telling me that a big bull never galloped. Then the moose disappeared at a trot round the bend. We waited a few minutes, cautiously landed, and started along the trail, watching to see if the bull was lying in wait for us; Arthur telling me that if he now attacked us I must shoot him at once or he would kill somebody.

A couple of hundred yards on the trail led within a few yards of the little river. As we reached this point a smashing in the brush beyond the opposite bank caused us to wheel; and the great bull came headlong for us, while Arthur called to me to shoot. With a last hope of frightening him I fired over his head, without the slightest effect. At a slashing trot he crossed the river, shaking his head, his ears back, the hair on his withers bristling. "Tirez, m'sieu, tirez; vite, vite!" called Arthur, and when the bull was not thirty feet off I put a bullet into his chest, in the sticking point. It was a mortal wound, and stopped him short; I fired into his chest again, and this wound, too, would by itself have been fatal. He turned and recrossed the stream, falling to a third shot, but as we approached he struggled to his feet, grunting savagely, and I killed him as he came toward us.

I was sorry to have to kill him, but there was no alternative. As it was, I only stopped him in the nick of time, and had I not shot straight at least one of us would have paid forfeit with his life in another second. Even in Africa I have never known anything but a rogue elephant or buffalo, or an occasional rhinoceros, to attack so viciously or with such premeditation when itself neither wounded nor threatened.

Gentle-voiced Arthur, in his delightful habitant's French, said that the incident was "pas mal curieux." He used "pas mal" as a superlative. The first time he used it I was completely bewildered. It was hot and sultry, and Arthur remarked that the day was "pas mal mort." How the day could be "not badly dead" I could not imagine, but the proper translation turned out to be "a very lifeless day," which was true.

On reaching Lambert's camp, Arthur and Odilon made affidavit to the facts as above set forth, and this affidavit I submitted to the secretary of mines and fisheries of Quebec, who approved what I had done.

On the day following that on which we killed the two bulls we went back to Lambert's home camp. While crossing one lake, about the middle of the forenoon, a bull moose challenged twice from the forest-clad mountain on our right. We found a pawing-place, a pit where one—possibly more than one—bull had pawed up the earth and thrashed the saplings roundabout with its antlers. The place smelled strongly of urine. The whole of the next day was spent in getting in the meat, skins, and antlers.

I do not believe that this vicious bull moose had ever seen a man. I have never heard of another moose acting with the same determination and per-severance in ferocious malice; it behaved, as I have said, like some of the rare vicious rogues among African elephants, buffaloes, and rhinoceroses. Bull moose during the rut are fierce animals, however, and, although there is ordi-narily no danger whatever in shooting them, several of my friends have been resolutely charged by wounded moose, and I know of, and have elsewhere described, one authentic case where the hunter was killed. A boy carrying mail through the woods to the camp of a friend of mine was forced to climb a tree by a bull which threatened him. My friend Pride, of Island Falls, Maine, was charged while in a canoe at night, by a bull moose which he had incautiously approached too near, and the canoe was upset. If followed on snow-shoes in the deep snow, or too closely approached in its winter yard, it is not uncom-mon for a moose to charge when its pursuer is within a few yards. Once Arthur was charged by a bull which was in company with a cow. He was in a canoe, at dusk, in a stream, and the bull rushed into the water after him, while he paddled hard to get away; but the cow left, and the bull promptly followed her. In none of these cases, however, did the bull act with the malice and cold-blooded purposefulness shown by the bull I was forced to kill.

Two or three days later I left the woods. The weather had grown colder. The loons had begun to gather on the larger lakes in preparation for their south-ward flight. The nights were frosty. Fall was in the air. Once there was a flurry of snow. Birch and maple were donning the bravery with which they greet the oncoming north; crimson and gold their banners flaunted in the eyes of the dying year.

# Roosevelt: Suggested Readings

THERE ARE A NUMBER OF ROOSEVELT BIOGRAPHIES, but the most thorough, and also the best, is the two-volume work of Edmund Morris, *The Rise of Theodore Roosevelt*, which covers his life to the Presidency, and *Theodore Rex*, which brings Roosevelt's life through the Presidency. Whether there will be a third volume taking the story to the end of his life, I do not know. A book by Patricia O'Toole, *When Trumpets Call: Theodore Roosevelt After the White House*, does just that, however. It scants the two expeditions, one to Africa, the other to South America, but it is quite good on his continuing involvement in politics.

For a book that covers Roosevelt's life in the outdoors, I can recommend H. Paul Jeffers, *Roosevelt the Explorer*. Jeffers has written a number of books about different aspects of Roosevelt's life; this one, though it suffers from more than the usual number of misprints, is well-informed and engaging. Joseph R. Ornig's book *My Last Chance to be a Boy* is a thorough, detailed account of the South American expedition.

Roosevelt wrote his own *Autobiography* in 1913 and it is available in the Library of America collection of his writings in two volumes. One of these volumes is devoted to the *Autobiography*, to a reprint of *The Rough Riders*, and to a useful chronology. The other contains a gathering of his letters—he wrote thousands and thousands of letters—and a few speeches. His speeches do not stand up well, but the letters are fascinating and take up most of this volume, which is well worth owning.

Roosevelt is a wonderful character and a vitally important President. More books about him appear all the time. These suggestions are just a beginning.

# NATIONAL GEOGRAPHIC
## ADVENTURE CLASSICS

### 20 HRS., 40 MIN.: OUR FLIGHT IN THE *Friendship*
Amelia Earhart • ISBN: 0-7922-3376-X • $14.00 U.S./$22.00 Canada

Amelia Earhart's high-spirited account of her first crossing of the Atlantic by airplane in 1928, as a co-pilot aboard the *Friendship*, rich with autobiographical information and a discussion on the future of flight—including the important role she expected women to play.

### THE ADVENTURES OF CAPTAIN BONNEVILLE
Washington Irving • ISBN: 0-7922-3743-9 • $15.00 U.S./$24.00 Canada

Capt. Benjamin Louis Eulalie de Bonneville, U.S. Army, explorer, fur trapper, and trader, was one of the most colorful figures in the history of the American West and an irresistible subject to Washington Irving, who purchased the captain's journals and wrote this engaging historical account of Bonneville's death-defying experiences across the American West.

### THE ADVENTURES OF THEODORE ROOSEVELT
Theodore Roosevelt • Edited and with an Introduction by Anthony Brandt
0-7922-9346-0 • $16.00/23.00 Canada

Adventure Classics series editor Anthony Brandt focuses his attention on Roosevelt's robust and adventurous spirit, and treats readers to an engaging assortment of Roosevelt's far-flung adventures including African safaris, ranch life in the American West, and a peril-filled trip down Brazil's legendary River of Doubt. Drawn from Roosevelt's numerous journals, letters, articles, and books, The Adventures of Theodore Roosevelt is an unforgettable chronicle of the life of a naturalist, outdoorsman, and gifted reader and writer, who also happened to be the 26th President of the United States.

### THE CRUISE OF THE *Snark*
Jack London • ISBN: 0-7922-6244-1 • $13.00 U.S./$21.00 Canada

In 1907 the author of The Call of the Wild and The Sea Wolf decided to undertake his own grand adventure: a seven-year, round-the-world cruise aboard the *Snark*. From Hawaii to the Marquesas to the Solomons to Bora Bora, the story of the voyage is one of excitement and spirit, occasional leaks, and London's own hilarious attempts to understand the mysteries of navigation.

### THE EXPLORATION OF THE COLORADO RIVER AND ITS CANYONS
John Wesley Powell • ISBN: 0-7922-6636-6 • $14.00 U.S./$21.50 Canada/£8.99 U.K.

John Wesley Powell, the legendary one-armed pioneer, led the first expedition down the Colorado River into the Grand Canyon. Powell and his crew faced forbidding rapids and scarce food, all of which are documented in thrilling detail in this harrowing saga of strength, determination, and perseverance.

### INCA LAND
Hiram Bingham • ISBN: 0-7922-6194-1 • $14.00 U.S./$22.00 Canada

In 1911, Yale University scholar Hiram Bingham set off for Peru with the goal of climbing Peru's highest peak. Along the way he discovered Machu Picchu, an ancient Inca stronghold high in the mountains. Bingham's wonderfully literate account of the extraordinary find is preceded by an engaging description of his own freewheeling adventures in Peru.

## The Last Voyage of Captain Cook
### The Collected Writings of John Ledyard
Edited and with an Introduction by James Zug
ISBN: 0-7922-9347-9 • $16.00 U.S./$23.00 Canada

A firsthand account of the last voyage and murder of Captain Cook, one of the earliest crossings of Siberia, and personal correspondence with Thomas Jefferson are among the treasures to be discovered in this unprecedented collection. John Ledyard may be the greatest and least-known traveler in the history of the United States. James Zug, author of *The American Traveler*, vividly brings this 18th-century traveler to life with an introduction and annotated text.

## The Journals of Lewis and Clark
### Meriwether Lewis and William Clark
ISBN: 0-7922-6921-7 • $16.00 U.S./$25.00 Canada/£9.99 U.K.

This newly abridged and edited edition of Meriwether Lewis and William Clark's unprecedented a two-year, 5,000-mile journey through the heart of the unknown American West to the Pacific Ocean includes a modern English "translation" that corrects the duo's famously poor spelling and grammar, making for a truly readable account of the journey.

## My Life as an Explorer
Sven Anders Hedin • ISBN: 0-7922-6987-X • $16.00 U.S./$25.00 Canada/£9.99 U.K.

An adventurer with a capital "A," Sven Hedin explored the parts of Asia marked "unknown" on the maps of the 19th and early 20th centuries. His delightful memoir is filled with dangerous situations, the discovery of lost cities, and exotic lands and people, all brilliantly illustrated by the author.

## The North Pole : A Historical Reader
### Edited and with an Introduction by Anthony Brandt
0-7922-7411-3 • $15.00/$22.00 Canada

The fascinating saga of tragedy and triumph in the quest to reach the North Pole is expertly told in this sweeping history of the quest for the North Pole. Series editor Anthony Brandt deftly presents the story of the exploration of the Arctic through selected passages from explorers, interweaving the words of the adventurers with his own contextual material and expertly carrying the story from the 15th century to the 20th. Featuring selections from Frijtdof Nansen, Adolphus Greeley, Robert Peary, and dozens more.

## The Oregon Trail
Francis Parkman • ISBN: 0-7922-6640-4 • $14.00 U.S./$22.00 Canada/£8.99 U.K.

The first historian of the American frontier left his home in Boston in 1846 to travel west with the Conestoga wagons along the Oregon Trail. Parkman encountered a truly wild land fraught with danger, starvation, and marauding Indians, all of which he recorded in the classic account of America's move west.

## Sailing Alone Around the World and
### The Voyage of the *Liberdade*
Joshua Slocum • ISBN: 0-7922-6556-4 • $13.00 U.S./$21.00 Canada

Joshua Slocum's 1899 account of the first solo voyage around the world has been treasured by sailors for more than 100 years. This Adventure Classics edition of Slocum's thrilling chronicle of raging storms, threatening pirates, and treacherous reefs includes another harrowing tale of hardships along the coast of South America.

### SCRAMBLES AMONGST THE ALPS

Edward Whymper • ISBN: 0-7922-6923-3 • $14.00 U.S./$22.00 Canada/£8.99 U.K.

Before thermal clothing, even before reliable ropes, Edward Whymper braved the Alps with energy and determination as he pioneered modern mountaineering. This classic account of his adventures recounts Whymper's many attempts to climb the Matterhorn and the shocking tragedy that befell his companions when they finally achieved their goal.

### THE SILENT WORLD

Jacques Cousteau • ISBN: 0-7922-6796-6 • $13.00 U.S./$19.50 Canada

This 50th anniversary edition of Jacques Cousteau's thrilling memoir includes his charming story of the invention of SCUBA from spare automobile parts in the 1940s and details the adventures that followed as he and his team tested the limits of endurance and pioneered ocean exploration.

### THE SOUTH POLE: A HISTORY OF THE EXPLORATION OF ANTARCTICA
Featuring Shackleton, Byrd, Scott, Amundsen, and more

ISBN: 0-7922-6797-4 • $15.00 U.S./$22.50 Canada

Through the words of the famous—and not so famous—explorers the challenges and hardships of reaching and exploring the South Pole are documented through journals, ship's logs, and personal accounts that tell the extraordinary story of the exploration of the frozen continent.

### THE TOMB OF TUTANKHAMUN

Howard Carter • ISBN: 0-7922-6890-3 • $14.00 U.S./$22.00 Canada

The 1922 discovery of the undisturbed tomb of an Egyptian pharaoh gave the world its first glimpse into the splendor of ancient Egypt. Carter's account, published for the first time as a single volume, deftly conveys his own amazement as he uncovers priceless treasures, including the pharaoh's intact mummy.

### TRAVELS IN WEST AFRICA

Mary Kingsley • ISBN: 0-7922-6638-2 • $14.00 U.S./$21.50 Canada/£8.99 U.K.

Defying Victorian conventions, Mary Kingsley traveled alone to West Africa in 1893. Kingsley was often the first European to enter remote villages, but she made fast friends with the tribes she encountered while collecting priceless samples of flora and fauna. Kingsley's engaging book records numerous obstacles and challenges, including a hilarious encounter with a panther. She faced each one head-on, and always dressed as a lady!

### VOYAGE OF THE *Beagle*

Charles Darwin • ISBN: 0-7922-6559-9 • $13.00 U.S./$21.00 Canada

Charles Darwin's 1845 account of a five-year journey to South America as the naturalist aboard the HMS *Beagle* is a wonderfully told tale of a marvelous journey, rich with vivid descriptions of the natural world, the observations of which would lead to the publication of *Origin of Species*.

### THE WORST JOURNEY IN THE WORLD

Apsley Cherry-Garrard • ISBN: 0-7922-6634-X • $16.00 U.S./$25.00 Canada/£9.99 U.K.

While Robert Falcon Scott and his party set off on an attempt to be the first men to reach the South Pole, Cherry-Garrard and companions set off in search of the never-before-seen breeding grounds of the emperor penguin, a miserable assignment that the author dubbed "the worst journey in the world"—until he returned and discovered the shocking fate of his expedition's leader.